℞: SPIRITIST AS NEEDED

A STUDY OF A PUERTO RICAN
COMMUNITY MENTAL HEALTH RESOURCE

Contemporary Religious Movements:

A Wiley-Interscience Series

Edited by IRVING I. ZARETSKY

Hebrew Christianity: The Thirteenth Tribe
By B. Z. SOBEL

On the Margin of the Visible: Sociology, the Esoteric, and the Occult
Edited by EDWARD A. TIRYAKIAN

Trance, Healing, and Hallucination: Three Fields in Religious Experience
By FELICITAS GOODMAN, JEANNETTE H. HENNEY AND ESTHER J. PRESSELL

Hare Krishna and the Counterculture
By J. STILLSON JUDAH

Changing Perspectives in the Scientific Study of Religion
Edited by ALLAN W. EISTER

Case Studies in Spirit Possession
Edited by VINCENT CRAPANZANO AND VIVIAN GARRISON

Rx: Spiritist as Needed A Study of a Puerto Rican Community Mental Health Resource
By ALAN HARWOOD

℞: SPIRITIST AS NEEDED

A STUDY OF A PUERTO RICAN
COMMUNITY MENTAL HEALTH RESOURCE

ALAN HARWOOD
University of Massachusetts–Boston

A WILEY-INTERSCIENCE PUBLICATION

JOHN WILEY & SONS, New York • London • Sydney • Toronto

Library of Congress Cataloging in Publication Data

Harwood, Alan.
Rx: spiritist as needed.

(Contemporary religious movements)
"A Wiley-Interscience publication."
1. Faith-cure and spiritualism. 2. Psychotherapy—New York (City) 3. Puerto Ricans in New York (City) I. Title.

BF1275.F3H37 615'.852 76-54841
ISBN 0-471-35828-2

Printed in the United States of America

10 9 8 7 6 5 4 3 2 1

TO JUDY

Preface

The initial impetus behind this book was my desire, after completing graduate training in anthropology in 1967, to discover if anything I had learned during my long years of schooling had any practical use in the world. My training at the University of Michigan and Columbia had been in the academic tradition of the major graduate departments in this country at the time, with a heavy emphasis on preparation for university teaching and basic research and a devaluation of applied aspects of the discipline. During my own preparation for the graduate degree I had followed the "approved" line and not taken any course work in applied anthropology, although I was dissident enough to have come out of both the Michigan and Columbia departments with a theoretical bias toward British structuralism and ethnoscience—to my mind a happy combination for which I can mainly thank David Aberle and Harold Conklin.

Thus, in spite of the raised eyebrows of my professors and fellow students at Columbia, I searched for my first employment as a full-fledged anthropologist in applied settings in New York City. Since my job quest corresponded to the period of generous government expenditures for social research in the late 1960s (a fact which had influenced my decision in the first place), there were a number of opportunities to choose from. In planning my search for a program in which research might have the greatest likelihood of producing results, I had decided that the organization which I joined should have three characteristics. It should be relatively small with decision-making powers vested on site and not in some remote bureaucracy; it should have some mechanism for community input into decision-making; and the administration should be knowledgeable about or at least sympathetic toward research. I found this happy combination in the Health Center for which the study reported in this book was done. As added bonuses, the Center also had an unusually stimulating and innovative Director in Harold Wise and a Director of Research, Ronald Brooke, who not only had a background in anthropology but also some clear notions of the kind of research that needed to be done for the program.

Brooke's plan was to develop three divisions to the Research Department: one to assay the existing health level and medical practices of the community served by the Health Center; a second to evaluate the quality of care rendered by the staff of the Center; and a third to examine the results of the Center's treatment program on the Community (Brooke, 1968). He planned a "community ethnography" as the research strategy for providing basic data on the community and had already begun work on certain aspects of the study (spiritist healers and a household census) when I came on staff in August 1967.

I spent my first year at the Center getting acquainted with the area and the staff, doing some preliminary participant observation, investigating the medical and psychological services provided in local schools to determine what kind of relationship the Health Center might develop with them, and writing a proposal for outside funding of the ethnography. This proposal, approved by the Community Advisory Board of the Health Center, was funded by the Carnegie Corporation of New York in mid-1968. After a period of recruiting and training staff, systematic observation began in the fall of 1968 and lasted until December 1969 in most households but was continued in a smaller number into the spring of 1970. (Additional information on the research method may be found in Chapter 1.) In 1970 I wrote reports for the Health Center on the application of my research findings to its program and an article on the implications of the hot-cold theory of disease for treatment of Puerto Rican patients. In addition, I spent much time discussing my results and suggestions with members of the Health Center staff and residents of the community—in a word, politicking for change.

In the upshot did my research have any effect in the world, as I had so ardently hoped in my initial resolve to work in applied anthropology? Within the Health Center a number of small, though to my mind, significant effects occurred. First, data we gathered on dietary practices in the community led to a revamping of the dietary information distributed to patients at the Center. In addition, our investigation of local terminologies for diseases alerted the medical staff and Spanish-speaking translators to certain divergencies in usage that detracted from clear communication in the treatment situation. Our findings on the relationship between housing and health in the area (Harwood, 1971b) also led to a local renovation program and an (unfortunately) abortive attempt to develop new housing. Finally, feedback from individual physicians, nurses, family health workers, and other medical personnel at the Center indicated that the in-service lectures I gave did have an impact on the way at least some individuals interacted with families at the Center. Apart from this kind of informal (albeit gratifying) feedback, the effect of the research on the behavior of the many individuals in the area who became aware of its findings is difficult to judge.

As is so often the case with applied research, however, forces outside the immediate situation exerted the strongest influence on the effects which the research might ultimately have on the Health Center's program. By 1970 when the research was completed, funds for the social and residential development of "poverty areas" in this country were severely curtailed, and the program of the Health Center cut back to little beyond the delivery of medical care to the sick. Efforts to mount programs to deliver truly comprehensive care were moribund. The Community Advisory Board, for reasons connected with political developments in the city and the nation at large, remained an ineffective force for change. And so the organization for which the research had been designed no longer had the financial or administrative capability to attempt to implement some of the research findings' more innovative implications for action. One lesson of this foray into applied research would thus seem to be that anthropologists might better direct their studies to the institutions of this society where high-level policy and funding decisions are made.

As for the implications of the research outside the Health Center, this is even more difficult to assess, particularly at such short range. We applied researchers publish our results with a faith that someone will read and be influenced, and it is with this faith that the following book has been written.

In the course of my research there have been so many people who have in one way or another assisted me that I can only begin to express my gratitude to all of them. First, I wish to thank the residents of the research area and the families who participated in the study. It is their lives and cooperation that made my job and this book possible, and I can never repay their generosity. I owe an equal debt to the many spiritist believers who welcomed me so hospitably to their consultations and *centro* meetings and patiently answered my questions. I have attempted to protect the identities of all these people by disguising personal names and omitting geographical references that would identify the research area.

Without the assistance and encouragement of various members of the Health Center staff, the research project could not have been completed. I would especially like to thank Harold Wise for his efforts in securing the grant for the project from the Carnegie Corporation but most of all for his counsel, friendship, and sincere efforts to implement the research findings. In this regard I would also like to thank Ronald Brooke, who as Director of Research gave me tremendous support and freedom in carrying through the research design. To members of the research staff who helped gather and process the data of the study—Gloria Alston, Delia Betancourt, Olivia Castaldo, Maria Cuevas, Beverly Davison, Juanita Hamilton, Rose Henriquez, Esther Hernandez, Iola Jordan, Mariana Morales, Etervina Ramos, and Juanita Torres—I am indebted for their inestimable contribution to my understanding of the life and people of the area. To Evelyn Eason, Marilyn Tindall Glater, Josephine Juan, Diana Paul, Sonia Valdes, and many other members of the Health Center staff too numerous to mention, I am also indebted for the many forms of assistance they provided in bringing the research to completion. Finally and most appreciatively I would like to thank the Community Advisory Board of the Health Center for their permission to carry out the study.

My particular thanks are also due to the Carnegie Corporation of New York which financed the research and later awarded me a grant to write a book on the findings. The thoughtfulness of Margaret Mahoney (formerly Associate Secretary and Executive Associate), Avery Russell, and their assistants helped make my relations with Carnegie the most pleasant and efficient I have ever experienced with a funding agency. To Dr. Martin Cherkasky, Director of Montefiore Hospital, I owe a similar debt of gratitude for committing the hospital to act as administrator of the grant and kindly easing some of the burdens entailed by that administrative relationship.

For clerical and bibliographic assistance in the final stages of preparing the manuscript I would like to thank Hope Brand, Leola Fitzpatrick, Kathleen Kelleher, Marcia Sorcinelli, John Tuma, and William Warriner.

In dedicating this book to my wife, I wish to express my appreciation to her for her forbearance, support, honesty, and critical judgment—all so important to me when I write. It is largely to these qualities (and her efficiency) that we owe our ability to pursue independent careers and simultaneously to manage a marriage, a household, and a family.

ALAN HARWOOD

Boston, Massachusetts
November 1976

Contents

Tables and Diagram

TABLE

DIAGRAM

℞: SPIRITIST AS NEEDED

A STUDY OF A PUERTO RICAN

COMMUNITY MENTAL HEALTH RESOURCE

Introduction

In the last fifteen years two trends in contemporary American medicine have led to an increased professional interest in healers from other cultural traditions: first, the renascence of the comprehensive health care movement and second, a shift in some medical quarters from an exclusive focus on curing disease or relieving symptoms to the broader theoretical issue of how healing occurs.

The first of these trends, the comprehensive health care movement, is an approach to the delivery of medical services that has its roots in philosophical currents in American medicine dating back to the beginning of the century.[1] Comprehensive care has two aspects. First, it in-

[1] See Stoeckle (1969:300–314) and Seipp (1963:3–6, 21–24) for discussions of the early history of comprehensive health care in general medicine, and Caplan and Caplan (1967:1499–1512) for the development of this mode of patient care within American psychiatry.

volves complete health services, from education and health maintenance to disease prevention, diagnosis, treatment, and rehabilitation. And second, it involves an approach to patients that goes beyond their organic condition to a concern with the many other factors that contribute to their well-being: emotional makeup, familial and other social relations, economic status, and cultural background (Somers and Somers, 1962: 31-32).

In the 1960s this approach to the delivery of medical care received renewed impetus with the passage of the Community Mental Health Centers Act and the funding of Neighborhood Health Centers by the Office of Economic Opportunity. As a result of this federal support, by the second half of the 1960s comprehensive health centers were established in many parts of the country, mostly among ethnic minorities in low-income urban and rural areas. In the course of setting up these comprehensive community health centers, two problems had to be confronted: (1) the inadequate supply of health professionals, and (2) the recognition that most health professionals were neither trained nor particularly skilled to deal in a truly comprehensive fashion with populations whose class and ethnic origins differed from their own (Strauss, n.d., 1970:11).

One of several proposed solutions to these problems was, and still is, to make contact with and in some way utilize the skills of healers who already function within the communities designated for comprehensive health service. The feasibility of working with such "indigenous therapists" has been particularly attractive to psychiatrists in community mental health centers (Bolman, 1968; Fendall, 1972:45; Torrey, 1969, 1970), who for various reasons have expressed an awareness that their therapeutic techniques are not always suited to the populations they serve. Some, who have been trained in modes of psychotherapy that stress insight, long-term treatment, and verbal skill on the part of patients, see these techniques as largely inapplicable to a lower-class clientele (see, for example, Kaplan and Roman, 1973:218-219; Prince, 1969:22-29; Riessman et al., 1964). Others (for example, Pattison, 1973) maintain that using psychiatric therapy with some populations involves translating patients' problems into a wholly different belief system, and they concede the difficulty and even impossibility of doing so. Particularly with populations who speak a language different from that of the therapist, when the therapist and client have very limited command of each other's language, the verbal techniques of psychiatric professionals are of limited use. In view of these problems, many mental health professionals have been open to developing training schools or special relationships with local curers. (For example, see Luce, 1971, on the school for Navaho healers funded by the National Institute of Mental Health, or Pattison, 1973, on the collaborative treatment of a Yakima Indian patient by an indigenous healer and himself.)

In short, an important force behind the contemporary medical interest in healers from other cultural traditions has been the very practical one of providing comprehensive services in the various community health centers established during the 1960s. The other major force behind the recent interest in indigenous curers among medical and psychiatric professionals has been more philosophical than practical—a shift in some medical quarters from an exclusive focus on curing disease or relieving symptoms to the broader theoretical issue of how healing itself occurs. This shift in perspective is connected with the comprehensive health care movement as well as with the involvement of social scientists in medical research. Both these influences direct attention to the psychological, social, and cultural aspects of illness and health and thus strongly emphasize the importance of understanding not only the means by which a patient's physical system can be restored to normal functioning, but also the way in which the patient comes to feel well again and is reintegrated into his or her society as a full participant.

In searching for answers to these broader questions about healing, physicians (particularly those trained in psychiatry) have turned to the comparative study of religious healers and curers in peasant and tribal societies in an attempt to abstract what is common and therefore presumably basic to their methods of changing people's behavior and attitudes and restoring patients to full social life. Sargant (1957) and Frank (1961) in pioneering works and more recently Kiev (1964, 1973) and Torrey (1972) have closely examined the similarities and differences between Western psychiatry and the psychotherapies of nonliterate peoples and religious groups. These studies have documented important commonalities among many traditions of curing and have thus furthered the general understanding of psychosocial aspects of healing considerably.

Both the practical problem of providing comprehensive services to low-income ethnic minorities and a theoretical concern with healing have animated the research and writing of this book. Faced initially with the practical task of assisting a Neighborhood Health Center in evaluating the health resources of the predominantly Black and Puerto Rican population which it was mandated to serve, I undertook an investigation of spiritist beliefs and practices among the Puerto Rican segment of that population as part of a larger health study of the area. As an anthropologist, I assumed that every society has certain institutions that function, at least in part, to minister to the sick, and several suggestive but incomplete reports available in the literature at the time (Bram, 1958;

Padilla, 1958:291-292; Rogler and Hollingshead, 1961, 1965; Wakefield, 1960) indicated that the *espiritista* was an important institution of this type among Puerto Ricans.[2] Indeed, subsequent data from surveys in the South Bronx and Washington Heights sections of New York (Garrison, 1968:4–5, 1972:256–257, on a random sample of 63 adults from the South Bronx; Lubchansky et al., 1970:313, on a probability sample of 52 adults in Washington Heights) indicate that approximately one-third of all Puerto Rican adults seek help from a medium at some time in their lives. Given the very limited psychiatric service available at the Health Center (in spite of its commitment to comprehensive care) as well as the lack of any Spanish-speaking member of that service (although Spanish was the only language spoken in 39% of the Puerto Rican households of the area[3]), it was important to understand the role of spiritism and spiritist therapy in the lives of the Puerto Rican population served by the Health Center for the purpose of possibly developing some kind of communication or relationship with these local healers.

The primary focus of my research was thus to gather basic data on the etiological and nosological system underlying spiritist therapy, the kinds of problems brought to these therapists, their treatment procedures, and many other pieces of information necessary to an understanding of their activities in community health. The study was intended primarily for two audiences: (1) Puerto Rican community leaders and advisors in community health programs, as an aid in assessing existing resources within their community; and (2) medical and psychiatric professionals, as a source of information basic to working with Puerto Rican patients who may have received spiritist treatment in the past or are receiving it concurrently with other therapy. In the course of pursuing this practical goal, however, I became increasingly interested in the larger theoretical issue of healing itself. In the concluding chapter of this book, I therefore examine the basic data on spiritism as it sheds light on both the practical and theoretical issues that inspired my investigation.

The argument of the book develops in the following manner. Chapter 1 describes the methods used in the study as well as the nature of the geographical area and the sample from which the data on spiritists and spiritism come. Chapters 2 and 3 turn to the central topic of the book and present basic information on the ideology, social organization, and

2 After the study began, a number of additional papers on Puerto Rican spiritists as psychotherapists appeared in print (Lubchansky et al., 1970; Purdy et al., 1972), and a few papers were read at professional meetings by Koss (1967; later published 1970) and Garrison (1967; 1973).

3 Household Census of Health Center Target Area, Research Department of Health Center (1967).

ritual procedures of spiritism. This material provides essential background for the discussion of spiritist diagnosis and treatment of psychological and social problems, which follows in Chapters 4 and 5. Chapter 6 shifts focus away from the formal organization of spiritism to the use of spiritist concepts and rituals in ordinary social interaction. After exhibiting the basic data on spiritism in this way, I return in the final chapter to the two fundamental issues that motivated this investigation: the practical concern with possible relationships between therapists of the spiritist tradition and health facilities that serve a Puerto Rican clientele and the philosophical problem of the nature of healing. In short, the plan of the book is to describe the research method and evaluate the sample in Chapter 1, to present the data on spiritist belief, ritual, and therapeutics in Chapters 2 through 6, and finally to offer a discussion and some conclusions concerning the implications of the data in the final chapter. For the reader who prefers conclusions to data, I therefore recommend a dip into Chapter 7 before proceeding.

ONE

Fieldwork: The Setting and the Sample

The material reported in this study was gathered largely by the research method termed "participant observation." Thus the research involved direct participation in and observation of the activities of people living in a particular geographical locale, formal and informal interviews of respondents and informants, analysis of documents pertaining to the research area, introspection by researchers on their experiences in the area, and creation by them of hypotheses for later examination in natural settings of areal life. To draw wider inferences from research data of this type, it is necessary first to place the research locale, as well as one's respondents and informants, within the general context of the society and culture one is studying. Therefore, this chapter begins with a description of the area of New York City in which the research was undertaken and then proceeds to an analysis of the demographic characteristics of the Puerto Rican households and spiritist churches that contributed to the study.

THE LOCALE OF THE STUDY

The research described in this book was carried out within a section of New York City defined by the boundaries of two adjacent service areas of the city's Department of Health. The residents of these two Health Areas had been designated as the target population for a Neighborhood Health Center funded by the Office of Economic Opportunity (OEO), and the findings reported here were part of a wider investigation into the health beliefs and practices of that population.

The two Health Areas had been chosen for special medical attention partly because of their poor showing on various health indices in comparison with other Health Areas in the borough. In 1967 when the Health Center first opened its doors, for example, the infant mortality in one of the two Health Areas ranked fourth highest in the borough (41 per 1000); the tuberculosis rates in the two areas ranked sixth and tenth in the borough; and the rates of venereal disease were fourth and fifth highest. In addition, there was only one physician in private practice per 4812 residents of the vicinity, a ratio 4½ times greater than the comparable figure for the borough as a whole.[1] In view of these statistics, as well as some political considerations on the part of the affiliated hospital which need not concern us here, the Health Center was created to provide, according to the OEO mandate, "comprehensive, family-centered medical care" to the two Health Areas, with the standard stipulation that there be "maximum feasible participation" in the program by the residents of the target area. This latter provision thus created, besides the health facility, a Community Advisory Board which, as we shall see, became one more addition to a plethora of politically active councils in the region, all of which received what little power they had from higher administrative bodies.

THE PHYSICAL SETTING

The two Health Areas, which we shall call the "research area" or simply the "area," consist of 42 square blocks set off from the rest of the borough

[1] Figures supplied by the New York City Department of Health.

by several distinct geographical features. To the west, an escarpment prevents easy access to streets and facilities beyond. Only two roads and a number of steep stairways penetrate this divide between the lower-lying area of our study and the higher-elevation, higher-income region to the west. The northern boundary of the area is formed by that pervasive feature of all "renewed" American cities, the Expressway. Although the highway itself is elevated, the no-man's-land created by the uninhabited, somewhat forbidding area beneath the causeway forms an effective boundary to communication between the research area and streets to the north. Along the northeast border of the area lies a park. With its swimming pool, baseball fields, and tennis courts, it is one of the major recreational facilities of the region. At the same time, however, it effectively limits access to streets on the other side. Only the southern and southeastern margins of the area are without distinct geographical features, and neither the population nor streets of this end of the area differ in any way from those adjacent to it to the south. Indeed it is through this southern corridor that new groups have repeatedly moved into the area.

Pedestrian traffic within the area centers around two major shopping districts. The northerly one is located along one of the two principal arteries that cross the area from east to west and on two streets that run perpendicular to it. One of the latter streets has an old-world quality with polyglot signs hanging in shops windows and open-air stalls offering clothing, food, and hardware. Since streets around this shopping district have a heavy concentration of Puerto Rican residents, many of the shops and stalls cater to the needs of this ethnic clientele. To cite an example pertinent to the subject of this book, this district contained during the period of the study a total of six herb shops (*botánicas*) and three well-marked spiritist "churches" (*centros*). (Other *centros* existed in the area but were not apparent from the street.) For reasons discussed below, the housing around this northern shopping district, and concomitantly the shopping facilities themselves, were undergoing marked and rapid deterioration during the time of the study. The second major shopping district is located at the southeastern periphery of the area and is more obviously Black in orientation, with Moslem and soul-food restaurants as well as the store-front headquarters of important Black community organizations in evidence. Most residents of the area depend on these two shopping districts only for food and travel by subway or bus to larger retail districts elsewhere in the city to purchase clothing, household furnishings, and entertainment.

DEMOGRAPHIC CHARACTERISTICS[2]

Historically the research area was part of a larger sector of the city inhabited until the late 1940s almost exclusively by lower-middle-class Jews. At that time American and West Indian Blacks began moving into the area, and in the 1950s Latins from the Caribbean, mostly Puerto Rico, began settling there in large numbers as well. By 1970 the two Health Areas contained close to 40,000 residents, approximately 46% of whom were Black; 36% Puerto Rican and other Hispanic ethnics; 16% White of various ethnic origins; and 2% Chinese American, Native American, and other non-White ethnic categories.

Residents of the area, compared with New York City as a whole, were characterized by youth and low income. Thus, 52% of the population was under 21, compared to approximately 33% for the city as a whole. The median family income in the area was $6000, about two-thirds the median for the city, and 55% of the families received some form of public assistance, as opposed to 20% for all New York City families at the time. (In the midst of this general poverty, however, it is worth mentioning that 5% of the residents reported incomes in excess of $15,000). Most people from the area who were employed found jobs as low-paid clericals, factory operatives, or service workers in the cleaning, food, and health industries.

Various characteristics, typically correlated in census figures with low income and high rates of public assistance, also obtained in the area. Thus 32% of the households were female-headed, compared with 17% for New York City as a whole. Educational attainment was lower than city and borough figures: only 28% of area residents over 24 years of age had been graduated from high school, compared with 47% for the city, and 40% for the borough. The median number of school years completed differed from the borough median, however, by only 1 year (10+ for the borough; 9+ for the area.)

These statistics thus portray an area of low-income families with young children and few of the educational credentials that are generally considered necessary for material advancement in this society. Many residents were dependent on public assistance and thus subject to the capricious

[2] Unless otherwise noted, all demographic data quoted in this section are from the 1970 Decennial Census and thus represent the demographic picture of the area as the research terminated. Figures on ethnicity, mobility, income, and employment are projections based on questionnaires administered by the Census Bureau to a sample of the censused population; the remaining figures are full counts. I would like to thank the Department of City Planning for its assistance in providing these statistics.

regulations of that system. As we see in the following sections, this general economic deprivation was accompanied by poor housing and political ineffectuality, both induced and supported by administrative or financial decisions that were completely outside the control of area residents.

HOUSING

Buildings in the area ranged from private dwellings and four- and five-story walk-ups to large apartment complexes of 50 to 100 units and the high-rise structures of a city housing project. Excluding the housing project, the median building size for the area was 13 apartments, and most families lived in four- and five-story tenements that housed from 8 to 30 families. Apart from the project, which was less than 10 years old, most of the buildings in the area were constructed from 50 to 70 years ago and were in varying states of disrepair.

When asked what the major health problems of the area were, families in the study mentioned housing as the second most critical. (The first was drugs.) The housing problem was characterized by two features: deterioration of existing buildings through neglect, and a net loss of housing stock through fire and abandonment by landlords. Beyond the deteriorated living conditions, however, the significance of the housing problem for area residents lay in the clarity with which it revealed their inability to influence appreciably the conditions under which they lived.

Deterioration of Existing Buildings

As is described more fully in the section on research methods, 11 buildings were randomly selected for collection of the health data that constituted the focus of this study. Nine of these buildings, all of the four- and five-story tenement type, were observed throughout the study and thus provide a sample of housing conditions in the most common type of building in the area.

All nine buildings sustained malfunctions in basic services which caused residents persistent discomfort and stress throughout the period of study. Complaints, which ranged from leaky faucets to bathtubs and toilets that drained into apartments below, were answered, if at all, with superficial repairs. As a result; conditions worsened—in two buildings to a point where the plaster between several apartments had deteriorated sufficiently to allow neighbors to peer at one another through the disintegrated walls. Because six of the nine buildings had lead-base paint on all surfaces, the flaking plaster associated with leaky plumbing presented a significant health hazard to children living in these buildings. (In a five-month campaign to test area children for lead poisoning, the Health Center found almost 11% of those tested with lead levels sufficiently elevated to warrant close monitoring or hospitalization for detoxification.)

During the winter of 1968-1969 the researchers kept records on the provision of heat to eight of the buildings in the study. During that period only one of the buildings had constant service. The rest had no heat at all for periods ranging from 2 to 15 days. In three of the buildings, furthermore, the heat was on for only a few hours a day, so that room temperatures were below the legally established minimum during most of the day. Neglect of basic services also meant that hallways were often repositories for garbage. As a result, all nine buildings were infested with roaches, mice, and rats.

In addition to the physical discomfort that accompanied these housing conditions, residents of the study buildings experienced the frustration of knowing that they had little power to change the circumstances in which they lived. Even when tenants, through the various educational organizations established during the "Great Society" era, knew the proper legal methods for seeking redress of their housing problems, no substantial improvement was forthcoming. In most cases tenants reported complaints not only to their building superintendents and landlords but also ultimately to the City Department of Buildings. In August 1969, for example, the Department of Buildings had a total of 211 violations on record for the nine buildings in the study. The median number of violations per building was 19, and the figures ranged from 5 to 88. In six of the nine buildings (including all those above the median in number of violations), over half the violations were "major" in terms of the Department of Buildings classification, involving leaky roofs or broken flooring, toilets, fire escapes, stairs, electrical fixtures, steam boilers, and windows.

As dangerous and inhospitable as these figures make these buildings appear, the reality was much worse. Landlords and superintendents put pressure in various ways on tenants and building inspectors to reduce the number of violations on record, so that these recorded figures are without question underestimates. Furthermore, reported violations represented only the most persistent and vexing problems that tenants experienced. The important point to be drawn from these figures is that even though complaints of major violations were on file with the proper authorities, the necessary repairs were made in only one of the nine study buildings. The legal provisions for redressing housing problems did not work for most of the tenants in our study.

A particularly telling example of this last point is provided by a rent strike action that was undertaken in one of the study buildings. Conditions in this building became so intolerable that tenants, in coordination with the Health Advocacy Department of the Health Center, initiated a strike under the provisions of a New York State statute which empowers the Department of Social Services to deposit rent payments in an escrow account for use in repairing buildings with uncorrected violations. Since most residents of the building were welfare recipients, this law seemed specifically addressed to their needs, and the required proceedings were initiated with both the New York City Department of Social Services and the Department of Buildings. Yet when research in this building stopped 11 months after the tenants had filed the requisite petition indicating their willingness to strike, no rent had ever been withheld from the landlord by the Department of Social Services, nor had repairs been made. Furthermore, it is unlikely that any improvements ever resulted from this action. Thus, although legally appropriate action had been taken, the tenants were still suffering substandard housing.

Diminishing Housing Stock

Neglect of the kind just described, along with a number of other factors, was leading to a rapid decline in the number of older housing units in the area. When the Health Center began operation in mid-1967, there were approximately 11,860 units in the area—4190 in the project and 7670 outside it.[3] The 1970 Census, only three years later, reports a decrease of 723 units. Since the number of units in the housing project remained constant in that period, this figure represents a loss of 9% of the housing stock outside the project. This may not sound like a sizable decrease; but in proportion to the number of square blocks of nonproject housing in the area, it represents the loss of almost two tenement buildings per square block in the short period of three years.[4]

[3] Figures on the number of units in the housing project were supplied by the management office, and those on the nonproject area were assembled by the Research Department of the Health Center.

[4] Of course this computation assumes the comparability of the original Research Department figures and the federal census data on the number of housing units in the area. In the absence of any compelling reason to question this assumption, I have compared the two sets of data.

It should be pointed out, however, that the federal census figures do not fully reflect the housing loss to the low-income residents of the area because they include approximately 150 units of a middle-income high-rise apartment house that was built between 1967 and 1970 on land formerly used for low-income dwellings. Because the high-rise

This pattern of decrease in housing was not uniform throughout the research area. Around the northern shopping district it was particularly acute. In this sector 531 housing units (15%) were lost between June 1967 and January 1970. A major cause of this severe reduction in housing can be traced to the designation of this subsection of the area as a possible site for redevelopment under the federally funded Model Cities program. Faced with the likelihood of condemnation proceedings, landlords completely stopped repairing their buildings. As tenants moved out for lack of services, suspicious fires became rife. Whole blocks were abandoned or fire-gutted long before the wreckers came to prepare the locale for redevelopment. Funds were never forthcoming for the rejuvenation project, however, and the district remains a wasteland.

Effects of Deteriorating and Declining Housing Stock on Residents

One of the most obvious effects of declining housing on the area was a high mobility rate. According to the 1970 Census, 42% of the inhabitants of the area had been living at other addresses five years previously. Information gathered in the nine sample buildings in the study indicates, furthermore, that the turnover rate among tenants was, as one might expect, directly correlated with the condition of the building—the more dilapidated the structure, the greater the turnover.[5]

The trend toward high mobility in a building would often begin when only a few apartments had been poorly maintained. When plumbing started to deteriorate, a number of vertically adjacent apartments would become affected. Movement in and out of these deteriorating

was set on a large plot in order to provide parking facilities, the loss in four- and five-story units was about equal to the number gained in the high-rise structure. Thus although the net loss from this middle-income high-rise, as reflected in the census figures, was roughly zero, the real loss in housing to low-income residents was an additional 150 units, which would bring the loss to 11% over the three-year period.

[5] Researchers visited the nine buildings in the study almost daily to gather various kinds of health information from residents and at the same time recorded data on housing conditions. Twice during the course of the year's observations, researchers rated the housing quality of the buildings on an interval scale of 1 to 4 (1 representing the best conditions and 4 the worst). These ratings were based on observations of the following: the state of the plumbing, electrical fixtures, plaster, windows, and other structural features; the cleanliness and maintenance of public areas; and the presence of vermin. Researchers also kept a continuous record of tenant turnover in the buildings under observation. From this record a turnover rate for each building was computed. This rate equals the total number of moves from a building divided by the total number of apartments in it. The data on quality and turnover are found in Table 1, see footnote on page 14.

apartments then created a sense of impermanence about the building among the remaining tenants whose apartments were still adequately maintained. These tenants found it difficult to develop a sense of trust in their transient neighbors, and public areas in buildings came to be perceived as unsafe. Indeed they may in reality have become so, since drug addicts frequently squatted in the run-down apartments, which were essentially unrentable and thus empty for long periods of time. Under these circumstances the long-term tenants, some of whom preferred to remain in their still-adequate apartments, would nevertheless begin to move. Since new tenants who might continue to maintain such apartments also started to shun the building, an almost irreversible downward spiral had begun.

Once this spiral had started, the perceived and real dangers of living in a deteriorating building were added to the frustrations, mentioned above, of badgering landlords and city bureaucrats about repairs. Addicts who camped in empty apartments were feared not only because they were likely to burglarize the legal tenants but also because, having to rely on candles for light (since there was no electricity in the apartments they frequented), they were often responsible for fires. During the course of a year's research, three of the study buildings had fires caused in this way.

In sum, deteriorated housing was not only a source of physical and psychological stress for many area residents, it was also a constant demonstration of the ineffectiveness of their power to alter their living conditions.

TABLE 1 QUALITY RATINGS AND TURNOVER RATES IN STUDY BUILDINGS[a]

Building	Quality Rating	Turnover Rate
A	2.5	.50
B	1.0	.12
C	1.0	.00
D	1.5	.13
E	1.0	.00
F	1.5	.33
G	4.0	.45
H	1.5	.14
I	4.0	.33

[a] The correlation between turnover and dilapidation is +.61 (Kendall's Rank Correlation Coefficient) and is significant at the .02 level of probability.

POLITICS IN THE AREA

The housing situation and its supposed remedies were symptomatic of conditions in the area and of the governmental measures designed to improve them: although more money than heretofore was available for social services to low-income people during the "Great Society" period of our research and "maximum feasible participation" was the byword, residents still had minimal power to change their circumstances. Most of the administrative and economic decisions that intimately affected their lives were made by people with different life styles and different life opportunities from their own. As a result, residents repeatedly faced the problem of living out their own life styles and taking advantage of their own life opportunities within the structure of laws and social institutions designed and ultimately controlled by outsiders. Nowhere was this more evident than in the political structure of the area.

The borough in which the research area lay was heavily Democratic. Party leaders came from and drew their major support from voters in the higher-income districts to the west. In the recent past the regular Democratic organization had sent a representative to the local clubhouse of the party once a week to handle requests from residents of the area, but with the advent of the various New and Great Society programs during the Kennedy and Johnson administrations, the formal Democratic organization became less and less directly involved in the problems and needs of the lower-income areas of the borough and by and large yielded local control to community boards, particularly the OEO Community Progress Centers.

The problem with this reallocation of power was that almost every New and Great Society program created not only a new community board but also a new constituency, since funds for different social purposes were almost without exception allocated to different but overlapping geographical areas. Moreover, some of these areas were preexisting units within the city administrative structure and had not been designed to serve as a basis for local representation in decision making. The Health Center itself is a good example of this phenomenon. The Center's target population, as mentioned earlier, was delimited by Health Area boundaries that had been drawn up decades before for a different purpose. Nevertheless, a board intended to represent this "community" was established to advise about program and policy at the Center. Community Action Programs funded under the Economic Opportunity Act of 1964 present a similar situation: the boundaries of Health Districts, the next largest geographic unit in the Department of Health's administrative structure, were used to demarcate "communities" for allocation of these funds.

Since the boundaries of various sectors of the Department's delivery system had not been drawn with a view toward local participation in the development and administration of programs and funds, internecine factions within the newly established local Boards (largely between Blacks and Puerto Ricans in the vicinity under consideration here) stalemated many of their activities and reduced their effectiveness.

It is important to appreciate, furthermore, that during this period OEO was not the only governmental agency that contributed to the creation of these new "communities" with their "representative" boards. Similar or related community services were often funded by different governmental agencies along different geographical lines. Thus money for mental health services was allocated to Mental Health Catchment Areas, divisions of the city which corresponded to neither Health Areas nor Health Districts, even though the functions that these units served were closely related. Similarly, City Planning Districts, concerned with urban planning and renewal, did not correspond to Model Cities Areas, which were established under federal auspices to deal with the same issues.

In addition to these new "communities" established between 1964 and 1967 largely through federal intervention, the area contained many preexisting administrative subdivisions, none of which was delimited by the same boundaries. While the research was under way, the School District, which covered a much larger area and included a sizable sector of middle-income residents to the west, gained political significance through the establishment of a Local School Board with limited hiring and firing powers. Election districts for city, state, and congressional offices each followed yet other boundaries, most of which trisected the research area and bound it to contiguous regions, often with quite different needs and socioeconomic composition.

This phenomenon of overlapping and heterogeneous administrative units would undoubtedly have had little political significance so long as the residents of these units had not been granted decision making or advisory powers. However when the old units (like Health Areas and Districts and School Districts) were endowed with these functions and other new units were created under various federal programs, politics became highly fragmented and characterized by a great number of leaders with few followers. Each centrally administered service that required a "representative" local board aroused both politically ambitious people of the area and residents who were concerned about the particular problem that the service was designed to ameliorate. These people ran for board seats, necessarily seeking support within the geographical boundaries of the particular administrative unit in which the service was established.

Because the geographical boundaries and therefore constituencies shifted for almost every administrative function, it became particularly difficult for local leaders to amass the widespread, permanent support that might impel them into positions of real power in the city.

To cope with this situation, ambitious political leaders could use their constituencies in part of one administratively defined geographical unit to secure votes to seat themselves on the boards of overlapping administrative units. Some also tried, usually unsuccessfully, to establish residency in several such units. These strategies resulted in a pattern of interlocking board memberships in the area. Once seated on several boards, politically ambitious leaders would then create alliances with fellow board members whose constituencies lay in administrative units outside their own. In this way leaders might be able to influence policy not only on the boards on which they personally sat, but also on those of their allies. For some, the goal of this strategy was to gain sufficient renown and influence to secure nomination for office in regular party politics; for others, the goal lay outside the regular party system.

Whatever effect these strategies might have had on the political fortunes of individual leaders, they often led to the inaction of local boards. For alliances and interlocking memberships meant that agreement on an issue under debate before one board presupposed agreements on how members would vote on issues pending before other boards. Thus, while votes were being lined up to decide an issue before one board, the work of other boards often became stalemated. The effect on ordinary residents of the area was hopelessness; even when local people had some decision-making power, leaders could not organize themselves well enough to use it. Many city officials also maintained the same view. I am suggesting, however, that the situation was partly the result of the way in which the city and federal administrations themselves allocated power and money to the area. (See Jones, 1972 for a similar observation in relation to voluntary organizations among Blacks.)

For the purposes of this book, the main point to be observed regarding housing and politics in the area is that many residents experienced major problems in their lives—for example, housing and medical care—as insoluble through prevailing legal and administrative arrangements. In spite of a *Zeitgeist* that favored political solutions to social problems, many people in the area expressed feelings of futility about change through governmental intervention. New Society "solutions" were experienced simply as newly-imposed conditions under which residents had to contend with the perennial problems of earning a livelihood and living decently.

SOURCES OF MEDICAL AND PSYCHOTHERAPEUTIC CARE FOR AREA RESIDENTS

In view of the statistical indications of poor health in the area, and the concern of this book with one form of health service used by local residents, it is appropriate to conclude our description of the research area with a survey of the various sources of medical care available to the population. We also begin to indicate in this section the different kinds of conditions brought to these various health care facilities, although we pay particular attention to this matter in Chapter 4. The following generalizations on local usage patterns are based on observations of the entire study population—that is, of both Puerto Ricans and Blacks.

The Health Center and Hospital Outpatient Clinics

Most families in the area received medical attention from either the Health Center or the emergency room and outpatient departments of two hospitals. The Health Center was designed to provide comprehensive, family-centered care free of charge to any family in the area that registered (up to a maximum of 7500 households). The Center itself gave primary care, and an associated voluntary hospital provided most specialty and inpatient services to registrants. In contrast to the services offered by the Health Center, the care received at the two hospitals most used by local residents (the nearest city hospital and a voluntary hospital located within the area) was of the episodic, noncomprehensive variety typical of all traditional outpatient departments. Because services were organized by medical specialty, people who used these hospitals either attended a single clinic, where they received care for one narrowly defined condition, or were forced to attend several different clinics to receive anything resembling comprehensive care. If they had a choice in the matter, most area residents went for inpatient care either to the voluntary hospital in the area or to several other well-known voluntary hospitals in the city. The emergency rooms of the hospitals were used for broken bones, serious falls, lacerations involving considerable loss of blood, unexplainable loss of consciousness, and, in children, high fevers.

Private Physicians

Nine private physicians practiced within the area, two of them elderly men who worked on a part-time, semi-retired basis. Additional physicians were available in the higher-income area to the west, and two group practices near the area, which were known to accept Medicaid reimbursement, were also used by a number of families. Although none of the families in the study population used private physicians exclusively for every member, approximately half the families used private doctors episodically—mainly for upper respiratory or urogenital problems or for conditions which they judged to have been treated unsatisfactorily at a public facility.

Pharmacies

Pharmacies in the area were an important source of medical care, particularly for problems of the respiratory and digestive systems. Customers would describe their symptoms to the pharmacist and usually receive an over-the-counter preparation, accompanied by cautionary advice to see a physician if the symptoms persisted. For easily diagnosed conditions some pharmacists also occasionally provided prescription medicines to their regular customers, and one pharmacy in the area was known to do so on a more liberal basis. An Hispano-owned pharmacy, which stocked many medicines commonly used by Puerto Ricans, was patronized especially for these products. [Examples are *alcoholado*; magnesium carbonate (*magnesia boba*); manitol (*maná de manito*); and a patent preparation called *Cerebrina la Francesa*.]

Special Pediatric Services

For children, in addition to the above facilities, there were two Child Health Stations within the area and an additional one a short bus-ride away. These were part of the city health care system and specialized in infant care and immunization. Apart from polio, smallpox, and diphtheria inoculations, little health care was delivered to children in the schools, in spite of elaborate provisions on paper for universal health screening (Swearingen, 1968: 12–13).

Folk Healers

In addition to spiritists, whose contribution to the health care of Puerto Ricans is the subject of this book, specialists in other forms of folk healing were also important in the area. Hispano and Black faith healers of various evangelical Protestant persuasions were available either in established churches or by private consultation. Because most of these healers consider spiritists to be agents of the devil, they banned their followers from using them. As a result, the clientele of spiritists and these sources of health care were, at any one time, mutually exclusive; over time, however, unsatisfied recipients of one form of healing often tried the others.

Herb shops (*botánicas*) also provided medical service to residents of the area. Although both Hispanos and Blacks patronized these shops for religious and magical wares ("good luck" candles, lodestones, various powders designed to produce good or ill), the most frequent customers for medicinal herbs were Hispanos and, to a lesser extent, West Indians—groups with a vital tradition of herbal medicine. Customers usually knew what herb they needed for each health problem and would ask for it by name, but proprietors of these shops sometimes also served as diagnosticians and prescribed for digestive disorders, general feelings of weakness or tiredness, menstrual problems, and asthma. In addition, many *botánicas* had a referral relationship with a spiritist, as seen in Chapter 3.

Another category of healers patronized locally by Puerto Ricans were *santiguadores*. From our observations children were the most common clients of these specialists, although adults went to them on occasion. *Santiguadores* specialize in setting dislocated bones and in curing a form of indigestion called *empacho*. Although Puerto Ricans recognize several different types of *empacho*, the one most commonly encountered (*de comida*, "from food") is attributed to an obstruction in the intestines caused by a bolus of undigested food. To treat this condition, the *santiguador* massages the victim's abdomen to dislodge the obstruction and, after it "falls," makes the sign of the cross and prays (*santiguar*) over the spot where it formed. The healer may also administer a cathartic. Children are often taken to *santiguadores* for treatment of this form of *empacho* as well as of another form purportedly caused by swallowing saliva while teething.

Psychiatric Services

Since spiritists function partly as psychotherapists, we conclude this review of health services by reporting on the formal psychiatric facilities in the area that partially parallel spiritists in function. The most common way for adults in the area to come under psychiatric care was to behave in a fashion defined as "crazy" by people around them. In discussing the meaning of this term with participants in the study, however, it became apparent that American Blacks and Puerto Ricans tended to emphasize different behaviors as symptomatic of this mental state. Among Puerto Ricans such actions as talking incoherently, appearing naked or half-clothed in public, making faces or laughing to oneself, attempting suicide—in general, acting unpredictably—constituted the syndrome labeled "crazy" (*loco*). American Blacks, on the other hand, stressed symptoms such as excessive worry, uncommunicativeness, pacing, and "thinking a lot." The typical consequences of persistently acting in either of these ways was that associates eventually either called the police or took the sufferer to an emergency room. From these points of entry into the health care system, suicidal, homicidal, or highly agitated sufferers would usually be sent to the city's major psychiatric hospital "downtown" for observation. After evaluation the patient might then be referred to either an outpatient mental hygiene clinic in the area (run by the local voluntary hospital) or to the nearest state mental hospital for inpatient care. Psychiatrists from the latter hospital also held office hours several days a week at the Health Center for evaluation and treatment of patients. In contrast to adults, children from the area usually came under psychiatric care through referral by the schools to a psychiatric outpatient clinic. (These patterns of psychiatric referral by police and schools parallel those reported by Hollingshead and Redlich, 1958:183–191, for people of similar socioeconomic status—i.e., their Class IV and V patients.)

THE RESEARCH SETTING: SUMMARY AND IMPLICATIONS FOR THIS STUDY

Besides providing a cursory description of the research area, the foregoing material indicates how little economic or political power area residents had to alter appreciably the material circumstances of their lives. For reasons outlined above, even in the "Great Society," with its apparent commitment to increased opportunity for the poor and community participation in decision making, many decisions that profoundly influenced the delivery of basic services such as housing and medical care (and one might add sanitation and education) by and large did not meet the area residents' felt needs. The prevailing sentiment was that because of their poverty and/or ethnicity, poor Blacks and Puerto Ricans were, more than others in the society, subject to rules made by people who did not have their interests in mind. Of course there were strategies for maximizing one's chances for a decent life even within or in spite of these rules, but many of these strategies (e.g., going on welfare to provide a stable financial base in view of marginal job opportunities) were censured either formally or informally by those in power.

It is within this context that institutions or attitudes that were felt to be one's own, like spiritism for many Puerto Ricans or "soul" among Blacks (Hannerz, 1969: 144–158), must be viewed. Such institutions, which are often of marginal interest to the economically and politically dominant in the society and thus subject to minimal interference from them, provide a strong sense of both identification and autonomy which participants do not gain through involvement with the institutions of the larger society. Indeed identification with other participants and relative autonomy from outside interference are part of what makes an institution like spiritism so important to participants from an area like the one we studied.

This fact, it must be admitted, creates an ethical dilemma in writing this book about spiritism as a form of psychotherapy or as a community resource among Puerto Ricans. By describing spiritism in this way to the various professionals who may read this book, I am exposing it to possible interference from outside, one of the very features the absence of which now makes the institution particularly important to participants. Knowing this, I have still decided to write about spiritism for two reasons. First, most mediums and many spiritists of my acquaintance were not averse to some form of "cooperation" with other psychotherapists or physicians, and given the current trend in psychiatry of searching out "indigenous healers," I prefer that any encounter between the two come with some prior knowledge of spiritist theory and practice on the part of mainstream psychotherapists. From this knowledge the respect that I came to feel for the institution and its practitioners may grow in others. Second, through explicating the beliefs and practices of spiritism as I observed it among the Puetro Ricans I studied, I hope to indicate how deeply intertwined these beliefs and practices are with the social relationships and fundamental attitudes not only of its devotees but of many of their coethnics as well. An appreciation of this complexity will, I hope, forestall any precipitate intervention into spiritist organizations or half-baked interpretations of its practitioners by psychotherapists of the dominant subculture.

In the foregoing description of the area I have also sought to place my material on spiritism in its historical and sociocultural context—viz., as data gathered among Puerto Ricans in a low-income, mixed ethnic area of New York City toward the end of a period of moderate reallocation of political power, increased attention to the legal rights of the poor, and enhanced funding of social services for the "underprivileged." I would not expect spiritistic practices to be precisely the same among more affluent Puerto Ricans; nor would I expect spiritistic ideas to be used in the social relationships of the affluent in exactly the same way. I would, however, expect that what I describe in this book about the beliefs and practices of the residents of the study area does pertain to Puerto Ricans of similar socioeconomic level in other areas of New York City.

RESEARCH METHOD

As mentioned previously, the study of spiritism reported in this book was part of a larger investigation into the health beliefs and practices of the residents of one sector of New York City. The principal methods used for the study were both participant observation and focused interviews. One aspect of the research concentrated on the health practices of people living in a sample of 11 buildings in the study area. This aspect of the research was carried out by community residents who had been trained by me in techniques of participant observation and process recording (see the Appendix for a description of the selection procedure and training of these researchers). A second aspect of the research focused on an examination of the health services offered by various formal and informal institutions in the vicinity (schools, Child Health Stations, spiritists, herbalists, and so forth). I carried out this part of the research in collaboration with community researchers and ad hoc graduate student assistants.

With regard to the study of spiritism, the community researchers concentrated on the role of spiritist beliefs and practices within the Puerto Rican families they were visiting in the context of the larger health study. I studied spiritist healers and groups within or near the study area. The resulting home-centered data highlight the place of spiritist practices in both normal and crisis situations in families, while the cult-centered material illumines the philosophy, ritual activities, and social ambiance of spiritist groups. The combination of these two kinds of data thus provides a picture of both structural and organizational aspects of spiritist belief and practice.[6]

The next two sections describe in somewhat greater detail the sources of these two kinds of data, to provide an understanding of the social characteristics of the specific households and groups that provided the qualitative information on which this book relies.

[6] The contrast invoked here between "structure" and "organization" was introduced into social anthropology by Raymond Firth (1956). "Structure" refers to those aspects of social relations that pertain to rights and obligations attached to specific social positions with respect to other social positions; "organization" refers to aspects of social relations that have to do with individual choice in the utilization of social ties to actualize concrete goals. With respect to the study of spiritism, for example, it is structurally the obligation of clients in a spiritist consultation only to affirm or deny the medium's divination truthfully; organizationally, however, clients may seek consultations from different spiritists and accept the divination they wish to accept.

HOUSEHOLD DATA

Sampling Procedure and Data Collection

At the outset of the study 9 buildings were randomly selected to provide a sample of 120 households or 1.6% of the total households in the study area, excluding the housing project. Random selection of buildings was modified by an additional proviso that at least 60% of the households in a selected building should consent to participate in the study before the building finally be included in the sample. This proviso was introduced to enable researchers to focus on relations among building residents with regard to health practices and mutual assistance, and to increase the visibility of the researchers so that they could more easily expand the sample to other households within buildings. Since one of the buildings in the original sample burned down four months after the study began, at that time an additional building was selected by the same criteria in order to maintain approximately the same sample size.[7]

To satisfy the second criterion for inclusion of a building in the study (60% participation of all households), six buildings had to be rejected before the requisite sample size was initially achieved.[8] Data from a household survey carried out by the Research Department of the Health Center in the year prior to the participant observation study indicates, however, that there were no significant differences in demographic characteristics (size of households, size of income, educational level of household head and spouse) between buildings where 60% acceptance could not be achieved and those that were included in the study.[9]

To secure permission for the study from building residents, researchers visited every apartment and explained the purpose and method of the study to whoever was home at the time. In addition, they left explanatory letters in either English or Spanish for the residents' further consideration. Several days later they returned to each apartment to inquire

[7] Another building was also selected seven months after the study was under way to offset attrition in the number of Black households in the sample. Since the present work deals only with Puerto Rican households, however, I shall not detail the selection procedure for this last building.

[8] In replacing the burned-out building, two more were also rejected because of insufficient participation.

[9] The Wald-Wolfowitz run test (Mosteller and Bush, 1954) was used to see whether the households from rejected and included buildings were drawn from a common population for each of the demographic characteristics listed above. For none of the three characteristics did the test indicate that the buildings constituted different populations. (Significance level = .05)

about the residents' decision concerning participation. Households that agreed to participate were advised that they could discontinue participation whenever they wished.

After securing permission from at least 60% of the households in a building, two researchers were assigned specific apartments for study. The researchers visited the building nearly every day and each household at least once every two weeks. Their basic task was to observe both health maintenance practices (for example, diet, use of medicines, herbs, and massage) and illness behavior in their natural setting. Some information (e.g., on diet, medicine kept in the house, the classification of diseases) was elicited through formal interviews. Other data were collected through observation of behavior as it unfolded, with further elucidation of such observations through immediate or subsequent questioning of the actors. Researchers wrote process notes on these data daily. In reporting the results, I have either changed personal names or otherwise disguised the identities of all individuals who participated in the study.

Nature of the Sample of Puerto Rican Households

The advantages of participant observation as a research strategy in studying a phenomenon like spiritism are clear. Besides enabling investigators to examine and experience the concepts by which this subculture structures the universe, it also and more importantly permits them to see how these concepts are used in natural social situations. Yet participant observation has often been criticized as a research method on the ground that its intensive analysis of one or a few cases, villages, families, or the like is insufficient to support generalization because of the likelihood of bias in the choice of so limited a sample (Denzin, 1970:200).

To meet this criticism, it becomes incumbent on researchers who employ this method to indicate as fully as possible the characteristics of the cases they have studied and to make clear what the possible biases of their data are and to what extent they believe their observations can be generalized to other populations. To this end, let us examine the characteristics of that portion of the health study sample that has provided information for this monograph, the 79 Puerto Rican households.

The 79 households ranged in size from 2 to 10 occupants, with a mean size of 4.8 and a median of 5. The heads of households varied in age from 22 to 72, and households in every phase of the developmental cycle were represented—from the expansion phase of the young, growing family, to the dispersion phase when children begin marrying and moving out, to the final replacement phase in which an elderly parent moves into one of his or her children's households. There was, however, a preponderance of households in the first developmental phase in our sample, a reflection of the youthful character of the area's total population. Of the 79 household heads, 67% were married, 5% widowed; 23% divorced or separated; and 5% single.

The median annual income per household was $7800, with a range from $1560 to $24,900.[10] A more meaningful index of the economic level of the sample, however, is provided by per capita income figures, since, as we have seen, household size ranged quite widely among the 79 households. Again the range is notable: from $13 to $160 a week per person with a median per capita weekly income of $26 (a figure that puts the yearly income of a family of four approximately $1000 below the "poverty line" for that period in New York City.)

Forty-six percent of the households received their major source of income from public assistance of various kinds (ADC, veterans' benefits, social security, etc.). In 21.5% of the households the chief breadwinner was a factory operative, deliveryman, porter, janitor, or other manual worker; in 10% of the households various jobs in the food service industry were the major source of income; and in 9%, earnings derived principally from skilled and unskilled trades (e.g., carpentry and truck or bus driving.) In the remaining 13.5% of the sample households the principal earners were in clerical or sales occupations, the merchant marine, or some technical or mechanical service (e.g., dental technicians or garage mechanics).

As this wide variety of occupations would suggest, the educational attainment of families in the sample also varied widely. Among all residents 25 years old and over,[11] 46% had attended high school, although only 17% had graduated. No one in this age range had gone to college,

[10] The fact that the median household income of the sample is approximately $1000 higher than the median figure for the area, reported previously, is undoubtedly due to their derivation from different sources. The sample data was based on either actual observation (of welfare checks, pay packets, etc.) or interview after many months of acquaintance with the researcher, while the area figure was derived from the federal census. It is likely that respondents underestimated their incomes for the latter source.

[11] The age category "25 years old and over" was selected for examining data on education in order to make the analysis comparable with federal census figures, which use this category. At the time I acquired 1970 census data for comparison, however, no breakdown of education by ethnicity was available, so that the figures used are for the whole area and thus include other ethnic groups besides Puerto Ricans. Comparison with these data indicates a lower educational attainment for our sample of Puerto Ricans than for the areal population, an expectable phenomenon in view of the fact that Blacks constitute over half the areal population and, as a group, New York City Blacks have more years of education than New York Puerto Ricans.

although several had received some form of technical training. Another 41% had not gone beyond sixth grade, and 12% had stopped formal education in the seventh or eighth grades. Women and people over 35 were more heavily represented in the group of primary school leavers, and men among the high school graduates.

Of the 79 household heads in the sample, 94% had been born in Puerto Rico, 4% in New York City, and 2% elsewhere in the continental United States. As might be expected with so large a proportion of Puerto Rican-born, 41% of the families spoke only Spanish in the home, and 59% both Spanish and English. (None spoke only English.) Among the household heads born in Puerto Rico, 42% were born in a city, 35% in a town, and 20% on farms. Most, however, were long-term residents of New York (67% for 10 years or more), and only 14% had been there less than 2 years .

In sum, the sample households from which the information on spiritism was obtained varied in size, composition, and income, although 40% of the households were below the established poverty line for the time. Household heads (and in general the parental generation) were overwhelmingly Puerto Rican-born, although most had immigrated to the mainland more than 10 years before our study. Spanish was still the language most commonly used in the homes, and in 41% of the households it was the only language. Educational level tended to vary with sex and age; males and younger people had higher grade attainment than women and older people. The median number of years of schooling for the group was seven years.

Characteristics of Spiritists in the Sample

We now ask whether the spiritists in the sample differed demographically from the nonspiritists. Before comparing the characteristics of spiritists and nonspiritists, however, we must define these terms unambiguously. Since the problem of differentiating spiritists from nonspiritists is considered at some length in the following chapter, for purposes of the present comparison let us simply adopt an interim, composite definition as follows. A spiritist is any person who exhibits at least one of four characteristics: he or she (1) identifies as a spiritist, (2) believes in mediumistic communication and the removal of harmful spiritual influences through the intervention of mediums, (3) regularly or in times of crisis visits a spiritist either privately or at public sessions, and/or (4) performs certain rituals in the home to cleanse the premises of harmful spiritual influences. For this comparison a nonspiritist, on the other hand, is someone who either declares that he or she is not a spiritist, or belongs to a sect such as Pentecostalism that prohibits the use of mediums and demands that its adherents belong to no other religious group. This definition thus requires an active demonstration of nonparticipation in the spiritist subculture, rather than simply the absence of the four positive criteria for assignment to the spiritist category.

This way of defining the two categories produces, as we shall see, the inconvenient result (from the statistician's point of view) of a large number of unassignable cases. I think that this outcome, however inconvenient statistically, nevertheless reflects reality. There were indeed many undeclared people in the sample who believed in spirits and their intervention in people's lives, and yet said they neither believed nor disbelieved in spiritism.

With these definitions and considerations in mind, we can compare the spiritists with the nonspiritists in our sample of households. Of the 79 households, 42 (53%) had at least one resident who was a spiritist, while 10 households (13%) had no spiritist. In 27 of the households (34%) there was insufficient evidence to assign people unambiguously. None of the standard demographic parameters differentiated households with at least one spiritist resident from those with none. Size, phase of development in the domestic cycle, marital status of the household head, amount and source of income, languages spoken in the home, and length of time in New York bore no relationship to whether a household had a spiritist member or not, although the small number of nonspiritist households in the sample (10) may call into question the reliability of these results.

Although statistical analysis of our data by individual is not strictly warranted in view of the absence of independent selection of individuals in our sampling procedure, the relationship between age, sex, and spiritist adherence among adults in the sample is nevertheless worth some attention (see Table 2). For the sample of 150 adults, 71 (47%) were spiritists, 19 (13%) nonspiritists, and 60 (40%) unclassifiable.

Before commenting on relationships among age, sex, and spiritist adherence, three characteristics of the sample require special notice. First, the higher proportion of adults in the younger age categories reflects the youth of the general population of the area, as reported earlier. Second, the higher percentage of males than females for whom insufficient evidence exists for purposes of categorization is, I suspect, partly an artifact of the research method (since the researchers were all women and male residents tended to be absent from the home, the place where most observations were made). My third comment about the sample is a caution. Given the small size of some of the cells in the distribution as well as the nonindependence of some of the units (as

TABLE 2 AGE, SEX, AND SPIRITIST ADHERENCE AMONG ADULTS[a]

Age Categories	Males			Females		
	S	$\bar{S}$	IE	S	$\bar{S}$	IE
Young adults (20–35 years)	12	4	26	24	3	18
% each sex	24%	9.5%	62%	53%	7%	40%
Early middle age (36–50 years)	6	2	6	13	3	6
% each sex	43%	14%	43%	59%	14%	27%
Late middle age (51–65 years)	3	2	1	6	4	3
% each sex	50%	33%	17%	46%	31%	23%
Elderly (over 65)	1	0	0	6	1	0
% each sex	100%	—	—	86%	14%	—
Total	22	8	33	49	11	27
% each sex	33%	12%	55%	56%	13%	31%

[a] S=spiritist; $\bar{S}$=nonspiritist; IE=insufficient evidence.

mentioned above), any projection of these data to the general population would be unwarranted. The analysis has value, nevertheless, in providing the reader with further insight into the sample from which our participant observation data came.

Three trends may be observed about the individuals in our sample. First, the percentage of male and female nonspiritists in each age category is approximately the same. In other words, roughly the same proportion of males as females openly reject spiritism. Second, in the younger age categories, higher proportions of females than males are spiritists; but with increasing age, the proportion of male and female spiritists tends to reach parity. Whether this trend is due to an increasing affinity for spiritist belief and ritual among males with advancing age, to a decline in the appeal of spiritism among the younger generation of adult males, or simply to an anomaly arising from the small number of cases in the age categories over 51 years cannot be definitely ascertained. Since I have no clear evidence to support either of the first two explanations, however, I tend to favor the last. The third relationship one observes from the data in Table 2 is that the total proportion of males who are spiritists is smaller than the proportion of females. This observation correlates with the preponderance of women at spiritist meetings, a datum discussed in the following section.

In sum, approximately half the households and half the adults in our sample were spiritists. Households with at least one spiritist member did not, however, differ with regard to any of the major standard demographic variables from households with nonspiritists. Individual adherence to spiritism, on the other hand, was related in our sample to sex and age, with women and older age groups having proportionately more spiritists than men and younger age groups. The proportion of nonspiritists in each age group, however, was roughly equal for the two sexes.

SPIRITIST HEALERS AND GROUPS: NATURE OF THE DATA

Sources of Data

Information on spiritist philosophy, ritual, and practice was gathered by participation and observation in spiritist "churches" (*centros*) located either within the study area or close by it. Over a period of 2½ years I participated in the activities of three such *centros,* two nominally of Santero persuasion and one nominally Mesa Blanca. (For a discussion of these two traditions of spiritism and the reason for terming these groups "nominally" one or the other tradition, see the following chapter.) My participation in these groups was as a member, not a medium, and at no time did I undergo training as a medium. As a member, however, I twice acted as *padrino* ("godfather") to people who were going through the ceremony of accepting the special protection of a saint, and became known sufficiently to be able to gather information from adults of all age ranges and both sexes. I never discussed spiritism with children, however, although the household data provide some information on its place in their lives.

In addition to the three *centros* that occupied my major attention, I observed meetings at two others (one Santero and the other Mesa Blanca) and got to know the leaders of these groups well. Further data derive from the work of a medical student (Stanley Fisch), who participated for a little more than a year as a member of a *centro* in the study area. Besides these data from Fisch and myself, who were obviously participant observers, five employees of the Health Center, all female, contributed additional information from their own experience in *centros,* both as members and as mediums.

The six *centros* in which Dr. Fisch and I participated were located either in storefronts or in basements, and the membership of each *centro* ranged from 6 to about 40. These figures were not constant throughout the period of observation, however, since the size of *centros* tends to vary through time, a feature we discuss at greater length in Chapter 3. The largest *centro,* for example, numbered only 10 members at the beginning of our observations and increased fourfold within eight months. But another group had 19 members when I started attending their sessions and fell to 6 within a year. In other sectors of New York City there are *centros* considerably larger than any of the ones in our sample. Although area residents occasionally visited these *centros,* I did not and, as a result, have no information on how this type of group either resembles or differs from the smaller ones that constitute the source of data for this book.

In addition to data derived from participation and observation in *centros,* Fisch and I obtained further material on spiritist beliefs and practices from open-ended interviews and discussions with mediums with whom we became well acquainted (Fisch, with one medium; and I, with three). Although we observed these mediums both in private consultation and while treating clients, we never saw them in the context of the *centros* to which they were attached. These mediums were the source of valuable personal data on mediumistic training and the role of the medium. Three of these mediums were female and one male.

Presentation of Self and Relationship with Informants

In *centros* and with mediums I presented myself as truthfully as I could —as a researcher interested in finding out more about how spiritists help people. Particularly in the Health Center's target area, I usually added that I was associated with the Center, which was planning to use my research to explore the possibility of developing relationships with mediums in the area. In the context of private consultations (*consultas*) with mediums, I also declared that I had problems for which I wished their help. I worked in either English or Spanish, whichever seemed appropriate for the situation.

If questioned whether I "believed" (that is, in spirits and mediumistic communication), I would say that I did not but that I did believe that these ideas were very important in shaping the lives of people who did hold them. This denial of belief was usually met first with accounts of incidents that the interlocutor found he or she could explain only by the work of spirits and then by the query, "Have you never experienced or observed anything similar?" I usually had to respond negatively, and if further amplification seemed warranted, I would admit that I could not explain the incidents recounted but was still reluctant to accept spirits as the cause.

An initial effect of my skepticism was that people attempted to enlighten me further about spirits and their activities, a result that naturally facilitated the research. In situations where I was later observed participating in spiritist rites, however, this action was often taken as belying my words, and people frequently remarked to me, "But of course you believe." As my knowledge of spiritist ideas increased, it became even more difficult to maintain a skeptical stance with people who knew me well, since they took my disbelief as a perversity in the face of overwhelming evidence and experience to the contrary. By that stage of our relationship, however, my sympathy for the cult, demonstrated by attendance at meetings and friendship with members and mediums, rendered this peculiar perversity of mine relatively unimportant in my friends' minds.

So far as I am aware, I was accepted by people initially and, in the case of those with whom I never developed a personal relationship, most saliently as a "sympathetic researcher," the role in which I cast myself. For those who viewed all researchers as spies, this identity foreclosed further communication, although I found this attitude to be rare among spiritists—partly because they viewed themselves as searchers into the beyond and thus also "researchers" of sorts. I found that a prior, friendly relationship with the head medium usually facilitated communication with the entire membership of a *centro,* and that by and large head mediums were very receptive to the study and the possibility of an association with the medical profession. My affiliation with the Health Center, however, often led people to assume that I was a physician, a status I denied except when denial seemed inappropriate at the time (for example, when a medium publicly chided her congregation to be more orderly, since a "*médico*" was present that night.)

My association with the Center was useful on several occasions in allowing me to repay kindnesses to informants by complying with their requests to arrange medical care for them. For the most part my indebtedness to informants was repaid with such personal services or gifts and not with money, which would have been seen as a lack of respect. Only when I enlisted someone to do a specific task did I structure the relationship as a job and paid the person accordingly. This method of handling the reseacher-informant relationship worked without incident.

SUMMARY

This chapter has been devoted to describing the methods by which this study was executed and to providing a background to both the area in which the research was carried out and the sample of Puerto Rican households and spiritist *centros* that furnished the information for the study. The data presented allow us to identify as precisely as possible the nature of the area and the social backgrounds of the people from whom the information on spiritism was gathered, so that we can evaluate its general applicability. On the basis of a comparison of the demographic profile of the sample with that of the Puerto Rican population in New York City, and of our data on spiritism with information available from similar areas of the city (García, 1956: Garrison, 1968, 1972, 1973; Lewis, 1968; Lubchansky et al, 1970; Wakefield, 1960), I venture that the following material is representative of spiritism as generally practiced by lower-income Puerto Ricans in New York.

TWO

The Subculture of Spiritism

In the previous chapter we defined a spiritist according to four criteria: self-identification; belief in spirits, mediumistic communication, and the regulation of spiritual influences through the intervention of mediums; consultation of mediums; and performance of certain rituals in the home. This composite definition recognizes three fundamental aspects of the phenomenon of spiritism: (1) spiritism as an identity, a way in which people can classify and define themselves for others; (2) spiritism as a subculture, a set of standards for what is (i.e., beliefs) and what one can do about what is (i.e., ritual); and (3) spiritism as a cult, a religious group with a certain structure of social statuses and roles revolving around the central status of medium. Although these three aspects are closely interrelated, they are separable both analytically and practically. (An example of their separability in practice would be embodied in the person who adheres to spiritist standards about the way the world is organized but does not participate in a spiritist cult.) In this and the following chapter we examine these three aspects of spiritism and their interrelations.

We begin by considering spiritism as a subculture. To do so, we shall adopt a perspective that views culture as a set of standards for organizing the real world into a phenomenal world of: (1) forms (objects and events, percepts and concepts); (2) propositions that link the forms into cause-effect, part-whole, and other kinds of relationships; (3) beliefs (propositions that are accepted as true); (4) values that codify hierarchies of preference among selected forms and beliefs; and (5) a series of procedures or recipes for operating with and on these forms, propositions, beliefs, and values in order to accomplish recurring tasks (Goodenough, 1963: 257–272; 1971:22–33).

To make this concept of culture somewhat more concrete, let us apply it to one aspect of American culture—medical therapeutics. Both medical experts and lay persons recognize certain *forms* that concern the physical state of organisms and their relationship with the environment. Most of these forms have linguistic labels, some of which ("pathogen" or "anorexia," for example) are used almost exclusively by experts. Other forms, such as "sickness," "cure," "symptom," or "medicine," are in general currency. These forms are set off from other forms and from one another by certain distinctive features that allow people who share the standards of the culture to discriminate them perceptually or conceptually and to recognize certain conditions in the external world as recurrences of the same form.

Forms may relate to one another in a variety of ways. One kind of relationship has to do with cause, so that some of the above terms may be linked into *propositions*: "Pathogens cause sickness," or "Cures cause pathogens." Utilizing another sort of relationship called "hierarchical inclusion," we might also propose the following: "Anorexia is a kind of symptom," or "Medicine is a kind of sickness." Clearly not all the above examples of propositions are true, and only those that for various reasons are accepted as true by the culture bearers would qualify as *beliefs*. Thus, "Pathogens cause sickness" would be a belief while "Medicine is a kind of sickness" is not.

Some beliefs are not only true, however, they are also *values*—that is, desired states of affairs. Certain forms, too, may be more highly valued than others. A "cure," for example, is generally preferred to a "sickness." Since "Medicine causes cures" and "Pathogens cause sickness" (two beliefs of medical therapeutics), "medicines" are valued more highly than "pathogens." Pursuing our example to the final aspect of Goodenough's conception of the contents of culture—*procedures*—we need only call attention to the many recipes that organize "pathogens," "medicines," and various other cultural forms into a series of actions designed to accomplish the valued therapeutic goal called a "cure."

A formulation of the contents of culture in this manner has four important implications for our analysis of spiritism. For one thing, this definition permits us to consider any shared set of standards that define forms, propositions, and so forth as a culture. Thus, according to this definition, spiritism itself is a culture or, more properly, a subculture, since its adherents share special competence in using certain standards and thereby identify one another as being of a kind with themselves. The reason that spiritism should more properly be considered a subculture rather than a culture is that spiritism does not provide a complete set of standards for living—for example, it does not provide beliefs or values that equip people to earn a living or to vote at the polls. Yet spiritist standards also do not interfere appreciably with adherents' abilities to interact in many social contexts with people who do not share their standards.

Indeed spiritist standards, as we shall see, do not even prevent adherents from interacting in many religious contexts with other Christians, particularly Roman Catholics. This point relates to a second implication of Goodenough's conception of culture for our own analysis—namely, that the forms and propositions of a culture (or subculture) are to some degree logically independent of their organization into beliefs and preference hierarchies. Thus some forms can appear as part of several subcultures. In *espiritismo,* for example, certain key forms—"spirit" (*espíritu*) or "envy" (*envidia*), to name only two—play a role in several sets of beliefs extant among Puerto Ricans. Thus when we examine a form like "spirit," we find that many of the beliefs concerning that form are asserted not only by spiritists (that is, those who publicly identify with the beliefs and values of the subculture and practice its appropriate ritual procedures and recipes), but also by Puerto Ricans who are not spiritists and even by many non-Puerto Ricans (for example, Roman Catholics of other nationalities). That is, elements of the subculture (certain forms, propositions, and even some of the beliefs) are shared among a much larger population than those who publicly espouse *espiritismo* (cf. Rogler and Hollingshead, 1965:255). The situation is similar to language, where certain forms (such as cognate words or grammatical categories) may be shared among several speech communities, although the entire lexical and grammatical configuration of the speech of these various communities sets them off from one another to such a degree that speakers from different communities do not understand one another. In such a case it is fruitful to analyze the various languages independently. Similarily, in treating spiritism we shall have occasion to point out certain forms or beliefs that spiritists share not only with other Puerto Ricans but also with non-Puerto Rican cultures, but the phenomenon of spiritism among Puerto Ricans is still analyzable as an entity in itself.

Of course this view of the sharing of cultural standards is oversimplified. That a particular form in spiritism has a role within certain propositions and beliefs, which are in turn part of an interrelated set of beliefs and values, means that the precise semantic value of the form may not in fact be exactly the same when used in nonspiritist communities. Within the spiritist belief system the form may entail certain distinctive features or connotations that are not contained in the form as used in another community. Nevertheless, the forms and beliefs that we shall specify as shared with a wider community are used in most communication between spiritists and nonspiritists as though these system-derived nuances did not exist.

An additional feature of Goodenough's conception of culture which influences the following exposition of the spiritist subculture is the consistent distinction he draws (1971:18–20) between culture itself (the standards for behavior) and the artifacts of culture (the products of these standards). Thus rules of marriage or the techniques for manufacturing a tool or a dwelling constitute culture in this view, while the statistical pattern of marriage arrangements in a society or its actual tools and houses constitute cultural artifacts (that is, concrete products of cultural standards as modified by material or other constraints).

For purposes of our analysis of spiritist subculture, this distinction between standards for behavior and concrete behavior itself permits us to examine the standards, at least initially, without regard to their manifestations in action. For example, we can state as a spiritist belief that "Spirits cause suicidal attempts," without reporting how frequently such attempts are actually explained by spiritual visitations. This procedure is not meant to minimize the importance of the latter kind of data but is intended to facilitate analysis by considering the shared standards independently of behavioral artifacts.

A final aspect of Goodenough's formulation that will guide our discussion of spiritism is his concept of "public culture" (1971:39–40), the standards that people who interact regularly with one another expect their fellows to use. As Goodenough expresses it, "a group's public culture consists of the individual versions of it held by those adult members of the group who are recognized by other adult members as competent in meeting their expectations of one another" (1971:39). The value of this concept lies in its focus on those standards that are either modal for the group or sanctioned by the group's recognized authorities, in contrast to individual versions of the subculture.

This formulation does not minimize the importance of individual variation but allows one to concentrate for analytic purposes on the standards most commonly accepted by competent members of the group. In the following exposition of spiritist forms, beliefs, and values, I therefore focus on this public aspect of the subculture by presenting standards that derive from the verbal and nonverbal behavior of self-identified spiritists I knew, as well as from expert sources on spiritism. The latter include not only practicing mediums but also writers of spiritist tracts that are widely known and frequently referred to by Puerto Rican spiritists in New York (namely, El Akoni, n.d.; Kardec, 1963a, 1963b).

SPIRITIST COSMOLOGY

MATTER AND SPIRIT

As mentioned above, spiritist beliefs share many features with other religious and philosophical systems prevalent not only in Puerto Rico but throughout the world. Like many of these cosmologies, spiritism posits a fundamental dichotomy between material forms or matter and non-material forms or spirits. Material substances are destructible and ephemeral; spirits, once created, are indestructible and eternal. Furthermore, matter is experienced by means of the five senses, but spirits are directly experienced by ordinary people only while in certain states of consciousness (such as sleep), or by other people who have special innate abilities called faculties (*facultades*) or who have developed a capacity for extrasensory perception through instruction and practice.

Incarnation: Union of Matter and Spirit

In spiritist belief the creator of the two basic constituents of the cosmos is God, an eternal, unchangeable, benevolent, wise, and infinite power. God, according to spiritists, chose man among all corporeal species to become the receptacle or envelope (*envoltura*) for the incarnation of those spirits to whom He gave moral and intellectual discernment. Mankind therefore combines two natures: animal (deriving from a bodily or material aspect) and spiritual (coming from the God-endowed spirit).

These two natures are said to become bonded together at birth by means of a substance called the *periespíritu* or, more commonly, *fluido*. In this moment of incarnation the spirit becomes a soul (*alma*).

As described thus far, spiritist doctrine does not differ appreciably from orthodox Christianity. It departs most conspicuously from it, however, in the value it places on possession as a mode of communication between incarnate spirits and incorporeal entities. According to spiritist doctrine, certain people (mediums) have the faculty of giving over their bodies (their material component) to incorporeal spirits who "possess" them for the purpose of communicating directly with incarnate spirits. Ordinary people without this special ability are also deemed capable of receiving messages from spirits, but they do this through dreams, daydreams, presentiments, and only occasionally through direct visual or auditory communication.

Belief in the possibility of communication between disembodied spirits and the living, although central to the spiritist subculture, is also widely held by Puerto Ricans who are not practicing spiritists. The generally accepted vehicle for this kind of communication is dreams, which are considered to be records of meetings with spirits. The soul, still connected to the body by *fluido,* is believed to journey anyplace on earth or in space to communicate with other spirits—good or bad, incarnate or disincarnate—while the body is asleep. During these wanderings the soul receives messages, particularly from incorporeal spirits who have a special interest in its well-being (such as deceased relatives or the guardians and protectors discussed below). Because these dream messages are believed to be motivated by beneficent intent, their interpretation assumes considerable importance not only for spiritists but also for the many nonspiritist Puerto Ricans who believe in spirit communication during sleep.

Death: Severance of Body and Spirit

Immediately on death, the soul is said to leave the body. The spirit, however, remains encased in *fluido,* which retains the form of the body to which it was attached. Although invisible under most circumstances, this *fluido* may be seen either by those in trance or occasionally by nonmediums as an apparition. Gradually, however, the soul "realizes" it is disincarnate and abandons earthly matter to rejoin the world of other incorporeal spirits. Before this reunion is achieved, each spirit is said to pass through a period of confusion (*turbación*), which is generally thought to last nine days (the period of the novena after burial, a custom observed by many non-Catholic as well as Catholic Puerto Ricans).

Spirits whose lives have been devoted to material and sensual activities, however, are believed to take far longer to quit the earth and may hover about as intranquil spirits (*espíritus intránquilos*), interfering in the affairs of the living.

THE SPIRIT HIERARCHY

The spirit world, as depicted in spiritist cosmology, is hierarchical in a dual sense. Spirits are not only ranked in terms of their moral perfection, but those occupying different moral ranks are also conceived as residing on separate spatial planes. This concept is accepted by all spiritists, although ideas about the number of ranks and the specific occupants of various ranks differ in the two major spiritist traditions, Mesa Blanca and Santería. The view depicted in Diagram 1 and described in the following paragraphs presents points of agreement in the two traditions. Differences are discussed in a later section.

The lowest level of the spirit hierarchy, which is conceived as starting only a few inches above the earth, is inhabited by spirits that departed from their bodies in an unsettled state—the intranquil spirits. These spirits may be bound to earth through a special attachment to the living which grows either out of inordinate love or an unmet obligation—for example, an unpaid debt. Spirits may also occupy this lowest rank because they have failed to fulfill their spiritual potential in life. People who have died prematurely (especially through suicide, a fatal accident, or violent crime) fall into this category, as do those who have devoted their lives to material pursuits.

To enable these "little elevated" spirits (*espíritus poco elevados*) to

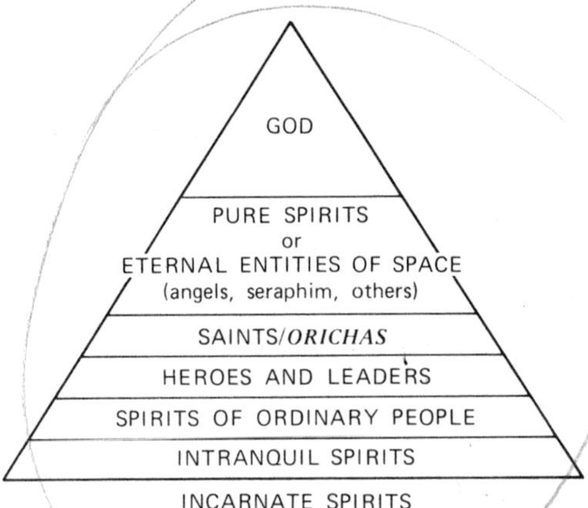

Diagram 1 The spirit hierarchy.

quit the earthly ambiance and ascend to the next spiritual rank, incarnate spirits (the living) must perform certain services in their behalf. These services, which include reciting prayers, lighting candles, and offering flowers, are spoken of as "giving the spirit light" (*darle la luz al espíritu*). If not "given light," these restless spirits may become subjugated to earthly malefactors (*brujos,* "sorcerers"), who use them in harming enemies. We return to the role of these "misguided" or "little evolved" (*poco evolucionados*) spirits in examining the practice of sorcery more fully in Chapter 4.

Above the lowest spiritual plane is one inhabited by the spirits of ordinary people, known relatives and friends, who are free of earthly attraction but nevertheless watch and protect their surviving loved ones. Although more elevated than spirits of the lowest rank, these spirits are still considered imperfect and may display many foibles of the living.

The next rank in the hierarchy contains the spirits of influential and just leaders, among whom an American Indian chief and an Arab figure importantly. More recently *Los Tres Difuntos* (John Kennedy, Robert Kennedy, and Martin Luther King, Jr.) have been added to this rank, and statues or pictures of these men occupy important places on the domestic altars of many Puerto Ricans in New York.[1]

Concepts about the composition of the spiritual hierarchy above the level of heroes differ among Puerto Ricans according to which of two predominant spiritist traditions one follows. It must suffice at this point to say that the remaining ranks are occupied by highly evolved (that is, morally perfect) spirits, such as saints, angels, seraphim, and *orichas* (the Spanish plural form of *orisha,* a deity in the Yoruba pantheon). At the pinnacle in both traditions is God. (Details concerning the hierarchy according to the two spiritist traditions are presented in the sections on Mesa Blanca and Santería in this chapter.)

RELATIONS BETWEEN INCARNATE AND DISINCARNATE SPIRITS

Superimposed on the hierarchical arrangement of the spirit world is a vertical partition into divisions or cadres (*cuadros*). Like a division in an army, each spiritual division consists of top-ranking spirits (the warriors, saints, and angels) on down the hierarchy to materialized spirits. In each division the higher-ranking spirits assist those below them in achieving moral perfection and thereby advancement in rank.

[1] In the early 1960s, when Rogler and Hollingshead observed spiritists in Puerto Rico in connection with their research on schizophrenia, Franklin D. Roosevelt and Mahatma Gandhi occupied important places at this rank in the spirit hierarchy (Rogler and Hollingshead, 1965:246).

Guardians and Protectors

At birth each embodied spirit is believed to receive a Guardian Angel (*ángel guardiano*) from the cadre into which the person has been born, who will give advice and help in making right decisions in life. Incorporeal spirits of lower rank within the same cadre aid the Guardian Angel in his task and are called protectors (*protectores*) or guides (*guías*). The angels and protectors act as intermediaries, carrying God's enlightenment and protection down the ranks to the living and bearing incarnate spirits' supplications upward to higher spiritual ranks.

Incarnate spirits cannot simply enjoy the assistance of their spirit helpers passively. The relationship between an incarnate spirit and his or her protectors is quid pro quo, and responsibility for initiating and maintaining the protective relationship rests with the living. Although the most common way of conducting this relationship is through prayer and such tokens of regard as flowers or candles dedicated to the protector, the ultimate means of confirming one's connection with protectors is said to be through development (*desarollo*) as a medium. Those who do this acquire at least one additional spirit or guide (called the *guía principal, cabecilla,* or *predilecto*), whose special function is to help control the entry and exit of spirits during possession. Relatively few believers attempt development, however.

Sympathetic Spirits

In addition to a Guardian Angel and protectors, a person may attract spirits with characteristics or tastes similar to his or her own. For example, a medical student who participated in the research was frequently told that he had the spirit of a physician beside him. Such "sympathetic spirits" (*espíritus simpáticos*) may be attracted either by a person's spiritual qualities or by that person's material, animal nature. Those whose sympathies are with the person's spiritual aspect are believed to exert influence toward morally right actions, while those whose attraction is animal turn the person away from the path of spiritual perfection. Sympathetic spirits, unlike the Guardian Angel, do not necessarily remain with a person throughout life, however, since their interest wanes when the person ceases to show whatever characteristics first attracted them.

SPIRITIST COSMOLOGY AND CHRISTIANITY: SIMILARITIES AND DIFFERENCES

Many notions about the structure of the universe that are found in spiritism are also part of orthodox Christian doctrine, particularly

Roman Catholicism. Common to both are the concept of the dual nature of man as material animal and eternal spirit, as well as the hierarchy of spiritual perfection in which higher-order, disincarnate members have special protective relationships with incarnate souls. Spiritism differs from orthodox Christianity, however, in the importance it places on direct communication between embodied and disembodied spirits and consequently in the value it places on the development and use of mediumistic abilities (hence the inclusion of this criterion in the definition of spiritists in the previous chapter). Although these elements are central to the spiritist subculture, systematic variations with regard to other beliefs and rituals may be found among Puerto Rican spiritists.

MESA BLANCA AND SANTERÍA: VARIANT SPIRITIST TRADITIONS[2]

The propositions about the spirit world, which were discussed above, were known to most Puerto Ricans in the sample and were espoused as beliefs by many who were not practicing spiritists. Among spiritists, however, these fundamental beliefs are incorporated into two divergent traditions of spiritism. One of these traditions, Santería, had its origin in Africa (Courlander, 1960; González-Wippler, 1973; Herskovits, 1937a, 1937b; Métraux, 1959; Simpson, 1962, 1965) and undoubtedly came into Puerto Rico by way of Cuba and Hispaniola. The other tradition, Espiritismo or Mesa Blanca (White Table), entered Puerto Rico from Europe during the upsurge of interest in spirit communication that accompanied the "crisis of faith" in the latter part of the nineteenth century (Koss, 1972:66–70; Macklin, 1974:388–393; Steward et al., 1956:88).[3]

The following two sections review the main ideological and ritualistic differences between these two traditions. In this review, however, we must recognize that variations in belief and knowledge exist among occupants of different social statuses in both cults. We therefore try to identify those aspects of the cosmology that are in general currency and those that are special to adepts or are found only in spiritist writings. This treatment of the two spiritist traditions concludes with a consideration of certain syncretic trends that are occurring in New York.

[2] Wakefield (1960:65–67) contrasts these variant traditions as beliefs in "spirits of the air" and "spirits of the water" respectively.

[3] Since the term "*espiritismo*" is used to label not only the particular tradition of spiritist belief derived from Europe but also the general belief in communication with spirits, I consistently refer to the European tradition by the alternative label, Mesa Blanca. Another term that has been used for this tradition in the literature is "Kardecism," because of the influence of the writings of the nineteenth century spiritist Allan Kardec on its introduction into Latin America (Macklin, 1974; Pressel, 1973:316).

MESA BLANCA

This spiritist tradition, introduced into Puerto Rico in the 1870s, was illegal under Spanish rule and only gained popularity in the post-Hispanic period during the early part of the century (Koss, 1972:66–70; Steward et al., 1956:88). Today at almost any *botánica* (herb shop) in New York City various editions of the works of the French spiritist Allan Kardec (pseudonym for L. D. Hippolyte Rivail) can be purchased in Spanish translation (Kardec, 1963a, 1963b).

According to Kardec and followers of Mesa Blanca, spirits pass through a series of reincarnations, each of which allows the spirit to enhance its moral purity by overcoming the suffering and ethical dilemmas entailed in life on earth. Life is thus seen as a test (*prueba*) of the spirit which, if passed satisfactorily, entitles it to ascend the celestial hierarchy. Failing the test entails no demotion in rank but may occasion a stiffer *prueba* in the next reincarnation.

This notion of life as a spiritual test is stressed more in the Mesa Blanca tradition than in Santería. Indeed in Mesa Blanca the whole ethical emphasis on good conduct as a basis for future reward seems a clear carry-over from its Christian origins. In conformity with this emphasis on future reward, furthermore, the major authoritative writings of the Mesa Blanca tradition hold that all spirits, even the most highly elevated, progress through every rank of the hierarchy (Kardec, 1963a: 96–97). Santería, on the other hand, posits the existence of certain very high-ranking spirits who have never been incarnate and never will be (El Akoni, n.d.:5). Although this is a minor philosophical difference, one which no practitioner of either tradition ever enunciated to me and which I learned only by reading spiritist literature available to Puerto Ricans, it nevertheless indicates the pervasiveness of the notion of progression through *prueba* in Mesa Blanca as opposed to Santería cosmology.

With regard to conceptions about the number of levels in the spirit hierarchy and their respective occupants, lay adherents to Mesa Blanca agree with the schema presented in Diagram 1, with the important omission of Yoruba *orishas* from the hierarchy. A different classification of spirits is found in the authoritative writings of the cult, however. Kardec's (1963a:85–98) taxonomy involves 10 "classes" of spirits, grouped into 3 "orders" labeled Imperfect Spirits, Good Spirits, and Pure Spirits. These terms for the orders are known to the lay public and are used by Mesa Blanca mediums, although the referents of the terms are not the same as Kardec's classes. Instead, the referents are the saints, heroes, intranquil spirits, and others mentioned in Diagram 1.

experiencing a *prueba* from God through generations of slavery and European domination. During this *Gran Prueba* (Great Trial), *orichas*[4] are said to have become incarnate in the bodies of Whites. Thus Jesus is the incarnation of Olofi, the highest *oricha*, while the Christian saints and some heroes are lower-order *orichas*. Santero doctrine further maintains that the present era is one of enlightenment in which people of all races are realizing the common identity of these two sets of spirits and learning to address them by their original African names. According to doctrine, the lesson to be learned from the *Gran Prueba* is that the flesh, with its various pigments, is simply the outward covering of the spirit and, as spiritual children of God, all men are brothers (El Akoni, n.d.:23–27).

In conformity with this view of history, the hierarchy in Santería is suffused with African spirits. Among the 15 or so saints who figure prominently in Santería, each has his or her corresponding African manifestation, as shown in Table 3. In addition, Africans appear as guides and protectors in the spiritual ranks below the level of saints and are called *congos* or *mandingas*, depending on the cadre from which they come.

Besides the African emphasis which differentiates Santería cosmology from Mesa Blanca, there is—as the name of the cult implies—an additional emphasis on higher-level spirits, the saints/*orichas*. Thus, although mediums within both Mesa Blanca and Santería communicate with lower-ranking spirits, only *santeros* serve as vehicles (*caballos*, literally "horses") for communicating with saints. In addition, the saints/*orichas* are highly elaborated symbolically in Santería. As in Roman Catholicism, each saint has an associated day as well as foods, alcoholic beverages, color and ritual objects, all of which usually derive from a legend about the saint. For example, St. Barbara's day is December 4, and she is associated with the color red, red apples, rum or red wine, blood, and a sword, cup, or tower. Yemayá's day is celebrated on September 8. She is associated with the color blue, salt cod (*bacalao*), white rum, seashells, and fans. Furthermore, certain saints and their cadres are grouped in association with certain natural features. Thus Regla (Yemayá), La Mercedes (Obatalá), and Caridad del Cobre (Ochún) are all associated with water, while Candelo, Changó, and Elegua are spirits of fire.

More significant for the psychotherapeutic implications of spiritism than these material symbols associated with the saints, however, is the

[4] When referring to African spirits in the context of Santería, I consistently use the Spanish form of *orisha*, *oricha*.

Discussions centering on such taxonomies and typologies seeme demic to my Mesa Blanca informants, however, since their major cern was the practical one of identifying a spirit that manifests during a séance (cf. Rogler and Hollingshead, 1965:246). For this pose voice level, intonation, accent, and vocabulary are importan dicators, and the primary classification is functional rather than for That is, in natural situations people are more concerned to kr whether a spirit is a protector or a "cause" (*causa,* a spirit who is sponsible for misfortune), rather than the spirit's exact status in t celestial hierarchy.

For most participants in spiritist meetings the style of mediumist performance, rather than ideological details, is what differentiates Mes Blanca most sharply from Santería. Unlike *santeros* (devotees of San tería), Mesa Blanca mediums communicate primarily with lower-ranking beings (*seres*) in the spiritual hierarchy. During meetings (*reuniones*) the head medium, called the *Presidente,* and his or her assistants sit around a table covered with a white cloth (hence the appellation "White Table"). A candle and a goblet of water are kept on the table. Mediums in training, regular attendants of the group's séances, and others who have come to a particular session seeking spiritual help sit in rows facing the table. The mediums, through prayer and concentration, summon spirits to the table to aid the assembled congregation in their relations with the spirit world. During this procedure the *Presidente* may assign a spirit to possess an assistant medium whose powers he considers adequate to the job. The *Presidente* then acts as interrogator of the spirit to learn more about the problems of specific congregants. During the course of the interrogation he may seek to persuade the spirit, if it is one that is tormenting a congregant, to depart and leave its victim in peace. This process of removing malevolent spiritual influences is known as "working the cause" (*trabajando la causa*) and is discussed further in subsequent chapters.

A book of prayers selected by Kardec (1960, 1964), often referred to as the *Colecto,* plays an important part in Mesa Blanca séances, since merely opening the book is believed to draw spirits to the table. In Santería, however, the book does not play an important role.

SANTERÍA

The ideology of this tradition differs from Mesa Blanca in a number of respects, the most important of which is the incorporation of African spirits into the spirit hierarchy. This incorporation is based on a view of history in which Africans are the chosen people and have been

TABLE 3 SPANISH AND AFRICAN NAMES OF MAJOR SPIRITS IN SANTERIA[a]

Spanish Name	African Name
The seven African powers *(Las siete potencias africanas)*	
Sta. Bárbara	Changó
San Francisco de Asisi	Orula, Orúnla
La Caridad del Cobre	Ochún
La Mercedes	Obatalá
San Antonio, San Benito el Moro, San Martín de Porres[b]	Elegua, Echu
San Pedro	Ogún
Regla, La Milagrosa	Yemayá, Yemalia
Other important saints	
San Lázaro	Babalú-Ayé
Sta. Marta	?
San Espedito	?
San Carlos Borromeo	Candelo
San Elias	El Varón del Cementerio
San Cristobal	Agayú, Bacoso
Sta. Clara	Odudúa

[a] The correspondences indicated in this table are those recognized by Santeros with whom I was acquainted. Different correspondences have been reported both in Puerto Rico and other parts of the New World (cf. González-Wippler, 1973; Simpson, 1962:1205–1206; St. Clair, 1971.)

[b] Certain *orichas* are identified differently by different informants. Some resolve the differences by saying that they are all reincarnations of the *oricha* in question; others maintain that only their own identification is correct.

fact that each saint has a unique personality and mannerisms, which are familiar to all cult members. St. Barbara, for example, is extremely aggressive and energetic and is also believed to be hermaphroditic—male half the year and female the rest. In fact her African manifestation, Changó, is a male *oricha*. When one of her devotees is seized by this saint, he or (usually) she becomes imperious and commanding in demeanor. La Mercedes, by contrast, is mild-mannered, calm, rational, and guiding rather than commanding. San Espedito, patron of drunkards and gamblers, slurs his speech and staggers as if intoxicated. San Lázaro walks on crutches and is shown the solicitude accorded a cripple, while he himself speaks words of encouragement to the sick. The psychotherapeutic implications of this diversity in saints' personalities is discussed in Chapter 4, when we examine treatment procedures in spiritism.

Unlike Mesa Blanca, séances in Santería take place in front of the cult's altar and not around a table. After an invocation and reading similar to a Mesa Blanca service, the head medium orders the lights turned out. While the mediums seek contact with spirits, the congregation claps and sings to the lively Latin beat of recorded songs honoring the various saints. As in Mesa Blanca sessions, mediums receive spirits of lower grades who may be harming or protecting those in attendance, but unlike Mesa Blanca one or more saints usually also manifest themselves during a session. A person possessed by a saint exorcises everyone at the séance and shows particular solicitude toward those present who are under his or her special protection. Also unlike Mesa Blanca, the head medium does not confine himself or herself to the role of interrogator during a session but takes spirits, just like other mediums.

The importance of saints in Santería makes for a much fuller ritual calendar than is observed in Mesa Blanca. Thus, in addition to their regular twice-weekly séances, *santeros* honor each major saint with a special ceremony on or near his or her Saint's Day. Periodically each cult group also holds a celebration called an *omblicht* in honor of the Seven African Powers, the major saints/*orichas* of the cult (see Table 3). At these celebrations each of the Seven Powers manifests himself or herself during the night and is feted with a characteristic beverage and foods.

A common conception about the difference between Santería and Mesa Blanca is that only mediums in the former tradition practice black magic (*brujería* or voodoo). While it is true that only *santeros* use certain techniques that are associated with voodoo, the use of magical practices to harm or influence others is by no means limited to them, and judgments as to whether a particular technique is *brujería* or not may vary among different observers who know the case being treated. Furthermore, some *santeros* dissociate themselves entirely from voodoo and name still other cults as perpetrators of the black arts. (See, for example, El Akoni, n.d.:63–68, and González-Wippler, 1973:30, 124, 145, who indict the Palo Monte and Palo Mayombe sects for this activity.)

An additional belief about Santería, common among nonspiritist Puerto Ricans, is that all *santeros* are Black. This belief is not supported by observations of *santero centros*. Since elements of Santería belief and ritual derive from Africa, and the cult was undoubtedly introduced into Puerto Rico by Blacks from Hispaniola, Cuba, or elsewhere in the West Indies, this opinion may have been true on the island at one time. It is certainly not the case in New York. However, since Santería abounds in African influence and views Africans as the chosen people, espousal of Santería does imply acceptance of its African heritage, a condition that is unacceptable to some spiritists who strongly identify as White. Indeed the only practicing spiritists I encountered who expressed the same view as the uninformed and identified Santería with Blacks were two White followers of Mesa Blanca who were outspokenly anti-Black and rejected Santería as an "African faith." If many White Mesa Blanca adherents were to adopt this view and reject Santería tenets and rites in order to keep their *centros* White, then a racial cleavage between the two cults could indeed emerge in New York—but not, as opinion would have it, with Santería uniformly Black. Instead Santería would be racially mixed and Mesa Blanca totally White. Although a few groups of Mesa Blanca mediums may indeed reject Santería on racial grounds in order to maintain a White cult group, the present strong trend toward syncretism, described below, makes widespread occurrence of this phenomenon seem improbable to me. Racial attitudes in this country as a whole, however, will undoubtedly play a determining role in the ultimate ideological blend and racial composition of the two cults and thus in their use as a source of identity for Puerto Ricans.

SYNCRETISM OF MESA BLANCA AND SANTERÍA

In New York today syncretism of the two spiritist traditions is rapidly taking place. Indeed if one were to take González-Wippler's (1973) description of Santería as the "pure" form of that tradition and Kardec's writings as "pure" Mesa Blanca, then every one of the four nominally Santería *centros* and two nominally Mesa Blanca *centros* that I observed embodied mixtures of ritual and belief from both traditions.[5] Since, moreover, the same individuals freely consult mediums of both traditions, the opportunities for learning and blending beliefs and procedures are frequent.

Many mediums, however, inveigh against visiting more than one spiritist for a single problem, particularly if the spiritists are of different traditions. As one medium phrased it, "A person can go in two ways: with the saints or with the spirits. One can't do both because that is dangerous. One gets confused." The rationale behind this interdiction is that in the course of treatment a person's protectors, having started to cooperate with the protectors of one medium and his assistants, will

[5] Of course the notion embodied in this terminology, that a religious system can have a "pure" form in the absence of a priesthood and formal rules for determining heresy, is misleading. The point is that the religious beliefs and practices described in González-Wippler and in Kardec are more different from one another than any rites labeled Santería and Mesa Blanca that I observed in New York.

become "confused" if they must suddenly switch to working with a new set of protectors. In fact, of course, the interdiction serves the interests of mediums by helping them retain clients who have begun treatment with them.

In spite of this injunction against consulting more than one medium, clients often visit several and go through diagnosis and early treatment with each one, testing until they find the medium whose interpretation and treatment of the problem suits them. Thus spiritist clients not only demonstrate a knowledge of criteria for evaluating their healers, but they also have the money and opportunity to choose the one with whom they feel they can work—two positive features of spiritist therapy that do not characterize the medically-based psychotherapeutic services available to most Puerto Ricans.

A belief that has developed among spiritists as an explanation for the existance of two traditions is that they represent progressive stages in the ability of mediums to contact spirits. Thus Mesa Blanca mediums, who, as we have indicated, work with intranquil spirits and protectors of lower orders, represent a first stage of mediumistic development, and Santería mediums represent a higher stage, since they are able to contact more exalted levels of the spirit world. A group of Mesa Blanca mediums I know, for example, collectively decided that they were "strong" enough to work with higher spirits and began incorporating *santero* rites into their séances. In addition, a woman who began developing as a medium in one of the Santería "churches" I attended was advised by the head medium to go to a Mesa Blanca group for awhile to learn their rites as a preliminary to deeper involvement in Santería. This concept, that Santería is a higher development of spiritism than Mesa Blanca, thus serves not only to unify the two traditions within a single cosmology but also to justify the right of mediums to mix traditions—a right which, as we have noted, they deny to laypersons. Since this concept legitimates the adoption of *santero* symbols and rituals by a medium as he or she develops, it effectively invests mediums with some, albeit limited, control over the amount and kind of syncretism that occurs.

It is interesting to speculate about the reasons for the current trend toward syncretism of Mesa Blanca and Santería traditions in New York today. In doing so, one must first view this syncretism as a particular manifestation of a general strain toward individuation that prevails among spiritist cults. As Koss (1972:71) has noted, "Each small religious group . . . seeks to construct its own ideological synthesis within the extraordinarily flexible frame of reference of spiritist doctrine as established by Kardec's [tutelary] spirits." Why cults in New York draw inspiration from not only Kardecist but also *santero* doctrine in this effort toward individuation, however, is the matter in question.

Some evidence that the demographic composition of spiritist cults is different in New York from what prevails or has prevailed until recently on the home island is suggestive in answering this question. Thus, although a belief in the existence of spirits and their ability to influence the activities of mortals seems to be widespread in Puerto Rico,[6] there is some indication that socioeconomic differences have distinguished adherents to the two spiritist traditions there, at least within the recent past. Thus Scheele (1956:452) has reported spiritist groups among the upper class of San Juan. These groups emphasize contemplation and experimental testing of psychic phenomena rather than mediumistic trance. Koss (n.d.) has been studying Mesa Blanca cults among middle-income groups in the capital. These groups are all Kardecist in belief and practice. According to Koss (1972:69), however, among the Puerto Rican "lower classes" Kardecist ideas became synecretized with Catholicism and indigenous curing practices. The synthesis of Catholicism and African beliefs must also have occurred in these strata because of the slave status of the bearers of the African tradition. But González-Wippler's statement (1973:10) that "contrary to popular belief, Santería is not confined to the ignorant and uneducated" would seem to indicate that this tradition of spiritism may no longer be exclusive to the lower classes on the island.[7]

Whatever the contemporary situation in Puerto Rico, in New York City a pattern of cult segregation along class lines is not apparent. In the low-income area where this study took place, both Santería and Mesa Blanca cults existed with no socioeconomic difference between people who attended the two kinds of group. Furthermore, most of the families in our household sample who visited spiritists had at one time or another consulted mediums of both persuasions. In addition, the social networks of devotees of both cults extended outside the area to middle-income counterparts who attended Santería or Mesa Blanca cult

[6] Spiritist beliefs and cult groups have been reported in both tobacco-growing (Manners, 1956:128) and sugar-producing areas of the island (Padilla, 1956:305–308; Seda, 1973) as well as among agricultural workers, small farmers, town laborers, and new members of the middle class living in a "traditionally-oriented" municipality (Wolf, 1956:245). Steward et al. (1956:88, 128, 245, 305–08, 452) see rapid change in ways of life as a common feature in all these communities in which spiritism has taken hold.

[7] Pressel (1973:316) has observed a similar contrast in the class membership of Kardecist spiritist cults and Afro-Brazilian Umbanda groups in Brazil.

groups elsewhere in the city. In short, Santería and Mesa Blanca do not seem to draw their adherents from different socioeconomic strata in New York City.

One might postulate that the syncretism of Mesa Blanca and Santería traditions in New York is related to the socioeconomic heterogeneity of the membership of cult groups there in contrast to groups in Puerto Rico, where adherents to the two cults have apparently been socioeconomically distinct. In the latter social situation the ideologies and practices have remained correspondingly more disparate, while in New York, where adherents to both of the cults are socioeconomically heterogeneous, the beliefs and practices of the two traditions have become blurred and syncretized.

Several additional factors in the New York situation undoubtedly contribute toward the unification of the two traditions. First, because of selective factors affecting migration to the continent (Sandis, 1970), the range of socioeconomic differences among Puerto Ricans in New York is narrower than that in Puerto Rico. Since the extremes in class variation that obtain in Puerto Rico are by and large not present in New York, people in the narrower socioeconomic range in New York may, in the absence of the extremes, interact more readily and thus opt for either tradition. This homogenizing trend is further reinforced by the social organization of New York City, where the salient status for Puerto Ricans, regardless of class origin, is their ethnic identity, and sociocultural differences that are relevant on the island become much less important in this new context. (Similar patterns of merging regional or socioeconomic differences when migrants become a minority group in a new setting have been observed almost worldwide—see, for example, Mitchell, 1956 and Cohen, 1974:92–98 on tribal identities in African cities; Suttles, 1968:especially 105–108 for Italians in a United States city; Gonzalez, 1975:113 for Near Easterners in the Dominican Republic; and Dirks, 1975:102 for "Garots" in the Virgin Islands.)

Whatever the specific reasons behind the growing syncretism between Mesa Blanca and Santería in New York, however, its effect is that many New York Puerto Ricans are competent in performing the rites of either tradition, and cults that go under the name of either Santería or Mesa Blanca (or *Espiritismo*) in New York are usually a blend of the two traditions.

THREE

An Introduction to the Social Structure and Ritual of the Centro

Spiritism, like most subcultures, not only consists of concepts that define the nature of the cosmos and the place of human beings within it but also contains standards that define right relations among human beings. These two components of subcultures are usually interrelated. In spiritism the latter are simply an extension of the former; just as the highest-ranking disembodied spirits assist those beneath them, so embodied spirits with strong spiritual power are obligated to help those spiritually weaker than they. The hierarchical and protective mode which, according to the cosmology, characterizes relations among all spirits thus finds its logical extension in relations among corporeal beings.[1] Family members with strong spiritual power (in practice often the mother, as we see in Chapter 6) are therefore believed to be morally bound to assist those weaker than they (usually children). Fully developed mediums must assist those who are beset by misguided spirits or who seek to increase their spiritual protection so as to become mediums themselves. Indeed this concept of the spiritually strong necessarily helping the spiritually weak provides the charter for spiritist cults (*centros*), which are constituted as organizations of spiritually developed people who seek to increase their spiritual faculties and help others with problems of a spiritual origin.

In this chapter I focus on the *centro*, examining its social structure and its most important ritual, the *reunión* (meeting). Discussion of the *reunión* focuses on its form and on its ritual paraphernalia. This material provides a necessary introduction to our central concern, an examination of spiritist therapeutics, which follows in Chapters 4 and 5.

THE SOCIAL STRUCTURE OF SPIRITIST GROUPS

STATUSES AND THEIR ASSOCIATED ROLES

The social structure of spiritist cults reflects the cosmological notion of spiritual gradations in perfection or power and thus parallels the world of disincarnate spirits in its hierarchical organization. At the top of the cult hierarchy stands the head medium, usually the founder of the group, followed by assistant mediums, mediums-in-training, and finally clients.

The head medium is the cult member whose spiritual protection is considered the strongest and whose mediumistic powers are most fully developed. In Santería this person is called the *Jefe* or Chief; in Mesa Blanca he or she is called the *Presidente*.[2] Assistant mediums, called collectively the *mediunidad* in both traditions, help the head in the spiritual work of exorcising harmful spirits and diagnosing clients' problems. One of their main functions is to "protect" one another while in

[1] This hierarchical structure, comprising both spirits and incarnate souls, exemplifies the "cone of authority" that Prince (1969:33–34) sees as characteristic of all "primitive" psychotherapeutic systems.

[2] Garrison (1972:279) reports that not all *Presidentes* are mediums. Although I did not observe any *centros* of this type, my informants also reported this possibility, in which case one of the *mediunidad* acts as head medium. The *Presidente* in such cults acts only as interrogator of spirits but is nevertheless believed to have very strong spiritual protection.

communication with spirits—that is, to see that a medium who is in touch with the spirit world returns to normal behavior. Unlike these assistants, who are full-fledged mediums, mediums-in-training are people adjudged to have mediumistic gifts but who are still developing them under the tutelage of the head medium and *mediunidad*. The remaining social status, that of "visitor" or client, includes all people who have come to a spiritist meeting for spiritual help but who are not in process of becoming mediums.

Since the above statuses derive from basic premises concerning relations among disincarnate and incarnate spirits, they pertain to all spiritist gatherings—from the formal rites of spiritist *centros* to the informal séances a medium may hold at home with the assistance of a few friends. In *centros,* however, with their special quarters and regularly scheduled meetings, there is an additional status, that of "member." Members pay dues to the *centro,* and *centros* in New York, like voluntary associations among urban migrants the world over (Abu-Lughod, 1961; Doughty, 1970; Freedman, 1961; Little 1965; Mangin, 1965), provide their members with important economic, social, and psychological benefits. Some *centros,* for example, use a portion of their income from dues to help members over financial crises. In addition, preparations for the twice-weekly meetings of the cult, numerous calendrical celebrations, intermittent crisis rituals (often held in the apartments of members), and picnics provide frequent occasions for members to socialize outside the family. For many members, the *centro* becomes the focus of social activity in their lives.

An important additional member of the role-set of many mediums and *centro* clients is the herbalist. As part of therapy, mediums usually prescribe herbs, oils, candles, perfumes, and various other paraphernalia for clients, which are obtainable only at herb shops (*botánicas*). A medium may therefore arrange to refer clients to a particular shop, in return for which the owner recommends the medium to his other customers and/or extends the medium credit on the purchase of necessities for the *centro*. Some herbalists also have a medium (often a friend or relative) in their shop who diagnoses and prescribes remedies which are then purchased on the spot. In such cases the profits may be shared by herbalist and medium, although in the case of mutual referral cash rarely changes hands between them. [It must be pointed out that although *botánicas* sell products essential to spiritist ritual and often have an affiliation with a spiritist, they also purvey herbs used in a tradition of folk medicine which functions independently of spiritism (Harwood, 1971a). Thus, the clientele of herbalists may include nonspiritists as well as spiritists.]

THE ROLE OF HEAD MEDIUM IN THE SOCIAL PROCESS OF SPIRITIST CULTS

In all secular as well as ritual activities of formally organized spiritist groups, the head medium assumes a dominant role. He or she controls *centro* funds and organizes all its activities. The head medium is also the primary source of command within the group as well as the focus for incoming messages from assistants and clients.

Because of the pivotal position of the head medium in the *centro,* the persistence of the group depends heavily on the members' continuing allegiance to the head. This allegiance is difficult to maintain, however, and a characteristic feature of spiritist churches is their cyclical growth and decline. Part of the reason for this cylical pattern lies in the ideology of spiritism itself. As Koss (1964) has noted, a member of the *mediunidad* who becomes a successful medium may begin to challenge the authority of the head and ultimately deplete the *centro* by luring adherents away to form a *centro* of his or her own. Dissatisfaction with a head medium's leadership in secular matters may also lead to a *centro*'s decline. In one such case that I witnessed, the defectors disagreed with the Chief's way of managing the secular affairs of the *centro,* although they justified their defection on spiritual grounds, by claiming that the leader's mediumistic performances were counterfeit.

This process of adherence and subsequent defection of assistant mediums and followers brings into focus another important element in the sociology of spiritist groups—the antagonism that may exist between them at certain stages of development. When defectors leave a *centro* to form a new one under the direction of a former assistant medium, or when the defectors join an ongoing *centro* that is known to members of the original group, the head mediums of the two *centros* often become involved in mutual accusations of sorcery. At this stage in the developmental cycle of these groups, the afflictions and problems of members (particularly of the defectors) are typically attributed to sorcery on the part of the head medium of the opposing group. Relations between the two groups become conceptualized in terms of a contest between the two chief mediums, both of whom are seen as summoning all their spiritual powers to protect their followers from the antagonist's sorcery. In some *centros* this confiict seems to decline as the group builds in numbers and develops its own internal structure. In other *centros,* however, the conflict persists. Further research into the determinants of the cycle of centro growth and decline would undoubtedly shed valuable light on the relationship between group dynamics and psychotherapeutics in these cults.

THE REUNIÓN, A MAJOR SPIRITIST RITUAL

Usually twice a week each *centro* convenes a meeting (*reunión*), which is the most important and frequent public ritual of the subculture. (Other terms for this ritual are *sesión,* "session," or *velada,* "vigil.") By the term "ritual" I mean, following Turner, a "stereotyped sequence of activities involving gestures, words, and objects . . . designed to influence preternatural entities or forces on behalf of the actors' goals and interests" (1973:1100; also Turner, 1964:20ff.). According to this definition, ritual encompasses the sterotyped activities undertaken cooperatively by a set of actors who attach shared meanings to these activities; it does not include the private obsessions of individual neurotics. As Freud told us long ago, there are many important parallels between these two kinds of activity; but in using the term "ritual" to describe the spiritist session, I decidedly do not wish to imply a neurotic obsession as its source. (Readers who subscribe to the assumption that the concept "neurotic" is applicable to whole cultures or subcultures may judge the ritual on these grounds for themselves. I find the assumption neither warranted nor fruitful. Compare Fromm, 1967:105ff., on this same distinction.)

The utility of Turner's definition for the following analysis is to focus attention on the two most clearly observable characteristics of the ritual: (1) the "stereotyped sequence of activities"—that is, the patterned and therefore predictable series of events which occurs at all sessions; and (2) the activities themselves—the "gestures, words, and objects" which comprise the ritual.

DESCRIPTION OF A SANTERO MEETING

The following account of a *santero* meeting is part of a more complete description from my field notes. At the time of this observation the *santero* group was in a phase of expansion and had become fairly well known in the vicinity in which the study occured. The *centro* was located in the basement of a building on a main shopping street. The only evidence of its existence to passersby was a small sign indicating the name of the group, *Iglesia de Elegua,* and the hours that the head medium was available for private consultation.

I was introduced to the *centro* by a Puerto Rican co-worker at the Health Center who lived in the area. At the time of the following observation, I had twice consulted the head medium privately and had attended one other session of the group. I had also consulted two other mediums and was familiar with sessions at their *centros.* On the basis of this prior experience and subsequent attendance at other spiritist meetings, I consider the following description, apart from the few exceptions noted, typical of *santero* gatherings.[3]

The meeting falls into five segments, which are indicated by number in the account. As noted, some of the segments are identified and named by the celebrants; others are unnamed but recur consistently at all meetings. The five segments are: (1) the *invocación* or summoning of good spirits to the meeting through prayer, a portion of the *santero* rite similar to Mesa Blanca practice; (2) the *despojo* or removal of evil spiritual influences from the congregation; (3) preparations for attracting good spirits; (4) *buscando la causa* or spiritual diagnosis (literally "searching for the cause"); and (5) *trabajando la causa* ("working the cause") or spiritist treatment. In a typical session stages 4 and 5 may be repeated a number of times with different clients, although I have omitted these recurrences in the account. Most meetings also end with another exorcism *(despojo)* of the entire group to prevent anyone from leaving the premises under the influence of a misguided spirit. Meetings in nominally Mesa Blanca *centros* usually also contain the above segments, although the activities comprising each segment may differ.

The meeting was held in the largest room of the *centro's* basement quarters. About 30 folding chairs were set up around the room—some toward the front, facing the center, and those toward the rear, facing the altar, which was located against the wall opposite the entrance from the street. Statues of several saints (La Mercedes, Regla, La Caridad del Cobre, Sta. Bárbara, San Antonio, and San Martín), several pitchers and goblets of water, and vases of flowers were placed on the altar. On the walls were drawings of several other saints with candles burning beside them. On the floor by the entrance were a bowl of ice and several vases of greenery.

When I arrived, the head medium, several assistant mediums, and a few congregants were already present. Several young boys were talking quietly among themselves, and the medium busied herself with preparations for the coming event. After turning on the phonograph and lighting up a cigar, she began greeting new arrivals. While doing so, she reminded people of a novena the group was having for a sick member and of a meeting of members the following Sunday. The congregants discussed the condition of the sick member and expressed concern at the head medium's report of a recent decline in his condition.

A discussion between the head medium and one of the members gradually captured the attention of everyone present. The substance of the discussion was the

[3] For a detailed description from Puerto Rico of a meeting in the Mesa Blanca tradition, see Seda, 1973:119–131.

relative cost of the various pictures and statues in the room and whether they were owned by the medium herself. She said that all the paraphernalia was hers and that the pictures cost $2 to $4. There followed an exchange of information about shops where ritual objects could be purchased most cheaply. All stores mentioned were in the Barrio (Spanish Harlem). The medium then pointed to a new statue of St. Martin and fondled it reverently, exclaiming "*¡Qué precioso!*" She volunteered that she had paid $15 for it.

The subject of moving the *centro* to larger quarters also came up at this time. The medium claimed that bigger places cost about $100 a month. She now pays $50, she said, and "only because I fought for that." She thought that it was not worth all that extra money for a larger place, since the quality would not be much better.

During these discussions people began lighting cigars. As newcomers arrived and found seats, many began taking off or putting on clothing. The clothing was special to the occasion, and each individual wore the color associated with his or her guardian. The medium was wearing a cloak of coarse brown cotton with a deep-hooded collar—the vestments (*vestuario*) of Elegua, patron of the *centro*. Around her head were a brown and a purple scarf knotted together. Prior to the opening of the session, everyone removed his or her shoes.

When the flow of newcomers had subsided, the head medium signaled for the door to be locked. By that time the congregation numbered 23—16 adults (9 female, 7 male), 6 teenagers (2 female, 4 male), and 1 female child. The nine mediums occupied the chairs in front facing the center of the room. Ana, the head medium, began by announcing several coming events: the fiesta of St. Martin to be held on November 4, a members' meeting, and the fiesta of St. Barbara on December 5.

1. The session opened with a recitation of the Lord's Prayer by the entire assemblage. One of the assistant mediums then read an invocation to good spirits, after which the congregation recited a Hail Mary. This sequence of recitations by a reader, followed by the congregation in unison, continued through several additional prayers. A basket was then passed, in which about $10 was collected (including eight $1 bills). After this, the celebrants rose with arms aloft to recite another invocation to the spirits, led this time by Ana. When this was over, Ana clapped her hands, and the lights went out.

2. In the center of the floor in front of the altar was a pail of flaming alcohol or lighter fluid. The head medium, puffing on her cigar, stepped over the pail four times: back and forth in one direction, then back and forth in the direction perpendicular to the first, thereby completing a cross. She then knelt beside the pot and began moving her arms back and forth between her face and the fire, as though wafting in some essence from the pot. Gradually her movements became more and more frenzied, and she began breathing deeply. She then arose and called others to repeat what she had done. As each congregant approached, Ana fumigated them with the smoke from her cigar and guided

them in stepping over the flaming pot the required four times. She then sat them before the pot to make passes as she had done. Some made cursory gestures and appeared unaffected by the whole procedure, while others shook violently and fell back rigid after waving their arms over the fire. Among the latter a few recovered almost immediately and walked back to their chairs; others had to be assisted and apparently remained dazed for a few seconds.

3. After everyone had gone through this procedure, the medium took a glass of cold black coffee mixed with rum, made a prayerful obeisance in front of the altar, and then took a drink. The glass was then passed for everyone to take a sip. The medium then circulated through the congregation with a bottle of cologne, *agua florida*, stopping to pour a little into each person's outstretched hands. The congregants rubbed the cologne on their hair and the backs of their necks. Meanwhile, a record (*Santeros Auténticos*) of songs for Elegua, Changó, Yemayá, and other saints/*orichas* was played.

4. As the music continued, people began clapping, and certain participants assumed an attitude of concentration with head in hand or performed characteristic gestures. (The man next to me, for example, would periodically take several deep gasps and then put his hands together in an attitude of prayer near the side of his head. After maintaining this posture for some seconds, he then snapped his fingers and assumed his normal sitting position.) When the music stopped, three of those who had been concentrating began relating messages which they had received from spirits—statements about the family life or habits of someone in the assemblage or about a spirit hovering beside a member of the audience. Each person to whom remarks were directed responded "yes" or "no" to each statement, indicating whether he considered what was said as true or false. Ana, and later several other mediums, noted the presence of a "misdirected" spirit hovering around Jorge, one of the *mediunidad*. After all who had received spiritual communications had spoken, the process of concentration, followed by revelation of messages, continued several more times.

5. During one revelation Ana suddenly began fanning motions with her arms at the sides of her head (spirit-inducing movements) and fell to the floor. One of the other mediums passed her a pitcher of water. Ana placed both hands over the mouth of the pitcher and revealed that she was possessed by her protective spirit who was going to retrieve a "job" (*trabajo*) sent against Jorge, the assistant medium. A woman, the spirit explained, had taken seven pieces of ice, a kerchief with seven knots in it, and seven bones from a cemetery. With these she had gotten a spirit to begin harming Jorge. Several times during her possession the medium moaned, breathed heavily, pounded her hand on the pitcher of water, and fell back motionless on the floor. When this would happen, one of the other mediums adjured the other participants to say the Lord's Prayer. Sometimes the medium herself (that is, the spirit) would call for help before falling mute and inert. If at the conclusion of the prayer the medium still did not speak, the prayer might be repeated or the group would sit in utter silence until she spoke again. On arising, Ana would wretch, reach

for her pitcher, and talk again. During the course of the possession the "spirit" produced all the objects which it had said were used in the "job" against Jorge.

When the possessing spirit, who was Ana's protector, had completed his mission, the medium arose (still possessed) and called several people up to her seriatim. She fumigated each one with cigar smoke and whispered messages to a few of them. Then, taking hold of each person's hands, drew the person toward her, pulled his or her arms out to the side, raised them, and snapped them down. After this the person began spirit-inducing movements, as described above. Some, but not all, became possessed.

Next followed the removal of evil spiritual influences from Jorge (the *despojo*). The head medium had him kneel in front of her and placed a wreath of rhododendron around his head, rubbing the branch into his forehead. She then took a coconut and encircled his head with it three times. At her command two assistant mediums then removed the statue of St. Martin from the altar and passed it up Jorge's back and over his head. The medium blew cigar smoke at him as he began to shake. The two went through the arm motions mentioned above, after which they stood back to back, arms linked. The medium then picked Jorge up and carried him laid out flat on her back.

Later in the session another cause was found and "worked." A few other people were told of problems and told to return to the next meeting for work. To close, the medium requested everyone to stand for a final prayer, after which the lights were turned on.[4]

RITUAL PARAPHERNALIA

Before discussing the sequence of events at the session, it is important to understand the significance of some of the ritual objects found in the *centro* as well as the paraphernalia used by the congregants throughout the session.

Preliminary Cleansing of the Premises

In an interview with one of the assistant mediums, I learned that during the afternoon before the meeting the *centro*'s quarters had undergone a "spiritual cleaning" (*una limpieza espiritual*). This procedure is used to prepare any premises where a session is to be held. It is also routine procedure in spiritists' houses on Tuesdays and Fridays, days of the week when malevolent influences are thought to be strongest.

A spiritual cleaning usually consists of two activities: fumigation

[4] This description was composed the day following the session on the basis of notes taken at the *centro* and at home immediately following the meeting.

(*sahumerio* or *desahumerio*) and washing (*riego*). Although various substances may be used in both these activities, in this particular case the fumigant was concocted of charcoal and crushed garlic, while the washing agents were holy water and the all-purpose cologne *agua florida.* The ingredients used betoken the dual purpose of the rite: the fumigation with noisome substances is designed to drive off evil influences; the lavation with salubrious agents is to attract benevolent spirits. Besides the spiritual cleaning, the medium and her assistant performed a service (*servicio*—prayers and appropriate offering) to Elegua, a preliminary designed to invoke his help in protecting the doorway from intranquil spirits.

Statues and Pictures of Saints

Every spiritist *centro* as well as the houses of all practicing spiritists contain an altar with basically the same range of objects as the one described in the *centro* above. In *santero centros* the statues represent the saints who are the protectors of the *mediunidad.* Similarly on home altars, the statues of the protectors of each family member figure prominently. In addition to statues of saints, most altars contain effigies of important spirit guides who act as intermediaries with higher-ranking spirits (for example, Congos, an Indian chief, and John and Robert Kennedy). Before placement on the altar, a statue is usually blessed by a medium while under possession by the saint represented.

Water

Water (either blessed, unblessed, or in the form of ice) is an important item in spiritist ritual. Its main function is to trap and hold malicious spirits. For this reason it is kept not only on altars but also near doorways to entrap spirits who try to enter by the door (witness the ice in the above account) and under beds to ensnare misguided spirits who might harm a sleeper during that particularly vulnerable period of dreaming, while the sleeper's spirit roams elsewhere. Water also functions during séances as a receptacle for the evil spirits and influences that mediums remove from clients.

Candles

Spiritists light candles principally for three purposes: to help dispell an intranquil spirit from the house, as part of a rite of sorcery, and in connection with a request to a saint for help. In each case lighting the candle must be accompanied by appropriate prayers and occasionally by additional activities which, in the case of the first two uses, must be learned from a medium. For petitioning a saint, however, lay believers can purchase both the candle (which must be the color associated with the saint) and the appropriate prayer at herb shops without special instruction from mediums.

Flowers

Flowers may be used in conjunction with or as substitutes for candles in petitions to saints and other spirits, although to my knowledge they are never used in sorcery rites. As with the candles dedicated to a saint, flowers must also be the color associated with the saint being addressed.

In recommending private rituals to their clients, some mediums express a preference for candles or flowers. The preference is personal and not associated with any generally accepted beliefs about the relative efficacy of the two. One medium, for example, preferred flowers because she considered them a bigger sacrifice than candles. They not only cost more but often require the petitioner to search from florist to florist for the correct variety of flower in the proper hue. The fact that flowers are a "creation of God" also gave them added appeal over candles in her judgment.

Herbs

Herbs are an important element in Puerto Rican folk medicine (Harwood, 1971a; Padilla, 1958) and are used by spiritists and nonspiritists alike for curative purposes. Certain herbs, have, in addition to their medicinal uses, particular functions in spiritist rites. The vases of greenery described as being beside the door in my account contained *pasote* (*chenopodium ambrosioides*), an herb used as a cathartic in folk medicine but used in spiritism as a sort of broom for cleansing a room of malicious influences in "spiritual cleanups." For the most part, however, herbs do not play a major role in spiritist ritual and function mainly within a separate tradition of folk medicine.

Agua Florida *and Other Essences*

Agua florida is one of many colognes and essences used in spiritism to attract favorable spirits. Unlike many essences, which are specifics, *agua florida* is an all-purpose agent. It is applied either to the forehead or, as in the instance above, to the back of the head *(cerebro)*, where spirits are believed to enter.

Essences used in spiritism bear names betokening their various purposes, like *Aceite Dominante* (Dominating Oil) or *Yo Puedo y Tú No* (I Can and You Can't). They are usually purchased by clients at the behest of a medium who then "prepares" them for use in a private ritual, typically designed to increase the client's control over someone.

Cigars

Cigar smoke is believed to repel malicious spirits, and is used specifically in exorcism rites (*despojos*), which are part of every spiritist meeting. (See 2 in the account above.) In Mesa Blanca groups usually only the mediums who actually perform the *despojo* smoke, but in Santería many members of the congregation also light cigars to deflect evil spirits. This practice, coupled with the custom of closing all windows and doors during a meeting to bar the entry of evil spirits, means that in time the air in a *santero centro* becomes dense and oxygen-deficient, conditions which favor trance.

Clothing

During *santero* meetings the protégés of each saint dress in some article of clothing in their protector's color. The clothing may range from a scarf, usually blessed by the saint at a previous session and put around the neck or forehead after arrival at the *centro*, to the complete vestments of the saint. The latter, however, are usually bestowed only on mediums as part of a ceremony to celebrate their attainment of a certain level of expertise in mediumship. In the meeting described above, the head medium appeared in the vestments of Elegua. Candelo, on the other hand, would wear a red cape and Cardinal's hat. A nonmedium may simply wear an important item of personal clothing (a dress or shirt) in his or her protector's color. The distinctive clothing serves both the social function of indicating to others the identity of the wearer's protection and the ritual function of attracting that protection during the séance.

Besides wearing specially colored clothing to *centro* meetings, some women may for a period of time wear an outfit known as an *hábito*. The *hábito* consists of a modest dress in the color associated with a saint and, more noticeably, a sash (*cordón*) decorated with pompons, also in the saint's color. This ensemble is worn as a result of a promise *(promesa)* to the saint by the wearer. The *promesa*, a pervasive feature of Latin culture, is a contract in which the promiser vows to perform certain acts in the saint's honor if the saint responds to his or her petition for help. These petitions, which may be made on behalf of oneself or a loved one, usually involve recovery from an illness or success in a particular undertaking (getting a job or becoming pregnant, for example). Besides wearing the *hábito,* the contractor may offer to recite a certain number of prayers to the saint, to light candles, or to perform any of the other acts designed to "give a spirit light." Among Roman Catholics, who also make *promesas,* the priesthood has tended to discourage wearing *hábitos,* so that contracts usually entail only the latter activities or a promise to attend mass daily for a specified period.

Like many believers in spirits the world over, spiritists usually carry or wear some objects to ensure their protector's watchfulness over them. The object may be a medallion or a small replica of something associated with the protector. Usually blessed or prepared by a medium, the object, once prepared, is known as a *resguardo* or *prenda defensiva.* The physical object, however, can never substitute for the assurance of one's guardians' protection, which one can acquire only through prayer and services for the guardian.

Shoes are removed during séances because they are believed to break the flow of *fluido* through the body. That is, spiritual influences are believed to enter the back of the head and emerge from the body through the feet. In relation to this belief, I have witnessed exorcisms in which the client was instructed to stand on the rim of a bowl filled with water while the medium stroked his legs downward in an effort to pass the *fluido* of the invading spirit out of the client's feet and into the water below.

SEGMENTS OF THE SESSION

1. Invocation of Good Spirits

This segment of the session is much like an orthodox Christian service in form and feeling. In addition to the reader-respondent pattern of worship, specific prayers from the Roman Catholic liturgy (the Lord's Prayer and the Hail Mary) and the institution of the collection have found their way into the ritual. The litany for invoking good spirits derives from a collection of spiritist prayers published in Mexico and attributed to Kardec (the *Colecto,* mentioned earlier).

2. Removal of Evil Influence from the Congregation

The tone of this and the following segments of the session contrasts markedly with the preceding one, as exuberant clapping and singing replace the reserve of the invocation.

In this phase fire is the major ritual object, although the flaming pail in the service described above was a particularly dramatic adjunct that I never saw used elsewhere. In fact, fire is not considered the operative element in the removal of evil influences, but is important for the vapor and heat it gives off. Thus cigar smoke is usually sufficient for the purpose, along with the passes (*los pases*) the medium makes over the client's body and the arm motions the client performs (the action I have labeled "spirit-inducing movements"). The latter motions, in which both arms appear to be fanning the air behind the neck, introduce beneficient spirits as well as drive off malicious spiritual influences. The movements are often a prelude to possession and may also be used in the exorcism of individual clients after their "cause" has been worked. (See 5 in the text, for example.)

3. Attracting Protectors and Other Beneficient Spirits

The third part of the session constitutes a peculiarly *santero* mode of invoking spirits, which contrasts with the prayerful and pensive invocation more characteristic of Mesa Blanca or of the opening segment of the meeting. Three activities carried out during this segment function to attract beneficient spirits: a service (*servicio*) for the patron of the *centro*, application of *agua florida* to all those present, and the playing and singing of songs dedicated to each of the major saints. The first and third of these activities are distinctively *santero*; *agua florida* and its functions, already discussed above, are part of Mesa Blanca ritual as well.

The service for the patron of the *centro* is one of a set of services for each major saint which is used in eliciting his or her help. The rite for Elegua consists in blessing and drinking the mixture of black coffee and rum, Elegua's special beverage. At other *centros* the corresponding service for the head medium's protector would be performed. By sharing in the service, the entire congregation comes under the protection of the saint/*oricha* for the period of the session and, by singing the various saints' songs, helps the mediums invoke their protective spirits.

4. Spiritual Diagnosis (Buscando la Causa)

After malevolent influences have been dispelled from the congregation and the *mediunidad's* protection summoned to the scene, mediums are ready to receive messages from spirits. Among Puerto Rican spiritists four methods of spirit communication are commonly used, and mediums generally specialize in one of these methods. The methods are also appropriate to different occasions and are ranked in terms of the mediumistic powers considered necessary to execute them.

The method that implies least power and is therefore often disparaged by heads of *centros* is cartomancy. I have never seen this method used in a *centro,* but it is often practiced by women who claim spiritistic powers and "throw the cards" for friends and neighbors in their apartments. These women (I have never heard of a man who practiced cartomancy) claim that their spirit guides enable them to read the cards by providing interpretations for the lay of the cards. Another method of contacting spirits, one which is frequently used in Mesa Blanca, is spirit writing. While possessed, the medium makes marks on a sheet of paper and later interprets the marks, which are conceived as a message from the possessing spirit. (For an example of the use of spirit writing, see the consultation on p. 79.) A method of spirit communication often used in private consultations involves concentrating on a vessel containing holy water in order to apperceive the spirits or *fluido* contained or reflected therein.

By far the most authoritative method of spirit communication, however, is possession. In this case a spirit, usually one of the medium's guides, speaks directly about the client's situation. As my account indicates, each medium tends to have a characteristic mannerism that indicates to the observer that he or she is in communication with spirits. Since mediums do not choose to diagnose by direct possession unless at least one other medium is present to offer "protection," this method is rarely used in private consultation. (Note the example in the following chapter, in which the divining medium calls in an assistant before undergoing deep trance.) After communing with spirits, the mediums state their observations, which are then subject to confirmation or denial by the individuals to whom they are directed. Other mediums may also enter into this colloquy by reinterpreting or amplifying another's insights. The goal of these joint efforts is to identify the spiritual cause (*causa*) of the client's problem.

In the *centros* with which I am familiar, it is usual for at least one member of every group of people which has arrived together at a session to be mentioned in a spiritual revelation during a session. Although many members of the congregation may therefore be addressed in this phase of the session, only a few will have their problems treated (literally "worked," *trabajado*) in the subsequent phase. Those treated will almost invariably be people who have attended several previous sessions of the *centro* and become known to the *mediunidad.* Many other participants will be told to come again for "work" or to perform a specific rite at home and then return. The following instructions to a new client are typical.

After a series of diagnostic statements from various mediums and responses from the client, the dialogue began focusing on the client's marriage. Finally the head medium summed up the problem and gave instructions, as follows:

Head Medium. You have a spirit-wife from another existence. She is clinging to you and won't let you live in peace with your wife. We must help you get rid of this spirit. You must come to our session this Saturday, but first you must do what I tell you. Buy a white candle that comes out of the glass and put a piece of paper with your wife's first and last names on it under the candle. Are you a Catholic?

Client. Yes.

Head Medium. Then you believe in the saints. You know you shouldn't be here; it is a sin. (Laughs.) I am a Catholic, too. You must also buy a charm (*ensalmo*) of St. Michael. You will also get some things so I can prepare the candle for you: Dominating Oil (*Aceite Dominante*), Tranquil Oil (*Aceite Tránquilo*), and liquid asafoetida. Then get asafoetida "in stone form" and burn it in your apartment in all the corners. Then wash down your house with *pasote, anumú,* and *yerba buena* (all herbs). Do that before you come on Saturday.[5]

The procedure outlined by the medium is designed to rid the client's apartment of any trace of the clinging spirit-wife in preparation for his return after the spirit has been "worked" (dispelled). Such private procedures are common preliminaries to the public treatment of a spiritual problem at a *centro*.

5. Spiritist Treatment: Working the Cause

After the mediums have analyzed a client's situation and diagnosed its spiritual cause, they may "work" the offending spirit. One medium may

[5] This excerpt is my translation of part of a consultation between a medium and an Hispano friend which the latter tape-recorded for me.

became possessed by the spirit so that the others can enlighten it about its wrongdoing and convince it to leave the victim in peace. Since Jorge's "cause" in the séance under discussion was due to sorcery, the medium's treatment consisted of sending her own *predilecto* (favorite guide) to retrieve the "job" (*trabajo*) that had been directed against him. After thus ridding Jorge's life of this impediment, she then performed a *despojo* to remove any residual evil influences from him. When the object of a *despojo* is an individual rather than a series of people as in the general exorcism discussed above, articles relating to the individual's own spiritual protection are used in the procedure. In this instance the medium used the statue of St. Martin, Jorge's principal protector, and rhododendron branches.[6] Only the coconut in this rite is an item in general use for removing malevolent spiritual influences in Santería.

The activities that occurred between the retrieval of the fetish that had been prepared against Jorge and his exorcism require some explanatory comment. In summoning a number of people from the congregation for exorcism, the medium, still possessed, was selecting those who shared her protector. The chosen few were thus being greeted and given special messages from the protector by the medium's *predilecto,* his emissary. This is a common procedure in Santería whenever a medium becomes possessed by a saint or one of his or her important messengers.

ADDITIONAL OBSERVATIONS AND COMMENTS

Attendance at Centro *Meetings*

Participants at *centro* meetings fall into two categories: those who regularly take part in spiritist activities as *centro* members or mediums (full-fledged or in training), and those who turn to the formal spiritist organization only at crisis periods in their lives. The second category may attend a number of sessions over several weeks and also consult the head medium privately during that time, then stop coming. From my observation between 20% and 40% of the people who attend any particular meeting of a *centro* fall into this category.

With regard to the age and sex of people who attend spiritist meetings, figures from 18 sessions at three different *centros* indicate that women above the age of 40 are overrepresented in proportion to their numbers in the general Puerto Rican population of the study area and the borough. Women also outnumbered men at 16 of the 18 meetings. Who.

[6] Since the use of rhododendron in this *despojo* is unique in my experience, I assume that it, too, must have had a specific connection with Jorge, although I unfortunately did not inquire into the matter.

The remaining 2 sessions had an equal number of adults of each sex, but the ratio of women to men was generally 3 or 4 to 1, with a high of 5 to 1 at one meeting. Children do not usually attend regular *centro* meetings, unless they are thought to require spiritual treatment. They may be present in considerable numbers at special celebrations for particular saints, however. The proportion of teenagers attending meetings seemed to vary considerably from *centro* to *centro*. For example, teenage attendance in one group was almost 20% at each of six meetings, while another *centro* averaged only 7% for the same number of meetings.

Another way of approaching the question of who visits spiritists is by specifying those times in the life cycle when people are most likely to seek spiritual help. Although a few infants receive baptism by spiritist rite, the earliest a child is usually brought for spiritist consultation is if he or she experiences nightmares and difficulty sleeping, typically betweeen the ages of 3 and 8. Pubertal girls are also frequently taken to spiritists. The next age group that frequently consults spiritists is young married couples, usually at the instigation of the wife. If the husband refuses to attend spiritist sessions, the wife may come alone at this stage. Menopausal women and the terminally ill constitute two remaining categories that tend to seek spiritist help.[7] In short, a common characteristic of times in the life cycle when spiritists are consulted is transition and social readjustment, an observation to which we return in Chapter 7.

The Role of Head Medium

In addition to describing the head medium's role in the ritual itself, the above account provides information on the medium's role in other contexts. As organizer of the *centro*, he or she negotiates contracts for the group (here, the lease on the premises) and sees that the quarters are furnished. The latter task may involve soliciting gifts, including ritual objects, from members. (Although I did not know it at the time, this medium's claim to ownership of all the *centro's* ritual objects was a source of vexation to some of the donors, who used this issue later as a justification for leaving the group. The issues at stake, whether the donated articles were *centro* property or the leader's personal property,

[7] Our data confirm those of Garrison (1972:282; 1973:22–23), who observed a bimodal distribution in the ages of both males and females who attended a single *centro* during one week. The highest frequencies were in the early 20s and the 40 to 49 age group—times when marital adjustment and menopause constitute significant problems.

highlights the inherent ambiguity in all cults in differentiating the leader's activities as a person from his or her role as head of the organization.)

Besides the head medium's business role, the pre-session conversations further illustrate the medium's pivotal position within the *centro* as recipient and source of messages. By announcing future *centro* events not only publicly at the start of the session but also privately in greeting members, the medium learned who would be coming and could better coordinate the activity. She also served as a source of information about the prices of spiritist articles and the health of the absent member.

Beyond these activities, the medium was also demonstrably a source of standards for the group by informing them of fair prices for ritual objects and exemplifying the importance of "fighting" with landlords to get what you want. This aspect of the Chief's role is particularly important in helping socialize recent immigrants to the ways of New York, and heads of *centros* in my experience have all been people who have lived in the city at least 10 years.

Centro *Economics*

The above account provides, in addition, a few hints about the economics of running a *centro*. Besides the income from collections at biweekly meetings (which, according to my observations, ranged from $16 to $20 in cash per week), members also paid monthly dues at $2. (An additional source of revenue for the particular *centro* described above was a lottery which often preceded the séance, although this practice was not followed at other *centros* I attended.)

Since this *centro* had approximately 15 regular members, the collections plus dues easily covered the monthly rent of $50. Furthermore, most of the expendables used in the rituals (flowers, *agua florida,* candles, and food) were either donated by members or procured through "professional courtesy" from a local herbalist. The balance from revenues, after rent, utilities, and other overhead expenses were paid, was used either for a slush fund to help members in need or for the medium's personal use.

In all cases I observed, donations received for private consultations (usually $2 to $3 a consultation) belonged to the medium personally, as did fees for performing sorcery, which may run to several hundred dollars. Although I do not have figures from mediums on their incomes from spiritist activities, my impression is that their gains are not sufficient to live on, since the six head mediums of *centros* whom I knew well all either held a regular job or had some other source of income (a working spouse or welfare). The earnings from heading a *centro* can serve the medium as an important financial supplement, however, so that he or she is (in the words of one woman who ran a *centro*) "never up tight for money." This fact does not of course imply that mediums are necessarily motivated to head *centros* for financial gain, just as an accounting of a physician's earnings could not be taken as evidence of his "being in it just for the money."

SUMMARY

This chapter and the preceding one provide an outline of the spiritist subculture, introducing spiritist cosmology, the social structure of formal spiritist groups, the essential features of the major spiritist ritual (the *reunión*), and the functions and symbolism of certain important ritual paraphernalia. This information serves as a background to the exploration of spiritist therapeutics that follows in the next two chapters. It is only against this background of the premises and standards of the spiritist subculture that the logic of its therapeutic system can be understood.

FOUR

Diagnosis and Treatment in Spiritist Psychotherapy

The psychiatrist Jerome Frank (1961:2-3) considers three features as characteristic of all psychotherapies: (1) "a trained, socially sanctioned healer, whose healing powers are accepted by the sufferer" and by at least a segment of the sufferer's group; (2) a "sufferer"; and (3) "a circumscribed, more or less structured series of contacts between the healer and sufferer through which the healer, often with the aid of a group, tries to produce certain changes in the sufferer's emotional state, attitudes, and behavior." Frank notes that although both physical measures and chemical agents may play a role in the kind of therapy he is describing, the healing influence in psychotherapy derives primarily from the words, acts, and rituals performed by the sufferer, healer, and group (if present).

Frank's description of the elements of psychotherapy applies to an important set of activities that occur in spiritist cults. To repeat an important point, this set is only a part of the entire concern of these groups. It is this part, however, which will dominate our attention in this section of the book. This chapter examines the diagnostic and therapeutic procedures of spiritist psychotherapy. The next chapter focuses on the effects of treatment by examining in detail the case of a hospitalized mental patient and her referral to a medium for treatment.

In describing the diagnostic and therapeutic procedures of spiritist psychotherapy, we first examine the kinds of "sufferers" who seek this mode of therapy and the occasions on which they do so. Next, we discuss the process by which spiritist healers diagnose problems that are brought to them and consider in some detail the range of causes that spiritist etiology permits them to assign to these problems. This leads to an examination of the treatment procedures used in spiritist therapy. The entire exposition presents the diagnostic and treatment alternatives available within the spiritist therapeutic system according to believers unsophisticated in Kardecist philosophy.

TURNING TO THE SPIRITIST FOR HELP

Since spiritism views man as composed of spirit and matter, problems may be attributed to a malfunction in one or both of these aspects. For malfunctions of the material component spiritists consider medical facilities (physicians, hospitals, pharmacies) as the proper source of treatment; for spiritual problems, however, the medium is the treatment of choice. Thus, although spiritist doctrine does not prevent believers from seeking medical help, the criteria that a spiritist uses to determine whether a problem is best treated materially or spiritually do not necessarily correspond with the criteria a person with medical training might use to decide whether a problem is best treated medically or psychiatrically. It is therefore important to consider some of the criteria spiritists use in defining the nature of a problem, an effort that necessarily directs our attention to symptoms and their evaluation.

SYMPTOMS, SPIRITUAL AND PHYSICAL

In spiritist belief certain symptoms are attributed exclusively to spiritual causes and are therefore referred to spiritists for treatment as a matter of course. Insomnia, suicidal urges, repeated nightmares (particularly if they involve deceased friends or relatives), unaccountable crying or silent brooding, and fugue states are all symptoms that imply spiritual causation.

Seizures may also fall into this category although additional discussion of this symptom is necessary in view of its special status in Puerto Rican culture. Because many Puerto Ricans, particularly women, exhibit seizures (*ataques*) at certain culturally approved and expected times and places, this phenomenon has received special attention in the medical literature, where it has been designated "the Puerto Rican syndrome" (Berle, 1958:158; Fernández-Marina, 1961; Mehlman, 1961; Rothenberg, 1964). Culturally appropriate times and places for seizures include occasions when a show of grief is called for (such as funerals) or when one has either witnessed or received news of a shocking event, particularly one affecting a loved one (Padilla, 1958:115). While not necessarily approved, seizures are also expected from some women when they do not get their own way. Seizures of these kinds, which occur under culturally predictable circumstances, are not referred to a spiritist for treatment. However, those which occur precipitously and repeatedly are likely to be referred to a medium, although the emergency nature of the symptom may influence the victim's friends or relatives to take him or her first to a hospital and thus bring the victim under medical treatment as well.

Although it is easy to enumerate symptoms that are believed to have a spiritual etiology only, those believed to be materially caused are somewhat harder to specify. This is because spiritists tend to assume that spiritual well-being is conducive to good physical health and may therefore interpret physical distress as a sign of spiritual problems. In spite of this tendency to seek spiritual causes for what would generally be considered physical ailments, spiritists almost invariably turn to medical practitioners as the first source of care for such ailments. If the condition is treated medically to the satisfaction of the sufferer, then the cause is generally conceded to have been material. This fact accounts for the difficulty in enumerating strictly materially-caused symptoms, since the criterion for considering them in this light is whether the sufferer has experienced relief and/or satisfaction through medical treatment. If medical treatment has not proven satisfactory or if the illness has been diagnosed as either chronic or terminal, the sufferer is likely to begin thinking in terms of either spiritual or dual causation.

The following account from a *centro* meeting illustrates an instance in which a client's condition is labeled as having both spiritual and material causes. The client was on old woman, the mother of one of the mediums of the *centro,* who had been experiencing fatigue and pains in her legs for some time. She feared that her condition was cancer and had not yet consulted a physician. The incident took place at a regular meeting of a *centro,* as described by one of the community researchers.

> Then B's mother got a very bad spirit, because somebody made voodoo on her. This spirit has been with her for a long time. She also has two other spirits, according to the mediums, so that one part of her sickness is physical and three parts spiritual. She said she didn't know why anyone would want to do voodoo against her, since she has never done anyone harm. The mediums said that she brought the spirits with her from the island. They said that the old lady had a domestic there who had an abcess on her leg which the woman used to look at all the time. That domestic has now made the pains in her legs come to the woman. One of the mediums then told the old lady that she has to say one Our Father and 10 Hail Marys at the same time every night for nine nights. Then after the nine days are up, she should go to a doctor. The mediums then exorcised the lady.[1]

This incident, in addition to illustrating a diagnosis of dual causation, also reveals the influence mediums can exert on the medical usage patterns of their clients. In this instance the mediums encouraged B's mother to consult a physician; at other times, mediums discourage clients from using medical services. Although this is important in understanding the role of spiritism in community health, it is not germane to our immediate concern with the circumstances that lead people to consult spiritists, and so is dealt with later (see Chapter 7.)

The incident also points out that fear that a medically undiagnosed physical ailment may be fatal may lead a client to turn to a spiritist. Rather than face the feared diagnosis of cancer, B's mother consulted a medium. Depending on the diagnostic acumen and persuasive skill of the spiritist, the consultation may lead to medical attention for the client. A striking example was provided by the mother of a co-worker of mine at the Health Center. The woman had been having pain in her breast and detected a lump there. She first consulted a medium, who, she contended, removed the pain, and then went to a hospital and had the tumor removed surgically. In short, sufferers may turn to the medium when they are not yet able to confront a frightening medical evaluation of a prob-

[1] This report is my translation from a simultaneous transcription on the typewriter of the researcher's verbal account of the meeting, which was provided in English and Spanish alternately.

lem, and the medium can function to prepare the client for medical attention.

Other symptoms that may be deemed jointly spiritual and material in origin are insanity (*locura*) and a chronic state of agitation (*manía*), marked by pacing and inability to concentrate. Both symptoms may be ascribed to physical impairment of the nerves, to troubled interpersonal relations, or to spiritual agents. *Locura* (adjective form, *loco*) differs symptomatically from the manic condition in implying either unpredictable behavior or complete lack of regard for self-preservation, two conditions that are neatly embodied in the common saying *"No es loco porque no come fuego"* (He isn't crazy because he doesn't eat fire). A person labeled "crazy" (*loco*) is generally believed to require restraint and confinement. Although both manic and crazy behavior may be attributed to either spirits or impairment of the nervous system, they are not usually attributed to both simultaneously. Which of the two causes will be applied depends on the sufferer's immediate personal situation. (Compare Rogler and Hollingshead's discussion of *locura* and "nervousness," 1965: 215ff, as well as their enumeration of symptoms for which mediums are consulted, 1965:299.)

INTERPERSONAL RELATIONS AS A STIMULUS TO SPIRITIST CONSULTATION

In addition to certain behavioral symptoms and refractory or feared physical ills, interpersonal relations in which one party wishes to influence the behavior or feelings of another are also deeemed manageable in spiritual terms and are frequently referred to a medium. Most commonly these interpersonal relations involve a lover or spouse, a boss or potential employer, or a judge in a court proceeding. The manner in which the spiritist handles such problems, either by strengthening the client's own spiritual forces or by attempting to undermine the forces of the other protagonist in the relationship, defines, as we shall see, the fine line between beneficent spiritism and sorcery.

THE DIAGNOSTIC PROCESS

Troubled by one or a number of the symptoms or conditions described above, a person may establish contact with a spiritist either during private consultation hours or during a public meeting at a *centro*. The decision to go to the spiritist, the precise spiritist selected, and the choice of a private consultation or public gathering for initial contact are matters that depend largely on the people most closely associated with the sufferer—family and friends. Their familiarity with spiritist ideology and their knowledge of various mediums' reputations are instrumental in influencing the sufferer to act.

The goal of initial consultations with a medium is twofold: (1) to determine the identities of the client's protective spirits, and (2) to pinpoint the client's problems and diagnose their causes. To diagnose a client's condition, the medium summons his or her spiritual guide to help make contact with other spirits who either are influencing or can report on the client. Messages from these spirits may be conveyed in various ways, and mediums generally specialize in one of the techniques of communication described in Chapter 3. During communication the medium makes statements about the client, ostensibly from spirits, with which the client must indicate agreement or disagreement. According to spiritist ideology, the client is dutybound to exercise this corrective function, which prevents malevolent or capricious spirits from interfering with the medium's clear view of the client's condition. In practice the comments help guide the medium toward matters that trouble the client. The diagnosis thus evolves out of a dialogue between medium and client, in which the former takes the initiative.

As an example, I quote from one of my own consultations with a medium, which took place early in the study. The format of the interview is fairly typical of consultations between mediums and clients. However, my status as a member of a different subculture points up an important additional feature of the diagnostic procedure and thus makes the interview particularly revealing. We shall consider this feature following the account of the consultation.

The medium began speaking, punctuating her statements with spastic movements of the arms, sudden clapping, and occasional hissing.

Medium. You go with a Latin American woman.

Answer. No.

M. I see a girl with dyed blonde hair. She is in love with you, but you won't go out with her. She is making you sick. In your job you feel nervous. You get sick to your stomach. Sometimes you have pains in your neck, back, and leg. The spirit of a woman is making you feel this way.

A. Sometimes I do have a pain in my back and leg, but I don't know any woman like the one you describe.

The medium then asked me to write my name and address on a pad which she had on her lap. After I did so, she scribbled on the pad and appeared to be interpreting the scribbling.

M. The woman's name is Carmen. Does Carmen mean anything to you?

A. No.

M. (suddenly clapping and shuddering) José or Joseph—who is that?

A. I don't know anyone by those names.

M. You are married.

A. Yes.

M. You have a child.

A. No.

M. There is a girl child.

A. No.

The medium then explained that she would have to go more deeply into trance and try to contact the spirit that was bothering me. She thereupon called her assistant into the room. [As mentioned before, when going into deep trance, especially to "work" misguided spirits, a medium requires an assistant present]. The assistant seated herself in a chair beside the medium, who began rubbing her hands together, hyperventilating, and spitting into her hands. She then began convulsive movements in her shoulders and afterward started describing circles in the air with her forearms and speaking in no language recognizable to me. After more convulsive movements, she grew limp and began talking in a voice slightly different from her normal tone. During the following conversation, she frequently rubbed her face with her hand and shuddered occasionally. She kept her eyes closed during the entire proceedings.

M. The woman who is bothering you is named Maria. She is Italian. Do you know such a girl?

A. No.

M. This girl was in love with you, but you married someone else and she went to a place like this [a spiritist's] and got something to harm you. She wants you to lose your job and go to the hospital and die. Do you ever have a dry throat when you talk?

A. No, not usually.

M. Do you cough?

A. No.

M. The spirit of your father is with you. Is your father alive?

A. No, he died a few months ago.

M. He is with you, and that is good. That woman Maria is making your wife frigid. She makes you start things and not be able to finish them [i.e., sexually].

A. No.

Following the dialogue recorded above, the medium responded to the only positive diagnostic clue I had given her (that my back and leg pained me) by rubbing my back with *agua florida*. She asserted, however, that my back problem was "not just arthritis" but had a spiritual component. She then removed a malicious spirit, all the while rubbing my back vigorously, and told me to come again in 15 days if my troubles persisted.

This interview demonstrates clearly both the goal of spiritist consultation (to diagnose the problem and identify protective spirits) and the method of statement and corrective response by which this is done. The account also illustrates two additional points about the diagnostic process.

First, statements by mediums, at least in the initial stages of a medium-client relationship, are general enough to apply to almost anyone in the client population. Thus nearly every Hispanic client would know a Carmen, José, Joseph, or María. In the course of the interview the medium also hit upon every major problem that might trouble a young man and lead him to consult a medium—unrequited love, job insecurity, vague muscular pains, marital problems, sexual difficulties, and problems arising out of a previous or extramarital affair (as evidenced by the medium's repeated assertion that I had a child).

The second point illustrated by this account is the important role the client's social relationships play in a spiritist diagnosis. The usual sequence in developing such a diagnosis is for the medium to begin by probing the psychological state of the client, then to move to social relationships, and finally to proffer a spiritual cause related to the social circumstances uncovered. Thus, in the above interview the medium explored my closest interpersonal relationships (family, job, love interests) in an effort to arrive at a spiritual and social assessment of the problem. As a member of a different subculture, however, I failed to respond positively to the social situations suggested and thereby frustrated the normal development of a "sociospiritual" explanation.

The following account of a consultation between a medium and a Puerto Rican client illustrates the more typical development of the diagnostic process. (See also the more typical outcome of Carmelo's consultation later in this chapter.)

A young woman, who had been seen at a meeting of this *centro* once before, fell to the floor in a particularly violent seizure during the general exorcism of the congregation. After reviving, she was seated on a chair toward the front of the room. One of the mediums then spoke to her:

Medium. You sometimes feel like going to a window and jumping out.

Woman. Yes.

M. When you are in the subway station, you sometimes feel like jumping onto the tracks when the train comes.

W. Yes.

M. Do you feel like sometimes getting a rope to hang yourself?

W. Yes.

Another Medium. When you have a knife in your hand, do you feel like putting the blade through you?

W. Yes.

M. Sometimes you feel like taking your bags and disappearing. You have enemies in your family.

W. Yes, everyone in the family.

M. You have a husband.

W. Yes.

M. Your husband had another wife before you. Answer me, don't be embarrassed.

W. Yes.

M. Well, she's the one that's doing voodoo to you. You have never been happy with him, right?

W. No, never happy.

Later in the séance, after something was done to the woman to remove the "voodoo," a different medium took the spirit of St. Martin and began another dialogue with her.

St. Martin. You are very love-sick (*enamorada*). I see you with a can of beer in one hand and a knife in the other. You make love to men, and they get pleasure out of it, but you don't. I am going to tell you something: you have to respect the husbands of other women [that is, don't commit adultery].[2]

The foregoing passage not only provides a spiritual cause ("voodoo," that is, sorcery) for the client's suicidal feelings but also locates social sources of strain in her life (an unhappy marriage, adulterous relations).

Since I do not know whether the client in this case was known to the mediums or not, I cannot judge how much of this diagnosis was due to "spiritual" inspiration and how much to common gossip. In my experience, however, such detailed diagnoses (especially somewhat slanderous ones like that by the medium St. Martin above) are characteristically given at public séances only after a person has been to the *centro* a few times and might therefore have become known to one of the *mediunidad*. In one of the *centros* I attended frequently, the usual procedure was for the medium to probe a new client's psychological symptoms and then advise the person to return to a later session for "work." The following excerpt from a meeting of this *centro* exemplifies the pattern.

Medium. Sir, you don't sleep well at night.

Client. No, I don't.

M. When you are at home, you feel like getting out of the house.

C. Yes.

[2] This account is by a Hispanic researcher, reporting in English. The translation of the term *enamorada* was discussed with me and the term used at the séance included in the report.

M. Do you dream a lot?

C. Yes.

M. You have a Congo [an African spirit] with you. It is a beautiful spirit, but some people are evil and are trying to harm you. You need to have a lot of work done to you. We do not "work the cause" on Wednesdays. If you want to come back on Saturday, we will work with you.[3]

The medium's question about the client's ability to dream reflects the importance of dreams in diagnostic procedure, although in this particular incident the medium did not follow through on this line of questioning. Analysis of dreams may be used to accomplish either task of spiritist diagnosis—to label the problem or to identify the client's protective spirits.

In my case the content of dreams was used in determining which protectors were working on my problem. For example, at my next visit to the *centro,* following the consultation described earlier, the medium asked me if I had dreamed about her or spirits since our last session. I related a dream I had had about a woman with black hair who was trying to lead me somewhere; the dream had taken place near a wharf. The medium then asked me to raise the curtain over the entrance to her consultation room and pointed out a picture of a woman dressed in blue and white, standing on the sea, with stars dropping from her hands. She identified the figure as La Caridad del Cobre, one of the seven major saints in Santería, and said she was working through her to help me. This identification thus not only singled out the protector involved in the cure but also confirmed the efficacy of the medium's efforts on my behalf, since the spirit she contacted was indeed entering into my life. In several of the examples below, we see additional uses to which dreams are put in spiritist diagnosis.

ETIOLOGICAL CATEGORIES IN SPIRITISM

As noted earlier, a medium may diagnose a complaint as physical, spiritual, or dual in origin. Although many spiritists say that they identify the cause of some of their clients' illnesses as exclusively physical, my impression is that this occurs with only a very small proportion of their clientele. Diagnoses of both physical and spiritual etiology are frequent,

[3] This is my translation of a dialogue I witnessed at a *centro* session.

however, and conjoint treatment often results. Entirely spiritual causes are nevertheless assigned most commonly. This does not mean, of course, that mediums necessarily treat a great number of physical complaints as though they were spiritual in origin, since, as we have already observed, many physical illnesses have already been selected out of the spiritists' client population by the lay diagnoses of potential clients themselves.

Once a medium diagnoses a client's problems as having a spiritual component, there are seven general causes that may be assigned.

1. *Envidia* OR *Mala Fé* (ENVY OR BAD FAITH)

Many Puerto Ricans believe that the unexpressed envy of one's close associates (relatives, friends, or neighbors) can bring misfortune to one's household. The particular household member who inspires envy is not necessarily the one who experiences misfortune, however. The injury is said to befall instead the member whose spiritual protection is weakest. This belief thus draws the entire household together in mutual concern over maintaining good relations with the spiritual protectors of all its members. Within the household the person who attends to these spiritual matters is typically the mother, a role assignment considered more fully in Chapter 6, where we examine the uses of spiritist belief in the home.

Although not universal in Puerto Rican society, belief in the noxious effects of unexpressed envy certainly extends beyond adherents to spiritism (Padilla, 1958:283; Steward, 1956). Many Roman Catholics and Pentecostalists in the study sample also directed prayers and offerings to spiritual powers as protection against *mala fé*. However, unlike the spiritists, who focused attention on the personal protectors of family members, Catholic families directed their observances toward favorite saints or the Virgin, and Pentecostalists petitioned Jesus.

There are several additional ways in which general ideas about *envidia* relate to spiritism. Some spiritists claim, for example, that the agent that causes misfortune in *mala fé* is the spirit of the envious person. To quote an herbalist who is also a practicing spiritist,

> Envy is a powerful thing. You've heard that envy is the worst sin? You can know this man, and if you envy him, your spirit can attack his spirit and make him sick—(snapping his fingers)—like that! At night when you are asleep, your spirit roams around. If you have envy for anyone, you have made a description of him in your mind, then your spirit will find him and attack him.[4]

[4] This quotation derives from a conversation in English between the medical student, Stanley Fisch, and his close friend and mentor. The conversation was reported by Fisch.

Not everyone cites the spirit as the malefactor in causes of *envidia,* however. Some spiritists say that unexpressed envy itself is sufficient to cause harm; others that only people with very strong protection can produce injury "through the mind"—that is, by simply having envious feelings.

Since the household member considered most susceptible to *envidia* is the one whose spiritual protection is weakest, and since animals are not normally thought to have spiritual protectors, many families keep a pet to serve as the first victim of any envy directed toward the household. The death or illness of the pet (usually a bird, turtle, or dog) is then taken as a sign that the household is the object of unexpressed envy. Indeed, since *mala fé* always implies a social relationship involving outward friendship but underlying unexpressed hostility, a palpable sign like the death of a pet is clearly necessary for its diagnosis.

2. *Brujería* (SORCERY)[5]

Closely associated with *envidia* in the minds of most people, sorcery differs from it in involving deliberate acts designed to harm a specific person rather than simply unexpressed feelings that are conceived as causing injury to a family member. Unlike *envidia,* sorcery presumes a social relationship already fraught with antagonism. Many people see a sequential relationship between *envidia* and *brujería,* however, and claim that envious feelings often eventuate in deliberate acts of sorcery.

To perform sorcery, one consults certain mediums who are believed to have a special relationship with "dark spirits" from the lowest level of the spiritual hierarchy. These spirits did not live up to their potential in life and have been coopted by sorcerers to do their bidding. In different traditions of sorcery extant in Puerto Rico, the spirit helper may be called variously "the servant" (*el criado*), "the dog" (*el perro*), or still other designations in an African-derived ritual language (such as *mbua, nkisi*). Mediums who develop relationships with these "dark spirits" are believed eventually to lose their beneficent spiritual guardians—a belief that deters some mediums from practicing sorcery entirely.

The technique of sorcery involves first making a charm (*hechizo* or,

[5] I have translated *brujería* as "sorcery" rather than "witchcraft," which is its usual translation in Hispanic literature, because the activities involved in *brujería* are closer to the definition of sorcery generally used by anthropologists (Douglas, 1967; Harwood, 1970; Mair, 1969:16–23; Middleton and Winter, 1963). That is, *brujería* involves the manipulation of material objects and spells to work harm, which is the defining property of sorcery, rather than a personal, psychic power which may be used to molest others (witchcraft). In the context of spiritism *envidia* is closer to the anthropological definition of witchcraft.

in ritual language, *masango*), which often contains either the exuviae or some belonging of the intended victim. The charm is taken to a crossroads, beach, or other outdoor location, and rites are held to summon the medium's spirit servant and direct it to carry the charm to its proper destination. The charm may be buried under a tree, deposited in a cemetery, or thrown into the ocean. The place of disposal determines the seriousness meant to befall the victim, burial under a tree implying the least malevolence and casting into the ocean the greatest. To retain their efficacy, these acts of sorcery (*trabajos infernales,* "infernal jobs") must be renewed periodically by additional rites.

Most people gain knowledge of sorcery techniques not so much through direct use, however, as through gossip and attendance at spiritist meetings. When a case of *brujería* is under diagnosis or treatment, the precise procedure used in ensorcelling a victim is usually described, as seen later in this chapter. To most people sorcery is thus a post hoc explanation of misfortune or unhappiness rather than a technique which they actively employ to manipulate social relationships.

3. *Mala Influencia* (EVIL INFLUENCE)

Of their own will, spirits from the lowest level of the spiritual hierarchy may attach themselves to a particular household, causing dissension and trouble, until someone in the household agrees to "give the spirit light." Thus *mala influencia* is like sorcery by contract with a lower-ranking spirit except that no human agency is implied in propelling the spirit into the home. According to one medium, *mala influencia* produces "a kind of feeling when you go into a house. You feel that the house is heavy or that the house is very cold. There is no good feeling in the house." Besides hovering within a household and causing general disruption, unelevated spirits may also attach themselves to individuals, either very briefly or for long periods of time. Such attachments are the most frequently diagnosed cause of spiritual problems.

Spirits that hover around houses or certain individuals are usually believed to have known a resident of the house or the person in a previous incarnation. Alternatively the spirit may be believed to have an unfulfilled duty that prevents it from quitting the earth. The following account of a private consultation illustrates a diagnosis of *mala influencia.* In this case the spirit involved is attached to the client from one of his previous incarnations.

The client is a Puerto Rican male, about 25, whom I knew through a resident of the study area. The man, whom I shall call Carmelo, had been thinking of consulting a medium, although he was somewhat skeptical of them. He chose this one at my instigation and the confirmatory recommendations of other friends and agreed to describe his consultation to me. Since I typed as he spoke, the account is a combination of his words and mine.

When I came in, M told me to sit down in a chair next to her table. She asked me if I believe in the spirits. I told her I wasn't sure. Before the medium began the consultation, she took a long drag on a cigar that was lying in an ashtray on her table. She then put my hand over a pitcher of water and put her two hands on top of mine. Then she bent her forehead over her hands and kept her eyes closed for awhile. Finally the medium raised her head and blinked her eyes.

Medium. Sometimes you are unhappy.

Carmelo. Yes.

M. Sometimes you find it hard to sleep and get up and walk around.

C. Yes.

M. Sometimes you are nervous.

C. Yes.

M. Sometimes you have headaches and the back of your neck hurts.

C. Yes.

M. Sometimes your eyes burn.

C. No.

M. Sometimes you walk the streets because of nerves.

C. Yes.

M. Sometimes you walk in the street and feel something or someone behind you.

C. Yes.

M. You have a girl.

C. No, I am married.

M. You are not happy with your wife.

C. Yes.

M. You come home and argue with your wife.

C. Yes.

M. You haven't been married long.

C. That's right.

M. She isn't the same person you knew before. Sometimes you go home, and she doesn't seem herself.

C. Yes.

M. Sometimes you go home, you fight, and you walk out.

C. Sometimes.

M. She is jealous. She gives you jealous nonsense.

C. Yes. . . .

After probing several other social relationships of the client and suggesting the identity of one of his protectors, the medium summed up the situation as follows.

M. Let's see, you are unhappy. I can see that. You are sorry now that you married. You have a spirit wife from another existence. She is clinging to you and won't let you live in peace with your wife. We must help you get rid of this spirit. You must come to our session this Saturday, but first you must do what I tell you.

Carmelo's failure to establish a harmonious relationship with his new wife was thus attributed to his spirit wife from a previous existence. To treat this case of *mala influencia,* the medium advised Carmelo to give his apartment a "spiritual cleaning" and urged him to return with his wife to have his "cause" worked. (The importance of joint treatment in this case is discussed more fully later in this chapter.)

Because the recently dead are believed to maintain strong attachments to loved ones, people frequently consult mediums after a death in the family, particularly if one of the members has dreams, nightmares, or just a "feeling" that indicate that the spirit of the deceased is attached to the household and has not found its way to a higher spatial level. Initially such a spirit may be considered an evil influence in the home, seeking to take one of its members with it to death, but through proper ritual acts the spirit may often be converted into a protector. For example, a young girl who experienced frequent nightmares after the death of her grandmother was taken to a medium for consultation. The medium divined that the grandmother was attached to the girl and had to be "given light" and convinced to go away. After the proper services had been performed, the medium announced that the grandmother was now the girl's very strong protector. Thus what is initially conceived as a negative influence in one's life may, through treatment, be converted into a positive force.

The term *mala corriente* (evil current) is often used synonymously with *mala influencia* but has the connotation of a rapid and passing spiritual visitation rather than prolonged interference. For example, in one of the families a researcher was visiting, a child who was usually will behaved started a fire in the apartment. When his mother caught him, the child said it was as though someone had been telling him to light the fire and he had not been himself until he satisfied the wish. The mother suspected *mala corriente* because of the impulsive nature of the act as well as the sudden change from the child's usual behavior.

4. *Facultades* (FACULTIES)

Faculties, a very important etiological category in spiritist diagnostics, implies that the sufferer has mediumistic abilities that have not been developed. The symptoms of the sufferer are seen as resulting from unwanted or uncontrolled possession by spirits. Particularly important among the symptoms indicative of possession are fugue states, unaccountable depression, suicidal feelings, certain kinds of dreams, and seizures. Fugue states are attributed to an intrusive spirit that impels the possessed person's body to do things that the person does not remember after the spirit departs. Unaccountable feelings of depression, often accompanied by vacant staring, are believed to reflect the sentiments of the spirit rather than the person possessed; suicidal urges are interpreted as possession by a spirit that wants to take the possessed person with it into death. Sufferers may also hear the voices of spirits, goading them to suicide. Any of these symptoms may also be attributed to possession through the agency of *mala influencia* or sorcery. A diagnosis of faculties is confirmed, however, by three additional factors: (1) the nature of the client's dreams, (2) seizures, and (3) the client's demonstrated sensitivity to other people's *causas*.

Dreams that indicate faculties usually focus on a dead relative, often one who was a medium, and the dreams may prophesy events that later take place. For example, a medium I knew recounted the dreams that had confirmed her possession of faculties. One night when she was feeling particularly restive, she dreamed she saw a friend dressed in a hospital gown who bid her good-bye. She felt a chill and sat bolt upright in bed. The next day she learned that the friend had died during the night. Her other dreams all involved her grandmother, who had been a medium. In a particularly important one, since it confirmed her calling as a medium, she saw herself seated beside her grandmother at the White Table as part of the *mediunidad.*

The seizures which, in addition to dreams, confirm a diagnosis of faculties typically occur in *centros* or other places where spirits are said to congregate. They are often violent. Clients may throw themselves down or career about the room, forcefully hitting themselves against the floor or walls. One medium aptly referred to these experiences as "party time" for the spirits, since the seizures are conceived as visitations of many spirits in rapid succession. The untrained medium cannot "control" these visitations, and the diagnosis of faculties thus implies a treatment procedure in which the client learns techniques of control.

The third indicator of faculties is the client's ability to "pick up" other people's spiritual problems (*causas*). Thus people may demonstrate their faculties publicly by announcing that they have felt malaise or a pain that they have picked up from someone in the room.

An important clue in the diagnosis of faculties is the repeated appearance of these three additional symptoms. Therefore, clients who know the ideology of spiritism and repeatedly display all or many of these above symptoms are in fact communicating their desire to develop their powers and participate actively as mediums.

Although some people evince a predisposition toward mediumship in this way, anyone is thought to be capable of developing into a medium. *Santero* doctrine holds that a person can strengthen his or her spiritual protection most by developing as a medium and becoming possessed by personal protectors (El Akoni, n.d.:42–43). As one medium explained after she had taken the spirit of her protector St. Barbara, "Every time you do this you get stronger and stronger." That is, with each possession the tie between the protector and her ward (*pupilo*) becomes more intense. Although most people who attend spiritist sessions hold the belief that they can increase their protection through possession by one of their protectors, relatively few seek to become mediums without first displaying evidence of faculties. Of the six mediums in training in one *santero centro* with which I am familiar, only one was attempting development without prior indication of faculties.

5. *Prueba* (TEST OR TRIAL)

Any difficulty in life may be interpreted loosely as a test (*prueba*) of an individual's spiritual or moral strength imposed by God or other spiritual beings. This diagnostic category may be applied to any problem brought to a medium and is therefore used quite frequently, particularly in the Mesa Blanca tradition. A *prueba* imposed by God, however, is used by mediums as a residual diagnostic category, applied to a client only after treatment under other rubrics has failed. For example, in the treatment of the hospitalized mental patient, to be described in detail in the following chapter, the medium finally concluded that the patient's condition was in part a trial imposed by God and that only God's intervention could bring the patient to repent her earlier renunciation of her protectors.

As a diagnostic category, *prueba* also carries a more specific meaning when applied to mediums in training and refers to hardships imposed on these mediums by their spirit guides during the period of development. Thus, during training the spirit guides and protectors of fledgling mediums test the novices' commitment by setting them difficult tasks or by placing obstacles in the way of further development. For example, one medium related how, among other difficulties, she experienced partial blindness in one eye while she was developing. Treated at an outpatient clinic for the condition, she had to wear a patch over the eye for two weeks. During this time she claimed to have developed greater sensitivity to clients' nonverbal messages, as conveyed in voice tone and volume. Surmounting the physical trial thus contributed ultimately to her development as a medium.

6. *Cadena* (CHAIN)

Literally a "chain" in Spanish, *cadena* implies a familial influence from the past which causes unhappiness in the present. Not all Puerto Ricans who speak of such chains or of living "an enchained life" (*una vida encadenada*) necessarily attribute intergenerational influences to spirits. The Biblical notion that the sins of the fathers are visited upon their children may also be used to explain such influences.

In spiritist belief, the chain is believed to derive from a spirit among the afflicted's ancestors who died in an unsettled state. It is the duty of the descendant to put the spirit to rest by "giving it light." If a descendant in one generation does not assume this duty, the obligation falls upon the next.

Various reasons may be given for the unsettled condition of the deceased ancestor. For example, if the ancestor committed an unjust act and was cursed by the victim, then the curse might pursue the family. Many mediums point to the Kennedy family's series of misfortunes as evidence of a familial curse. More often, however, ancestral unrest is attributed to an act of sorcery either committed by or directed toward the forebear. Since, as we noted above, such "infernal works" must be renewed periodically to retain their effectiveness, a *cadena* may come to light when the spirit servant who originally effected a "job" becomes disaffected because of the neglect of his or her master. The spirit may then reveal the ancient act of sorcery to a medium, who must then treat the entire chain.

Another reason why an ancestor's spirit might remain near earth to disturb a descendant is if the ancestor was a medium and wishes to pass on his guides and protectors to one of his kinsmen. In this form of *cadena* the victim is usually obsessed by dreams or fantasies about the deceased medium. The medium's dream, cited above, in which she was seated beside her grandmother at the White Table, indicates that her situation was a *cadena*. Since this type of *cadena* is simultaneously indicative of faculties, the treatment is the same as for a diagnosis of the latter condition alone, and usually quite different from the other types of *cadena* discussed.

7. *Castigo* (PUNISHMENT)

This term may be applied to both mediums and ordinary people, but with slightly different connotations. When used with reference to mediums, the meaning is similar to the psychoanalytic concept of regression. According to spiritist theory, persons with faculties who have developed their powers as mediums must continue practicing as mediums or at least pay honor to their special saints and protectors throughout their lifetime; otherwise, they may reexperience the symptoms that originally led them to become mediums. In the following extract from field notes, a *centro* leader reports to a medical-student researcher that one of the assistant mediums in his *centro* was taken to a psychiatric ward several days after revealing to him that she had given up spiritism.

Centro Leader. She threw all her [statues of] saints out the window. She became Pentecostal. I told her the Pentecostals were spiritual, too. She was giving up nothing. I warned her that she would be punished for throwing away these things like that. You can't quit this. If you want to stop, you put the saints on the side. Keep them. You will suffer punishment little by little.

Researcher. But why should she be punished? Would the saints and spirits really try to harm her?

Centro Leader. She loses her protection when she does that. No protection, she suffers. So yesterday her son comes and says, "The police came and took Mommy away in handcuffs to ——Hospital." She also had trouble with her husband.

Unfortunately the "trouble with her husband" in the above case was not probed further. However, the statement clearly indicates the close relationship spiritists see between family circumstances and spiritual well-being. From the viewpoint of preventive psychiatry, the act of throwing away or desecrating the statues of one's protectors may be seen as a sign (and hence a fairly good predictor) in spiritist subculture of impending mental breakdown.

The dialogue above clearly indicates that, although the diagnostic term *castigo* literally means "punishment," the causal nexus is more subtle. Since protectors do only good, they never in fact punish their protégés directly; instead, they abandon the protégé to the many, often evil spiritual influences in the environment. The developed medium thus experiences the same problem of uncontrolled spirit possession that untrained mediums suffer before they learn techniques of control. It is in this sense that *castigo* is a form of regression.

For ordinary people without faculties, *castigo* may occur when the person makes a promise (*promesa*, discussed in Chapter 3) to a saint and then fails to keep it. One can postpone such "punishment" for a time, however, by performing services to the saint (for example, lighting candles) until one is able to honor the promise fully.

ETIOLOGICAL CATEGORIES IN SPIRITISM: A SUMMARY

The technique of spiritual diagnosis, like psychiatric diagnosis,[6] is to assemble data on a client's psychological state and social adjustments and to apply to these a label that implicates a particular method of treatment. As in psychiatric diagnosis, any specific symptom may appear

[6] In general, I have adopted Torrey's terminology (1972:9) in this book and use "psychiatry" to refer to the types of psychotherapy practiced by formally trained professionals in the West (i.e., by psychoanalysts, psychologists, social workers, etc.).

as part of several different syndromes and thus receive different diagnostic labels. For example, dreams about a deceased relative, as we have seen, may imply faculties, *cadena,* or *mala influencia,* depending on the presence of other conditions.

Spiritual diagnosis differs from psychiatric diagnosis, however, in an important respect. In spiritism, clients do not play an active role in providing the diagnostician with information about their symptoms. It is the diagnostician's duty to uncover clients' symptoms. Indeed, clients evaluate the diagnostician's competence in spiritism on the basis not only of previous training and general reputation but also on an ability to provide an acceptable résumé of their conditions. On the basis of this résumé, the healer then assigns to the condition any of the seven diagnostic labels discussed above. Table 4 summarizes these labels in terms of the precise spiritual causes they implicate. Treatment procedures then follow from a knowledge of these causes.

SUMMARY OF LAST FEW PAGES.

TABLE 4 ETIOLOGICAL CATEGORIES IN SPIRITIST DIAGNOSIS

Etiological Category	Implied Spiritual Cause
1. *Envidia* (envy)	the unexpressed envy of incarnate spirits in close association with the victim
2. *Brujeria* (sorcery)	a disembodied spirit sent to harm the victim by an enemy working in league with a spiritist
3. *Mala influencia* (evil influence) or *mala corriente* (evil current)	a disembodied spirit of low rank seeking to be "given light"
4. *Facultades* (faculties)	spirits of various ranks who possess the body of a person insufficiently trained in controlling such seizures
5. *Prueba* (test or trial)	a. protective spirits who test a person while he or she is developing faculties b. God-predestined trials in a person's life
6. *Cadena* (chain)	the spirit of a deceased relative or other associate from the past who has done some misdeed
7. *Castigo* (punishment)	misguided spirits allowed to beset a victim who has neglected his relationship with his spiritual protectors

TREATMENT IN SPIRITIST THERAPY

As can be seen from Table 4, the problems brought to a spiritist may be attributed basically to four spiritual influences working either alone or in combination: (1) intranquil or other low-ranking, disembodied spirits; (2) the client's own spiritual protectors, if they have abandoned the client; (3) human envy or malevolence; and (4) God. Treatment procedures, as conceived in spiritist terms, focus mainly on the two goals of removing harmful spiritual influences from the client and strengthening the client's benign ones. This section describes the specific procedures used to effect these goals. While undergoing these procedures, however, clients may also receive direct advice or clarification about interpersonal relations, support and encouragement in facing difficult reality situations, bodily stroking or massage, and a variety of other therapeutic techniques that will be exemplified below in descriptions of treatment sessions.

These descriptions also show that the relationship between diagnostic categories and treatment procedures in spiritism is not one to one. That is, a single diagnostic category may implicate several different treatment procedures. Furthermore, mediums assert that to determine the specific treatment to be used for a client, the spiritual protection of both medium and client must be taken into account. For this reason different mediums may employ slightly different procedures with the same client for the same problem. They may prescribe different bath oils or prayers, for example.

KINDS AND COSTS OF SPIRITIST THERAPY

Spiritist treatment may take place either privately in the course of individual consultation or publicly at meetings of spiritist groups. In some cases the spiritist may require the client's family to be present and participate in the curing process. We have already recorded an instance of this in the case of Carmelo, who was having marital problems and was advised to bring his wife with him when the medium "worked" his cause. Spiritist treatment, in short, may take place in individual, group, or family settings.

The cost of treatment varies greatly, depending on the reputation of the medium, his or her relationship with the client, and the client's diagnosis. If the medium does not have a *centro* and is on friendly terms with the client (for example, if the medium and client live in the same building), payment may take the form of gifts or neighborly services. In the case of strangers, the standard practice is for clients to leave whatever they think a consultation is worth—usually \$2 to \$3 for diagnostic sessions and more for treatment, depending on the problem. Often, however, the treatment charge is negotiated and may vary from $10 for minor cures (such as a prescription or preparation for attracting benign spirits) to several hundred dollars reportedly charged for performing sorcery or removing it. In my own data, however, I have no direct statement from anyone that he or she had actually ever paid these higher amounts, although three people complained that spiritists "downtown" had requested them. It therefore seems doubtful to me that these fees are paid with any frequency.[7]

REMOVAL OF HARMFUL SPIRITUAL INFLUENCES

Three procedures are used for accomplishing the therapeutic goal of removing harmful spiritual influences from clients. *Despojo* (exorcism) involves certain physical acts designed to eliminate an offending spirit's *fluido* (semimaterial component) from the sufferer. *Trabajando la causa* (working the cause) consists of interviewing the spirit involved when it manifests itself through a medium and convincing it to leave the sufferer in peace. *Dando la luz al espiritu* (giving the spirit light) means saying prayers or making other offerings on behalf of a repentant, misguided spirit to assist its ascent to the spiritual realm.

Despojo

As we have noted before, *despojo* is part of every spiritist session and serves to remove harmful spiritual influences that clients have either brought to the meeting or may take away with them. The *despojo* is performed by a medium who fumigates the person being exorcised with cigar smoke and then runs his or her hands along the back of the sufferer's head and neck (the *cerebro,* considered to be the place where spirits enter) and then down along the person's shoulders and arms. (This stroking is called *pases,* "passes."). The medium then takes hold of

[7] Garrison's (1973:19) conclusions on this matter are similar. She makes the additional interesting observation that since high fees are invariably spoken of in critical fashion, such talk may in fact operate as a negative sanction against them.

In presenting material on spiritist psychotherapy to psychiatrists, psychologists, and other professionals trained in the mainstream Western tradition of therapy, I have found them particularly critical of the high fees occasionally charged by spiritists. Given the incomparably higher costs of treatment by these professionals and the opinion of many of them that their high fees are conducive to a cure, I find the criticism somewhat self-serving. The important issue seems to be whether and under what conditions either of these kinds of therapies works.

the client's hands, raises them above the client's head, and throws them down abruptly.

A *despojo* sometimes leads to the manisfestation of a spirit, as the following instance from a White Table *reunión* illustrates. This client was recovering from a heart attack, a fact which the researcher learned later in conversation with his wife. Compare the more elaborate use of *pases* in treating this individual with the general form of exorcism described above. The case is one of *mala influencia.*

Elena [pseudonym for the medium] said that the client had been very ill recently and was full of bad influences. She saw near him a spirit that wanted to help and protect him. She announced that she would pass this spirit and give it to him so that he could become strong. Then she took her guide and went over to the man and told him to take off his shirt, shoes, and socks. He did this, and she rubbed his shoulders and arms. She then told him to stand and rubbed his stomach and legs, always in a downward motion. Then she took his hands and began to shake. She twisted away from him and became possessed with the spirit that had troubled the man. The *Presidente* brought out a bowl of water, and Elena pounded on the rim, getting rid of the spirit she had taken from the man. Finally she advised him to pray to La Caridad del Cobre, his major protection.

A *despojo* may be used to treat *envidia* as well as *mala influencia,* as the following account illustrates. The account comes from a researcher who found preparations for a session in progress when she entered the apartment of one of her assigned families.

The medium, here called Julia, and client in this case were neighbors in the same building, and this incident was part of an ongoing therapeutic relationship between the two. The client (I shall call her Nilda) is in her early 30s and has five children. In the course of the last 12 years she has had relationships with several men, each lasting a number of years. After one of these relationships terminated, Nilda was hospitalized in a mental institution and her children placed in a home. She subsequently underwent periodic hospitalizations for asthma, during which times the children either returned to the home or were cared for by relatives. After her last marriage broke up, Nilda was again hospitalized in a mental institution, but at the time of this séance (several years later) she had established a new relationship with a man who wished to marry her. The couple had been together almost a year. Lately, however, Nilda had experienced pains in her legs in addition to her usual asthma.

[When the researcher entered, Julia told her she was giving Nilda's apartment a "spiritual cleaning" (*una limpieza espiritual*) in order to work on Nilda. Julia was washing the floor with water, ammonia, and probably other things like perfumes.] After putting the pail and mop in the corner of the living room, she took out a dish with incense and put it in the center of the room.

Julia's husband then entered, and Julia asked him for cigars. He distributed them, and everyone began smoking. Julia began blowing smoke on her husband and exorcising him so that he could leave. Julia explained that a priest protects her husband and that the priest does not get along with the Madama, who is her protector. [The Madama, represented on *santero* altars by a rag doll of a black woman, is an important figure in the cadre of *congos*.]

After her husband left, Julia began fumigating Nilda with cigar smoke. She then put a glass of water on the floor and began playing records of songs in honor of saints. She began to dance and clap and brought out a doll representing the Madama. She placed the doll and a vase of water on the phonograph and began exorcising herself, throwing the evil influences into the water [that is, tapping her hands on the edge of the vase after running her hands over the back of her head and shoulders.]

Afterward she took the spirit of the Madama and began to cry and speak in a slightly different voice, saying that people are envious of Nilda. Although the Madama did not say why they are envious, people want Nilda's children to be taken back to a home. This will not happen, said the Madama, while she is at her side. Nothing will happen to her. Nevertheless, people want Nilda to go crazy so that the children will be taken away for good.

Then the Madama left, saying, "I am leaving now because the Nun is coming. Remain here." [Besides the Madama, Doña Julia has a protector who is a nun.] Suddenly Julia began shaking as if she had a chill and complained of pains in her knees. The Nun said that Nilda's pains had taken hold of her. Nilda went into the next room to get some *agua florida*. While she was out of the room, Julia told the researcher that she was counseling (*aconsejar*) Nilda because she had a fight with her husband last night and was very sad and wanted to cry.

When Nilda returned, Julia rubbed *agua florida* on Nilda's forehead, back of the head, and legs, depositing the evil influences (*mala influencia*) in the vase. She did the same to the researcher and then served everyone black coffee [a drink attractive to good spirits].[8]

Here we see in context the use of many of the paraphernalia of spiritist treatment that are described in Chapter 3. The spiritual cleaning of the apartment before the session, as well as the cigar smoke and containers of water, rids the apartment and the participants of the *fluido* of wayward spirits. For attracting favorable spirits, incense, *santero* songs, *agua*

[8] This is my translation from Spanish of the researcher's notes on her visit. Remarks in brackets are explanatory notes provided by me.

florida, and black coffee were used. Julia's Madama doll was also taken from the altar during the séance to help the spirit manifest herself.

The description is even more important for our present discussion in exemplifying an exorcism in treatment of *envidia* (as diagnosed by the Madama). The medium, as the Nun, first took the noxious spiritual influences adhering to Nilda onto herself and then made Nilda attractive to favorable spirits with *agua florida* and black coffee. This procedure of removing harmful spiritual influences without regard to the individual identities of the spirits involved, and then increasing the client's receptivity to benign influences is the usual method of dealing with cases of *envidia*—a condition where the underlying cause is also somewhat vague and anonymous (see the discussion of *envidia* earlier in this chapter). This mode of treatment is also appropriate, as in the present instance, when only one medium is available. That is, a *despojo* may have to suffice as treatment for *mala influencia* and other spiritual causes until a meeting can be held with more than one medium present. For only in a group can a medium undertake the more potent treatment procedure for dispatching malevolent influences known as "working the cause."

Before providing examples of that procedure, a few comments on the verbal part of Julia's session are in order. The medium, after expressing some of Nilda's anxieties (about going crazy and having her children taken away from her), gave her reassurance that none of these fears would come to pass because she had good protection beside her. The reader will note that Nilda's fears were phrased as coming not from her but from outside sources—"people" want her children taken away, "people" want Nilda to go crazy. Since this phraseology is common in spiritist treatment and is antithetical to psychiatric procedure, we consider it more fully later, after we have seen more instances of its use.

Working the Cause

When specific spirits are implicated in the cause of a client's problems (as in diagnoses of sorcery, *cadena*, and usually *mala influencia*), and when at least two mediums are present, the more elaborate and more personalized treatment procedure of "working the cause" is employed. The following description, from a researcher's report of a *centro* meeting, exemplifies this type of therapy.

This Sunday, as soon as the head medium took [the spirit of] his Protector, Candelo, he said, "¡Carajo! There is a dead person here who is going crazy. Let me do a work of charity (*una obra de caridad*)." He then went over to a woman who had come to the *centro* for the first time. He told her to come up

> front with her daughter. The daughter had been in a mental hospital, but no one knew this until Candelo began exorcising her (*la despojó*).
>
> When he was exorcising her, he took the cause or, in other words, the bad spirit (*el mal espíritu*) that was with the girl and said to her, "¡Carajo! Who has brought you here? This isn't where you belong because you are mine, no one's but mine! I want to see you wearing a straitjacket, where I used to have you." In a very loud voice the spirit repeated this again until the assistant mediums began to say a prayer for the dead so that the spirit would know that he was dead and would stop harming the child.
>
> After the dead spirit realized this, he begged the girl's pardon three times. The mediums answered, "May God pardon you." The spirit then began to speak. "Pardon me, good spirit, for all the harm I have done you." The assistant mediums asked, "What kind of harm have you done to her?" The spirit replied, "Every time that she raised her hand to her mother, it was the work of my spirit. Every time she ran through the streets as though crazy, it was the work of my spirit."
>
> After recalling other deeds which he had prompted her to do, the spirit was "passed" into a jar of water by the medium, who then told the child that she would no longer be compelled to do these things. As Candelo, the medium then exorcised the girl again (*la volvió a despojar*) and told her to return to the *centro* the following week.[9]

The treatment procedure exemplified here (working the cause) contrasts markedly with the simple exorcism in Nilda's case. With Nilda there was no direct interrogation of the spirit nor ritual of pardon prior to passing the spirit's *fluido* into water, because the basic cause of her problems was not identified as a specific spirit. Her exorcism was simply to dispel any nonspecific bad influences that were around her as a stopgap before a proper *reunión* could be held. The procedure was designed to deal with a crisis in the course of an ongoing treatment relationship.

Besides cases of *mala influencia* like the above, "working the cause" is also the treatment of choice in cases of sorcery. During interrogation of a spirit sent through sorcery, however, mediums may probe the identity of the person who contracted to molest the victim. In addition they usually produce a charm (*hechizo*) that was purportedly used in the deed. To illustrate this procedure, we return to a case cited earlier in this chapter to illustrate spiritist diagnosis, the case of the young woman whose suicidal and depressed feelings were attributed to sorcery ("voodoo") on the part of her husband's first wife.

[9] This is my translation of the researcher's report.

After questioning a spirit involved in the sorcery, the *mediunidad* learned that an important agent used in the deed was black thread. One of the mediums then called for white thread. Warning her client not to be frightened, she proceeded to encircle the woman from neck to ankles with the thread. She then asked for a white and a red candle, lighted them, and inverted a glass of water on a plate. She gave the red candle (St. Barbara's color) to the woman to hold and passed the white candle (St. Martha's color) over her body.

One of the other mediums suddenly took one of his protective spirits and appeared to be in deep trance for about 15 minutes. He then began producing the things that were used in ensorcelling the woman: two candle ends, a green ribbon tied with seven knots, the spell that was spoken in preparing the charm, and finally the black thread. He also produced several prayers—one to St. Martha and one for the intranquil spirit that participated in the act of sorcery. The woman was instructed to say these prayers three times a day for seven days. After the components of the *hechizo* were deposited in a container of water, the other mediums removed the white thread from the client and instructed her to burn it and give it to her husband as protection.

Later, one of the other mediums under protection of St. Martin secured the final component of the voodoo charm, two dolls which had purportedly been tied back-to-back with the black thread.[10]

After this dramatic procedure the client was told that she was free of the sorcery that was coming between her husband and herself. They would no longer stand "back-to-back" but could face each other. She would not be "love-sick" any more (see case description above) nor driven to commit adultery. The woman was told to visit the medium during consultation hours and continued attending *centro* meetings for a number of months. Unfortunately I do not know the effects of this treatment on the client's marital relationship.[11]

The main therapeutic effect of exorcism and "working the cause" seems to lie in facilitating the client's alienation from certain patterns of behavior by attributing them to outside (spiritual) influences and then convincing the client, through dramatic enactments and suggestion within the framework of spiritist concepts, that these influences are no longer operative in his or her life. What the long-run effects of such treatment are, when coupled with follow-up sessions designed both to advise clients on changes they should make in their behavior and to strengthen their spiritual protection as a barrier to recurrent intrusion of outside influences (and thus recurrence of the unwanted behavior), was a matter

[10] This description is from my own notes of a *centro* session.

[11] For another example of the treatment of a case of sorcery see the recovery of the *hechizo* against Jorge, described in Chapter 3.

beyond the scope of our research, with its emphasis on the basic methods of diagnosis and treatment. It is clearly an important issue for further investigation.

Giving the Spirit Light

An additional method for removing a harmful spiritual influence is to "give it light," a technique described briefly in Chapter 2. This technique is used especially for cases of sorcery, *cadena,* and those instances of *mala influencia* in which the offending spirit has been specifically contacted and identified.

The treatment consists in setting the client a program of rituals designed to elevate the offending spirit and thus remove its harmful influence. The program usually consists of reciting a specific prayer several times a day for a set number of days, together with lighting a candle or placing a fresh flower either on an altar or in a spot associated with the spirit. As part of the previous account of a treatment of sorcery, for example, the medium produced a prayer to give light to the intranquil spirit who had participated in the deed and instructed the client to recite it for seven consecutive days.

The case of the attached grandmother (see pp. 88–89) also exemplifies the procedure of giving a spirit light. In this case all members of the deceased woman's household (her husband, son, daughter-in-law, and two granddaughters) attended a *centro* after her death. There they participated in a *despojo* and were also assigned a domestic ritual to perform. This ritual involved sprinkling holy water in the corners of every room of the apartment and placing a vase with a white carnation and a lighted candle beside the deceased's bed. When doing these tasks, the family members were to tell the spirit that it no longer belonged with them but must join other spirits (*ir por otra parte*). At a later session the head medium confirmed that the woman had indeed gone "to the other side" and was now a protector of one of the granddaughters. This method of treatment, commonly instituted for mourners, helped the family in the gradual acceptance of the death of an important member and then installed the dead woman in a perpetual protective relationship with one of the survivors.

As a treatment technique for depression or any other condition that may prompt a client to withdraw from normal social contact, "giving the spirit light" functions to force the client into ordinary social intercourse and establishes a pattern for his or her life by setting tasks necessary to elevate the spirit (for example, purchasing flowers, candles, or other ritual paraphernalia). The client, in short, becomes actively engaged in duties that contribute toward the cure.

Giving the offending spirit light in a case of *cadena,* however, usually involves more than just the prayers and offerings that ordinarily serve to elevate repentant misguided spirits or the spirits of recently deceased relatives. Since the ancestor in most cases of *cadena* is conceived as causing some misfortune to pass down through the generations, improvement in family relations is a necessary part of the cure. The following case illustrates this point.

Miguel is a man of about 45, the father of four children. He and the eldest child, a woman of about 20, have had a very stormy relationship ever since she entered puberty. His constant concern about her whereabouts led to persistent fights that continue even now, two years after her marriage and absence from his home. About a year ago father and daughter had a violent argument, after which she swore never to see him again.

After the argument Miguel began waking frequently at night and claiming to hear strange breathing. At his wife's insistence he consulted a spiritist who told him that the breathing he heard was either the spirit of his paternal grandmother or a spirit sent by her. Miguel's father had been very attached to his mother and in fact had left his wife when she was pregnant with Miguel to live with her. The older woman also succeeded in getting Miguel away from his mother and raised him herself. Miguel's mother reportedly tried taking him back with her several times, but he would always return to his grandmother. The medium claimed that the grandmother had performed sorcery on the boy to keep him near her, and it was her continued influence that came between Miguel and his own daughter. At the time the daughter was also having problems with her young son, which was attributed to this ancestor's sorcery as well.

To break this "chain," Miguel or the daughter would have to go to a medium and have the grandmother's hold on them removed. Only then, according to the medium, could the relationship between them be worked out. The only other solution would be for both to carry special protection against the grandmother's spirit their whole lives. When I heard about this case, Miguel's wife was trying to get him to the medium to have the grandmother's influence removed.[12]

As this case with its oedipal theme illustrates, interpretations of clients' problems in terms of *cadena* often come very close to psycho-

[12] This case was reported to me by a reliable informant who was a close relative of Miguel.

analytic interpretations. The mode of treatment of this type of *cadena* entails a symbolic working out of the relationship with the problem ancestor as well as an attempt to reconcile problem relationships within the immediate family, treatment goals close to those of contemporary psychiatric therapies.

DEVELOPMENT OF MEDIUMISTIC POWERS

This treatment procedure not only removes a client's harmful spiritual influences but ultimately also increases the client's spiritual protection. For that reason we are discussing it between the sections devoted to these two basic therapeutic goals. Development (*desarollo*) may follow either a diagnosis of faculties or the expressed desire of a client to become a medium. Although people who manifest the syndrome indicative of faculties are considered particularly appropriate candidates for development, any person, as mentioned before, is said to be able to become a medium with sufficient perseverance and training. Development is also part of the procedure used in treating *castigo,* the "punishment" befalling mediums who renounce their protection. Treatment of *castigo* involves removing all the evil influences that have adhered to clients during the period of renunciation and then redeveloping their mediumship by reviving their relationship with their protectors.

Writers on the subject of spiritism as psychotherapy (e.g., Bram, 1958; García, 1956; Koss, n.d.; Rogler and Hollingshead, 1961) emphasize the therapeutic procedure of development in their writings, and it is undoubtedly true that clients who display serious psychopathology (hallucinations, fugue states, suicidal tendencies) do receive this mode of treatment. It is important to note, however, that development is only one mode of treatment in spiritism and that the bulk of casual clients and even *centro* members neither manifest extreme psychopathology nor undergo mediumistic training. (For similar observations, see Garrison's material on spiritist groups in the South Bronx, 1968:4, 20ff. and 1973:17; and Rogler and Hollingshead's material on Puerto Rico, 1965:247–48). This point underscores once more a major thesis of this book: spiritism has broader relevance to the field of community mental health than simply the treatment of psychosis. We return to this point in the concluding chapter.

As indicated earlier, the syndrome labeled "faculties," for which spiritual development (*desarollo*) is the recommended therapy, includes fugue states, seizures, possibly auditory hallucinations, and other dissociative symptoms. Basically the therapy involves teaching the client culturally and ritually appropriate times and places for displaying dissociative reactions. This teaching occurs within the context of the hierarchical structure of the *centro,* under the tutelage of the head medium and his or her assistants. Thus the developing medium becomes a member of a primary group with a clear authority structure and the following definite role expectations. First, the leader and assistants expect clients to bring their dissociative behavior under control, not only within the *centro* but also in the outside world. They also expect them to live amicably with their family and other associates and to participate in the work of the *centro* both by performing assigned tasks in preparation for *centro* meetings and by using their mediumistic powers at meetings to help other clients of the *centro.*

The following notes from a series of open-ended interviews I held with a medium provide a sense of the development experience and its precursors. The medium, Juana, is an attractive, poised, always fashionably-dressed woman of about 35.

Juana began by telling me that her power to take on spirits was inherited. Her grandmother had been a great medium. She first knew that her destiny was to have such power in the course of a dream in which she was seated at a White Table with her grandmother. Suddenly a spirit moved in from behind her "from outer space." She woke up making the motions used to induce possession.

Since that dream, spirits have kept coming to Juana and visiting her, although her real dedication to development came later, about 13 years ago. At that time she was applying for a job and was having pictures taken for the application when she suddenly "blacked out" and didn't know where she was. She later went to a medium who told her that this occurrence was a sign that she should not take the job and should instead develop her faculties.

Juana said that when this sign came to her, she felt as though she was going out of her mind. She felt like packing her bag and going to a mental hospital. She felt as though her mind was going in different directions, that she was being directed by several forces. This is a dangerous time, she explained, because the person has to be taught to control the forces when this happens. Juana stressed the difficulty she went through in trying to control the visitation of spirits. She spoke about one night at a *centro* when she went from 2 A.M. to 7 P.M. the next evening taking one spirit after another, trying to learn to control this kind of thing—or as she put it, "learning to say 'I'm the boss' and not letting any spirit ride you."

During the course of development Juana also experienced *pruebas.* She had bouts of laryngitis; at one point she had to walk with her knee bandaged; another time she had a "cold" in her back; then she dislocated her rib. Finally, she "almost went blind."

To provide some idea of the nature of an uncontrolled possession like the one mentioned by Juana, we include the following description of the possession experience of a developing medium, Rafael. Rafael was about 30, married, with a young son. The possession occurred at a fiesta given by the medium S in honor of St. Barbara. Because this was a special occasion and not a regular session, other mediums and guests subdued Rafael but did not treat him.

S took up a red scarf (St. Barbara's color), waving it about the circle of people. Suddenly Rafael dropped to the floor and began rolling from one side of the circle to the other. His legs trembled. S pinned Rafael down and lay on top of him. She kept whispering to him and finally helped him up. Rafael's eyes were closed, and S opened them. He stood facing her, knees bent, arms hanging limply, slouch-shouldered and bug-eyed. S put her arms around him and danced with him. He spun away from her and lunged at a man, with whom he danced, then spun away and lunged at another man. Then he dropped to the floor again and rolled about so violently that several people had to restrain him. He was finally picked up, but as they stood him on his feet, he went limp. They sat him down, and in a few minutes he was able to stand again, very groggily.

On another occasion S commented that when she first took a spirit, it was fierce and terrible—like Rafael's. "Rafael has very strong spirits. They are still stronger than him. But now he is just beginning, so someday he will control them." Although S did not treat Rafael at length at the fiesta, her actions did constitute a brief form of treatment. In pinning Rafael down and speaking to him, she did for a time get him sufficiently in control to act the part of a protective spirit in a culturally appropriate manner (that is, by dancing with one of the guests as a form of blessing from the spirit.) The effect, however, was short-lived.

As in the brief treatment of Rafael, the fundamental therapeutic process in all development, according to Koss (n.d., p. 19;1970), involves the medium's first gaining control over the client's dissociative behavior (by forcing him out of trance through exorcism or by providing encouragement and the ritually appropriate atmosphere for trance induction) and then utilizing this control to elicit other changes in the novice's personal life. Koss sees this technique as providing the paradox which the psychologist Haley (1963:179) claims is essential to and characteristic of all psychotherapies—namely, the client is expected to develop control over his own behavior and at the same time submit to the control of the therapist.

This is by no means the only therapeutic technique embodied in mediumistic training, however, particularly in the Santería tradition. For, an important characteristic of the behavior of *santero* mediums is the degree to which it is patterned by the personalities ascribed to the major saintly spirits of the cult. As mentioned earlier, St. Barbara, for example, is aggressive, imperious, and hermaphroditic; La Mercedes, mild-mannered, soothing, motherly; St. Espedito, boisterous and drunken. When the chief medium names a particular saint as a spiritual protector of the novice and encourages the novice to "take on" the spirit of this saint in ritual contexts, the medium is not only encouraging dissociative behavior in a socially approved context, as Koss indicates, but is also directing the kind of behavior which is acted out. For example, when a medium indicates that St. Barbara is the client's protector and encourages the client to take the spirit of this saint at *centro* meetings, the medium is by this act channeling the client to become commanding and hyperactive in the ritual context.

Since the saints offer a range of personality types, the manner in which the head medium decides on the identities of the novice medium's protective spirits becomes an important therapeutic question. Does the spirit protector personify repressed impulses in the client, or does he or she embody overt problem areas of the client which, when acted out in the ritual context, become available to the suggestion and control of the medium? As the fledgling medium develops, of course, he adds new protectors to his spirit "crew." This permits the medium to work on different kinds of behavior as they become manifest in the client.

F. J. H. Huxley, in a stimulating essay on Haitian voodoo, attempts to understand this type of treatment by showing its relevance to neurotic conflict. Huxley locates the etiology of neurosis in the attempt to counter uncomfortable emotional states by muscular activity and suggests that the various patron gods enacted by a medium in voodoo rites express both the unacceptable emotions and the countervailing mode of muscular displacement. Thus, "a man may be possessed by a number of different gods during one ceremony, some of them energetic and outgoing, others withdrawn; some again fierce and tormented, others minatory and censorious. During possession, it seems, neuroses are dissociated into their positive and negative elements, and either of them can then emerge into physical action" (1966:426).[13] It is important to remember, however, that the medium's behavior would always be canalized chiefly by the personality and nature of his principal guide (*guía principal*), who is conceived as controlling the appearance of misguided spirits and other members of the medium's spirit "crew." Because of this controlling role of the *guía principal*, understanding the emergence of this force in the psychic life of the developing medium, as well as the personality and nature of

[13] See Wittkower (1970) for further discussion of the therapeutic value of trance states.

the particular guiding spirit, constitute important keys to comprehending the effects of spiritist psychotherapy. Unfortunately this and other interesting questions about the efficacy of spiritist treatment methods were beyond the scope of this exploratory study. Research into these questions by people trained in psychology or psychiatry would undoubtedly further our understanding not only of the spiritist system of psychotherapy but also of psychotherapy in general.

STRENGTHENING SPIRITUAL PROTECTION

The goal of strengthening the client's spiritual protection is central to all spiritist therapy. Although a specific treatment for *envidia* and sorcery, it plays a part in the treatment of all problems brought to spiritists. There are two ways of strengthening a client's spiritual protection. First, the medium can tell the client who his protectors are so that he can summon them directly in future; and second, the medium can make the client more pleasing to spirits so that he can attract additional protectors. After learning the identities of his protectors, however, the client becomes responsible for retaining their beneficence by remembering them through prayer and offerings of flowers or candles.

The following spiritist meeting described by the medical student Stanley Fisch, who attended sessions of this *centro* for a period of almost two years, demonstrates the identification of protectors as part of spiritist treatment.

> Later in the evening María (one of the mediums) became possessed. The *Presidente* motioned me to stand in front of her. She took my hands and began, "I am the spirit of a famous Spanish doctor, and I want to help you. You have shown much faith in spiritual things, and you want to help people with their spiritual problems. I am F—— de O—— of Spain. I died in 1897. I was a good doctor. You will be a doctor for children. When you need help, call me, and I will help you. Remember all the things you have learned here, and you will be a great doctor." Then she paused and rubbed my shoulders and arms and banged on the rim of the bowl. She made a few passes and then spoke again; "I am M—— S—— of Spain. I will also help you. When you need help, just call me, and I will come. You will be a great doctor, famous for medical and spiritual things. But remember, I am only for you. You must not tell anyone about me." Then she recovered.
>
> The *Presidente* repeated the last warning: these spirits are mine alone. I shouldn't tell anyone their names.

As the mediums explained, the purpose of learning the identity of one's protectors is to call upon them in time of trouble or uncertainty.

The second way of strengthening a person's spiritual protection—making the individual pleasing to spirits—has been partially demonstrated already in the use of *agua florida* on Nilda by the medium Julia. Baths scented with herbs or specially prepared perfumes or talismans may also be prescribed for this purpose. Honey or foods associated with particular saints may be eaten to attract protectors as well.

COUNSELING

In addition to dealing with the spiritual aspects of a client's problem, mediums also attend to the practical realities and interpersonal relationships of the client's life. This may be done either by the medium in person or by a spirit manifested through the medium. The former method is most frequently used in private consultations; the latter is typical of *centro* meetings.

The following passage illustrates advice given at a *centro* meeting by the spirit guide of a medium. Moving from one member of the audience to another, the medium stopped in front of two members of the *centro,* a mother of about 37 and her daughter, about 16. The daughter was known to the membership as a troublemaker—quick to take offence and frequently involved in arguments.

Medium. You'd like to be a boy, wouldn't you?

Girl. No.

Medium. You make love to the boys instead of them doing it to you. Don't look at me like that, or I'll tell your mother what happened. You know what happened. (To the mother) You are the man and the woman in your house. [She is separated from her husband]. Your children make you suffer a lot. You give them everything and don't get anything back from them. Why don't you go to a movie or a dance? You have to entertain yourself, have fun. Go out to a movie or dance![14]

Even if a client is not known to the mediums, as these were, the spirits often offer advice. A woman whose family was participating in our research project recounted to her researcher how she had gone to a *centro* she had heard about but never visited before. The spiritist at the *centro* had said that the woman's dead sister was protecting her. The sister's

[14] This is my translation of a community researcher's report of a session at a local *centro.*

spirit warned her to take care of her high blood pressure and not to take her children's problems so much to heart, because if she did it would cause her death. Since the woman had high blood pressure and her children were indeed going through several crises around that time, she was much impressed by the medium's accuracy.

The advice offered in these examples not only is typical of the direct counseling that takes place at *centro* meetings but also reflects some of the major themes of such advice. Anxious mothers are told not to worry so much about their children; young girls are cautioned about loose behavior with boys; married men and women are warned against carrying on extramarital affairs. Statements of public morality of this sort become more authoritative when they are articulated by a spirit, who purportedly knows more than he tells about people's behavior. In contrast to these public pronouncements, advice given at private consultations tends to be more analytical of the client's behavior in social relationships. In an open-ended interview with the medium Juana, whose developmental experiences were recounted above, she spoke of the kind of counseling she gives in private.

Juana began discussing the case of a woman coming to a spiritist because she wanted a boyfriend. "Many women come for that reason," she said. She would tell such a woman to bathe in a certain oil and build up her confidence. She would counsel the woman to buy a new dress. "Then if she went to a party, she would feel better about herself and undoubtedly attract a man." I asked if the medium would do anything with the woman's spiritual picture in an instance like that. She said no, not unless she saw some deeper trouble that the girl had. . . .

She then gave an example of a woman who came to her because she was "having problems with her husband." The man drank. Juana told the woman that the man was drinking because he wanted to. There must be something in the marriage and in her that helped lead him to it. The woman had to look at herself, too. She said that the man would not stop drinking until he wanted to, and Juana couldn't change him. The woman did not like this advice and went to another medium, who told her that she could make the husband docile and willing to do whatever the wife wished. [This pattern of behavior is expressed by the idiom, *sentado en el baúl,* literally "seated on a trunk," like a child.] The medium also told the woman that she would stake her herb shop on the effectiveness of her work. The woman, apparently conflicted over what she should do, came to Juana again and explained what the other medium had said.

Juana told the woman three things. First, she pointed out that a "job" like the one the other medium had suggested would cost her money and unless she was willing to pay, she'd better not start. Second, she asked the woman if she really thought she'd be happy knowing that her husband's attentiveness and love did not come from within himself but was caused by her voodoo. Third, she asked her if she were prepared for what might happen if her husband ever found out that she had "done a job on him." Juana told the woman that these three things were the ball park she would be playing in and that she should make up her mind in light of them.

These examples reveal a number of things about the advice given in private consultations. First, it tends to be direct and reality oriented. Second, as stated in Juana's first example, an important goal is to build up the client's self-esteem and confidence in his or her ability to function in the world. (This goal is undoubtedly aided by the spiritual practice of strengthening the client's protection.) Third, rather than giving direct advice, the medium may clarify the client's problem by indicating, as in Juana's second example, the implications of certain courses of action.

SUMMARY

The clientele of spiritist psychotherapy engage in either short-term, crisis therapy or long-term treatment in individual, group, or family-within-a-group settings. According to the spiritist etiological system, four factors work in varying combinations to produce the problems presented for treatment: intranquil or other imperfect disembodied spirits; the client's spiritual protection; the malevolence or envy of the client's kin, neighbors, friends, or other associates; and God. In arriving at a client's diagnosis, the therapists (one or more mediums) take an active role by stating presentiments about spiritual and social factors that might underlie the client's problem. The client must then either confirm or disconfirm the therapists' statements.

Problems that receive short-term treatment are usually either interpersonal or associated with periods of transition in life (puberty, early marriage, menopause, terminal illness). These problems are most commonly attributed to lower-order spirits and to human malevolence and envy, operating either alone (in which case the diagnoses are either *mala influencia* or *envidia* respectively) or in combination (*brujería*). Treatment typically involves removing the spiritual influences deemed to be causing the problem and increasing the client's spiritual protection. Direct counseling also occurs during this treatment.

Long-term treatment is usually initiated for more severe intrapsychic or familial problems. Suicidal feelings, silent brooding, fugue states, or recurrent nightmares constitute a syndrome ascribed to the effects of lower-order spirits who beset the sufferer because he or she has the faculty for serving as a vessel for communication with disembodied spirits. Treatment involves development of the client's ability to control the manifestation of these spirits (and consequently the symptoms) and to limit their appearance to appropriate times and places (such as, spiritist meetings). A history of intergenerational familial problems (a *cadena*), a condition conceived as the perpetuation of an act of sorcery, a curse, or some other evil spiritual influence through the generations, usually also receives long-term attention. Treatment involves removal of the spiritual influence and review of the client's past and present family experience.

Viewed as a form of psychotherapy, spiritism thus seems to address a wide range of interpersonal and intrapsychic problems by labeling them in terms of an etiological system that is widely known not only within the subculture of spiritism but also within the general Puerto Rican culture. The sufferer's problem thus becomes labeled but not stigmatized, as it would be after psychiatric diagnosis (see Rogler and Hollingshead, 1961:19), and the course of treatment implied by the spiritist label is plausibly and causally related to the etiology proposed within the logic of the psychotherapeutic system.

Thus far spiritist treatment fits Frank's definition of psychotherapy cited at the beginning of this chapter, and thus parallels other forms of psychotherapy. An apparent contrast with other psychotherapeutic systems—at least with Western medical models of psychotherapy—is the attribution of the etiology of problems to entities (spirits) outside the sufferer. This attribution appears to take responsibility for the cause of problems out of the sufferer's hands. Although such contrasts and similarities between spiritist and mainstream medical psychotherapies receive considerable attention in the final chapter, it is well to point out here that in my view the contrasts are superficial. Admittedly, however, areas of patient responsibility and nonresponsibility are allocated differently in the two therapies. Before taking up this issue at length, however, we examine in detail in the following chapter a case of spiritist treatment, and then look at how spiritist concepts are used in ordinary social life to render human motivations and actions comprehensible and manageable.

FIVE

A Case of Spiritist Treatment

Toward the end of the research project an opportunity arose to have a medium treat a patient hospitalized at an innovative state mental institution near the Health Center. The suggestion for this form of treatment for the patient apparently originated with a Puerto Rican ward worker, who believed in spiritism and learned from the patient that she had once been a medium. Since the patient, whom I shall call Clarita, had not responded to medication after several months of treatment in the hospital, the staff was open to a new approach for her case. With the approval of Clarita's family, the physician in charge therefore gave permission for a spiritist consultation.

Because I was known to be doing research on spiritism, I was contacted through the Health Center to locate a therapist for Clarita. Since I knew that the consultation was in the nature of a demonstration for the hospital staff, I decided to ask Juana to do it. Although not as experienced as some other mediums, I knew that Juana, articulate in both English and Spanish, was capable of explaining her methods to the hospital staff. Juana was eager to consult with Clarita, although she had considerable trepidation about doing so in the hospital, since, according to spiritist belief, many mental patients are in reality spiritually afflicted and she would therefore run the risk of taking on other patients' misguided spirits as well as her own client's. After conferring with friends and relatives who were also mediums, she decided to see the patient nevertheless.

PATIENT HISTORY

Our knowledge of Clarita's history unfolded slowly. At the time Juana agreed to the consultation, we knew only that she had been hospitalized twice in the previous six months, had not responded to treatment in the hospital, and had once been a medium herself. Since Juana was unwilling to work with Clarita if she were heavily medicated, we also learned that she was receiving tranquilizers (chlorpromazine and trifluperazine) and an anticonvulsive (diphenylhydantoin), prescribed because of reported "seizures." Juana requested that the patient be taken off medication, and the doctor ordered her morning dosage eliminated the day of the first session.

Only after that first session did we begin to piece together, from her family and hospital records, more data on Clarita's history. Even three months later, however, the history had many important gaps and inconsistencies. Each of our sources of information presented a somewhat different "truth" about Clarita.

At the time of treatment Clarita was in her late forties, alhough she appeared 10 years older. The earliest information about her went back around 25 years, when she was living in Puerto Rico. At that time she was married with four children (two girls and two boys), had been working for a number of years as a waitress, and began her development as a medium. According to Clarita's children, she became known as a spiritist and led an active life until her mother died about five years later. Although there are no data on the symptoms of Clarita's evolving illness, her first hospitalization reportedly occured five years after that, soon after she and her husband had separated. Since then, Clarita had spent several periods of time in mental hospitals, first in Puerto Rico and then in New York. In both places she received shock treatment for her illness; according to one of her daughters, insulin therapy was tried once in New York. Between hospitalizations she always lived with some member of her family—a sister in Puerto Rico and more recently with one or another of her children, all of whom were married.

Clarita's most recent episode of illness began about a year before Juana began treating her. She could not sleep, would not eat, and began staying in bed all day. She also suffered from "shaking spells and falling down," according to the hospital record—*ataques* in the terminology of her family. After several months of this kind of behavior, her youngest daughter (with whom she was living at the time) took her to the nearest city hospital.

At the initial hospital interview Clarita refused to answer questions in either Spanish or English, was characterized as walking "like a baby" (that is, clinging to staff members), and also displayed *flexibilitas cerea* (maintenance of imposed postures). She said she felt sad and very tired. After two weeks of observation Clarita was taken to the state hospital, where she was diagnosed as suffering from "schizophrenia, chronic undifferentiated type."

Clarita's behavior in the hospital was at first very active or, as the physician on the floor described it, "agitated." She changed her clothes frequently and was reported to pace the floor much of the night. On several occasions she fell to the floor as if in a faint and once took to her bed trembling after returning to the ward from a visit downstairs with her daughter. These episodes were all labeled "hysterical attacks" by the psychiatric staff. On one occasion during the first month, Clarita also ran away from the hospital but was soon found by the police and returned. During this period she also began a friendship with Fernanda, the ward attendant who later recommended her for spiritist treatment. Clarita confided to Fernanda that she thought her illness was caused by spirits who were castigating her for not performing *la obra* (that is, for not functioning as a medium). Occasionally Fernanda gave Clarita massages with *alcoholado* or *agua florida*.

On admission to the state hospital Clarita began receiving a moderately high dosage of tranquilizers—600 mg of chlorpromazine (Thorazine) and 10 mg of triflupcrazine (Stelazine) a day, as well as secobarbital (Seconol) as needed. Not unexpectedly, the daily ward record for Clarita's second month in the hospital reveals a change in her behavior. The patient was much more quiet, slept a lot, and complained of pains in her neck and back. Early in the month she suffered what was recorded as a grand mal seizure and was sent to another hospital for neurological examination. Although the electroencephalographic findings of this examination were negative, she was started on Dilantin. In spite of this medication, the staff continued to observe "trances" and "shaking spells" during the rest of the month. Before Clarita's condition became stabilized, however, she was sent home to live with one of her sons because the hospital staff went out on strike.

Four months later Clarita's son brought her into the Health Center in a very disturbed state. She was shouting abuses, especially at her daughter-in-law, and claimed that people were working sorcery against her. She was sent back to the state hospital, where she arrived "noncommunicative," according to the psychiatrist's report, and was put back on medication (Thorazine, 15 mg four times a day; Stelazine, 2 mg four times a day; and Dilantin, 100 mg three times a day).

The next three months showed marked deterioration in Clarita's condition, although her family reported that during their Sunday visits she conversed coherently with them and showed considerable interest in her grandchildren. On the ward, however, Clarita became more and more withdrawn. Except for periods of relatively normal behavior, in which she would eat and tend to her other bodily functions by herself, she refused to cooperate with the staff. She spent many of her days either lying in bed, if the ward staff gave up trying to rouse her, or huddled in a corner of the day room with eyes closed and arms covering her face. This was the condition of the patient when she was referred to Juana for spiritist treatment.

SPIRITIST TREATMENT IN THE HOSPITAL

Juana agreed to hold her treatment sessions behind a one-way mirror. The following report of these proceedings comes from my notes, which were later read and annotated by the medium. Additional explanatory information on the proceedings derives from direct discussions with her. Other material on the first consultation comes from notes taken by a medical resident on the ward, who witnessed the event. (This source is indicated as "M.D. observation" in the following text.) My own analysis or summary of the various events in the treatment process are contained in commentaries following each event.

FIRST CONSULTATION

Before the consultation began, Juana arranged a table with various ritual paraphernalia which she had brought from home: a white cloth to cover the table, a thermos of black coffee, holy water, and cigars. She asked for some ice, which was placed in a bowl on the floor. Supported by two orderlies, the patient was led into the room and seated in a chair on the opposite side of the table from Juana. Fernanda sat on the same side as Clarita but beyond normal conversational distance from the other two women. (Prior to the consultation Fernanda reported that she had explained to Clarita that the hospital was bringing someone in to help her spiritually and, contrary to her usual behavior when awakened, that morning Clarita had cooperated readily in taking her bath and getting dressed.)

At the consultation, however, Clarita sat slumped in her chair with eyes closed, almost inert. One of the first things Juana did was to prop her forward and upright on the chair. She then asked Clarita her name. When there was no response, she repeated the question several times and told Clarita her own name. The medium spent roughly the next hour trying by various means to get some response out of the patient. She fed her coffee, which the patient at first let dribble down her chin and after many attempts finally swallowed. Juana then tried to get Clarita to move her arms in the fashion typical of a *despojo*. If she let go of her hands, however, her arms would simply dangle limply. Juana rubbed the back of Clarita's head and neck, again with no response (although Juana later said she felt "vibrations" from the patient at that point). She also tried rubbing ice on Clarita's forearms and lower legs. She even laid an ice cube in the patient's hand. When this provoked no response, Juana forcibly pulled open the lids of Clarita's eyes. The pupils were rolled back, and she remained completely impassive. At this point Juana commented on how little the patient was responding and asked Fernanda how much medication she had been receiving. On hearing the amount, Juana seemed surprised and remarked on its excessiveness. MEDICATION.

Besides stimulating Clarita by touch and taste, Juana kept exhorting her verbally to speak to her, to say her name, and to tell her what her problem was. She repeatedly told the patient that she needed her cooperation in order to be of help. Gradually Clarita began responding to aural stimulation. When asked if her stomach hurt, for example, she rubbed her abdomen slightly. She also trembled faintly in response to Juana's rhythmic beating on a glass or the snapping of her fingers in an even beat next to the patient's ears. Since Clarita's response to auditory stimulation seemed greatest, Juana continued speaking to her, switching suddenly from a solicitous tone to one of impatience. Calling her *maricona* and other pejorative terms, Juana told Clarita, "Look, I'm leaving. Do you want me to come tomorrow? Do you want me to come Friday?" (At this point Juana asked Fernanda if Clarita responds to swearing and was told she does.) Juana therefore continued in a disparaging manner but switched her message to "Well, look, I've got all day. I'll just wait until you talk to me."

After almost an hour of this, with very little response other than some rhythmic shaking and rubbing of the stomach, Juana hit on a new tactic. Continuing her abusive language, Juana began accusing the patient of not being a medium. If she were really a medium, Juana challenged, she would have talked to her by now, because mediums talk and consult with one another. In saying this, Juana apparently noticed some response in the patient and again began tapping rhythmically. She continued for about a minute, still challenging Clarita about her claim to mediumship. Suddenly and very dramatically, Clarita's right hand shot out, and she took a spirit. Speaking very rapidly, she claimed that the spirit was that of José Cruz. She then fell silent, and Juana passed her the jar of water. Clarita exorcised herself and drew the spirit off into the water.

Juana made much of Clarita's performance, shouting *"¡Viva, Changó! ¡Gracias a Dios!"* Juana seemed to be on the verge of taking a spirit herself but was obviously fighting it by shaking her head. Soon Clarita took a second spirit, a protector, who announced that Clarita suffered a "chained life" (*una vida encadenada*). The spirit thanked Juana for coming to help her and said she wanted to cooperate with her. Clarita then drew this spirit off and deposited it in the water (*se despojó*). After giving up this spirit, Clarita sat up in her chair quite straight and smiled, although she never opened her eyes. Juana commented, "Uh-huh, now you're smiling!"

Juana then wrote down a prayer for Clarita to say every day for nine days. She advised that a bowl of ice be kept by the patient's bed and said that she would return at the end of nine days to perform a service with a rose and a glass of rum, which were then to be left beside the patient's bed. She also recommended that the patient be fed honey and black coffee, foods which she explained were both propitious for spirits and invigorating for the body.

After the consultation Clarita's frame of mind seemed quite different from when she came in. Although she still kept her eyes closed, she walked out of the room herself, feeling her way along the wall. Her posture was erect, and she retained a smile on her lips.

"I don't know what I expected of the session, but it was very striking to me. There was certainly nothing of sham or showiness about it, although I thought Juana might have been more than usually nervous because of the presence of observers. It seemed to consist of a sincerely applied set of techniques based on a system of beliefs about spirits—beliefs with which I am not familiar. The patient's response was very dramatic. She was pretty far regressed, and the session must have reached something very deep and important in her—some basic set of beliefs and fears—to rouse her in the way it did" (M.D. observation).

Commentary

The medium's major goals for this first session were the same as those which guide a therapist in the initial stages of any form of psychotherapy: securing the patient's cooperation, and convincing the patient that the therapist is indeed able to help. (Such phrases as "If you cooperate, I can help you" or "If you tell me your name and talk to me, I can help you" punctuated the consultation.) At the end of the session, Clarita's second spirit articulated her commitment to therapy precisely, by both thanking Juana for coming to help her and indicating her desire to cooperate. Judged by its realization of the major objectives of the early stages of psychotherapy, the session was therefore highly successful.

A noteworthy characteristic of Juana's method during the session was to test the responsiveness of Clarita's various sensory modalities. This procedure was conscious on her part, although the various tactics she used to stimulate the patient's senses were in part spontaneously chosen. That is, the props and verbal exhortations Juana used are all part of the cultural repertoire of spiritism, but the particular item from the repertoire and the exact moment it was used were not consciously controlled by her. It is this margin of choice in the use of specific spiritist techniques which, according to spiritist doctrine, becomes canalized during a consultation by the "vibrations" of the medium's and client's protectors. The tactics which seemed most efficacious with Clarita, for example, were the gruff talk of St. Barbara's cadre and Juana's ultimate challenge of Clarita's abilities as a medium. Juana initiated both these tactics spontaneously—in her terms, "through spiritual inspiration."

CASE CONFERENCE

methodology? – not really of spiritism

After the consultation the ward attendants, several social workers, and two psychiatrists met with Juana and me for a conference to discuss Clarita's treatment and prognosis. One of the psychiatrists asked Juana if she thought that Clarita's action of rubbing her abdomen had anything to do with ideas or fears of pregnancy. Juana replied that she thought not, that Clarita was rubbing her stomach because she was having her period. (Juana had been told this before the consultation by Fernanda, because it is reportedly difficult for menstruating women to pass spirits and she had therefore warned the medium that Clarita would be particularly hard to work with.) Later, when the discussion came around to the nine days during which Clarita was to recite the prayer, the doctor pursued his earlier line of inquiry by asking if the nine days had anything to do with nine months gestation period. Juana denied any connection between the two.

During the conference Juana advised the doctors that she could not continue working with the patient under so much medication. The physician in charge of the floor graciously ordered all tranquilizers stopped and the Dilantin tapered off over the next three weeks. In doing so he remarked, "We haven't seen any signs of improvement from the medication."

Another matter that Juana raised with the medical staff was the possibility of Clarita's discharge from the hospital. The physician in charge said that, so far as he knew, Clarita's family was willing to take her back and that he would recommend her leaving as soon as he felt she was ready. Juana pushed the point, suggesting that perhaps Clarita should have her own apartment rather than live with her family. The doctor agreed to discharge the patient as soon as was feasible. He also impressed upon the staff that the most beneficial thing they could do for Clarita at this point was to show her how important the medium's instructions and prescriptions were.

The staff expressed two concerns about following the prescribed regimen, however. First, they noted that keeping ice beside Clarita's bed might be difficult, since they had been having trouble with one of her roommates, who stole from her. This problem was resolved by deciding to move Clarita to a different room. The second obstacle the ward staff discussed was how to ensure that a Spanish-speaking worker would be present to help Clarita read the prayer. Schedules were checked and a verbal commitment obtained from various attendants to perform this task. In the event, neither of these problems was in fact overcome, and the regimen was followed only sporadically.

During the conference the chief psychiatrist on the ward asked Juana what she thought Clarita's prognosis was. "Juana said that no dramatic, sudden changes could be expected, but that hopefully after nine days little changes would become apparent. She hoped that the patient would begin to function at a slightly higher level" (M.D. observation). She explained that the degree of improvement depended a lot on the amount of time Clarita had been in mental institutions. The doctor thought this had been about 15 years. Juana said she had known mediums who had been in hospitals for one month or even six, but Clarita's 15 years was extreme. She explained that mediums frequently go through periods when they are "almost crazy" (the so-called *pruebas*). When pressed by some of the ward workers as to whether she thought Clarita would be cured, Juana admitted that she could not be sure, since a cure depends on so many factors. One of the psychiatrists supported Juana's opinion by saying that in his view Clarita's prognosis looked unfavorable, but that since psychiatric therapy had not helped her, they would try anything the medium suggested.

Commentary

In discussing the case conference later with Juana, I learned that she was considering the following diagnoses for Clarita's case: (1) *castigo,* the most obvious possibility, since Clarita had given up working as a medium; (2) sorcery, to counter a job Clarita may have done against someone while practicing as a medium; and (3) a *prueba* ordained by God. The latter two possibilities, she admitted, betokened a poor prognosis. She also reiterated her concern about Clarita's long years of hospitalization, during which time she would have become highly "contaminated" with the bad spiritual influences of other patients. These factors convinced Juana that Clarita's case was very "heavy" or "deep" (difficult to cure) and had led to her somewhat pessimistic prognosis when questioned by members of the staff.

The amount of medication that Clarita had been receiving also figured in Juana's cautious prognostications for the patient. Her concern, moreover, reflected an important tenet of spiritist therapy: that drugs of any type are contraindicated, particularly in cases (like Clarita's) of mediumistic development (*desarollo*). Since the goal of therapy for this diagnostic category is to enable the client to gain control over the comings and goings of errant spirits, any blunting of the natural functioning of the mind with drugs is seen as an impediment to treatment.

Thus from the spiritist point of view both hospitalization (where a patient may "pick up radiations" from the misguided spirits troubling other inmates) and the administration of drugs contravene standards of good psychotherapy. This helps explain Juana's request at the case conference for the doctor both to reduce Clarita's medication and to discharge her from the hospital as soon as possible.

FAMILY CONFERENCE

To provide more evidence for arriving at a diagnosis of Clarita's problem, as well as to see if she could identify José Cruz (the spirit who had manifested himself at the consultation), Juana arranged to meet with

Clarita's family. She managed to interview Clarita's youngest daughter and her daughter-in-law.

She first learned from them that Clarita had not actually been hospitalized for a full 15 years, although she had been in and out of hospitals for that period. Clarita's daughter claimed that so far as she knew, her mother had never practiced sorcery but only worked for good when she was a medium. Juana also learned that Clarita's estranged husband had died recently. In probing the circumstances of the couple's separation, Juana discovered that another woman had been involved.

The family identified José Cruz, the spirit who had presented himself at the consultation, as a friend of the family who had been "like a son to Clarita" and had died several months before. Several weeks later the family revealed that José was in fact Clarita's son-in-law, her eldest daughter's husband. The family claimed that they had never told Clarita of José's death because they had not wanted to upset her further. Juana advised the family to take a white carnation with them when they went to visit Clarita the following Sunday and to recite a prayer with her for José's spirit. (This ritual was designed to "give the spirit light"—that is, to help remove it from Clarita and the rest of the family. Since the family claimed never to have told Clarita about José's death, his spiritual visitation in the course of the treatment session constitutes what in spiritist terminology is called *comprobación,* proof or testimony to the existence of spirits or the correctness of a medium's words. José's materialization was therefore considered by the spiritist believers involved in the case as a major event, quite apart from its role in Clarita's therapy.)

In the course of her conversation with the family, Juana also suggested that Clarita get a separate apartment nearby when she was discharged from the hospital. She told the family that she did not think any couple should live with their in-laws.

Commentary

A spiritist diagnosis, it will be remembered from the previous chapter, entails both a spiritual cause and its relationship to the client's interpersonal situation. Juana thus sought an interview with Clarita's family to round out her data for the diagnosis. In addition to probing certain areas of Clarita's life that were obscure in the hospital record, Juana prepared the family for Clarita's discharge from the hospital. In doing so, she sensed some unwillingness on the part of the children to have their mother come live with them again. Clarita had been a burden in the last months before her hospitalization, and none of the children felt up to coping so soon again with the disruption she caused. In addition, the children's own lives had changed since Clarita's hospitalization: her eldest daughter's husband (José Cruz) had died, her youngest daughter had recently given birth, and her eldest son had returned to Puerto Rico. In view of this family situation, Juana suggested the separate apartment for Clarita and helped remove some of the family's guilt by invoking the normative rule in Puerto Rican culture that it is better for married children to live separately from their parents.

PATIENT'S REACTION TO THE FIRST CONSULTATION

The first few days after the consultation Clarita seemed much more alert and cooperative, although she did nothing that she had not done in the hospital on occasion in the past. She roused herself in the mornings, ate well on her own, and occasionally walked around the ward rather than sitting passively. Fernanda read the prayer with Clarita diligently, but on her days off no one carried through on the orders. Indeed, so far as we could determine, none of the regimen was followed completely as ordered. Within a few days Clarita's behavior was much as it had been before the consultation, a situation that Juana attributed to the ward staff's failure to carry through on her orders.

Commentary

It would seem that in spite of the genuine good intentions of many of the ward staff, structural conditions in the organization of the ward militated against compliance with a spiritist regimen. Work schedules meant that certain staff had never met the medium or seen the consultation and so were not familiar firsthand with the nature of the therapy. To read orders about keeping ice by the patient's bedside or feeding her honey without some insight into the purpose of these acts undoubtedly led to noncompliance—especially given the workers' responsibility for a full ward of other patients. Work schedules also meant that, in spite of the efforts made at the case conference to arrange for a Spanish-speaking staff member to be present on each shift, sometimes there was no one to read the prayer. Indeed even when there was a Spanish speaker on duty, there might be no one to read the prayer because of religious differences among Spanish speakers. Strict Roman Catholics and Pentecostalists, even though they may believe in spirits and know much about the subculture of spiritism, are enjoined by their churches not to participate in any spiritist rites, which they conceive as the work of the devil. Thus, sincere religious differences among staff members may also have prevented their compliance with the regimen.

Another factor in understanding the staff's role in complying with the regimen lies, I think, with Clarita's own behavior. Her developing pattern of dramatic improvement and equally dramatic lapses led to a cycle of aroused expectation among the staff, followed by frustration. The frustration led to anger, which some attendants expressed openly to Clarita and others acted out by avoiding her. As we shall see, Clarita's cyclical pattern began affecting many people involved in the case in a similar fashion (Juana included), in spite of genuine efforts on their part to understand the source of their anger and to control it. Clarita was, after all, a "difficult case" (as both Juana and the psychiatrist expressed it).

THE SECOND CONSULTATION

Juana had been planning to hold a second consultation with another medium present after the novena she prescribed was completed, but since her orders had not been followed, she decided to schedule the second session only six days after the first. She invited her friend Alma to accompany her in the hope that they might start "working Clarita's cause." The venue was the same as the first consultation with the same paraphernalia arranged on the table.

When I arrived with Juana and Alma, Clarita was in the day room sprawled across two chairs with her arm in front of her face. We had been prepared for her regressed behavior by the head ward attendant over the phone the previous day. Juana and Alma approached Clarita and coaxed her to get up. She was unresponsive for some time but finally acknowledged their presence. When they asked how she felt, she only murmured, "*Igual* (the same)," but managed to smoke a cigar which they offered her. The two mediums finally lifted Clarita onto a wheelchair to take her to the consultation room.

When the session began, Alma went over to Clarita and began talking to her in a very low voice. She took hold of the patient's hands by the middle fingers and squeezed them. She then stroked the back of Clarita's neck mildly (not in the more forceful fashion typical of a *despojo*). Meanwhile Juana lit a cigar and began blowing smoke in the patient's face. Juana also picked up some ice and then ran her chilled hands along Clarita's lower legs. Clarita grew stiff in her chair, and the mediums got her to sit forward. Alma then held the patient's hands up over her head, as mediums often do as part of a *despojo,* and Juana simultaneously rubbed the back of her head and began hyperventilating. She then began snapping her fingers rhythmically and trying to get Clarita to hyperventilate as well.

From this point on, there was a noticeable contrast in the way Alma and Juana each treated Clarita. Juana was boisterous, driving, and impatient; Alma was quiet, encouraging, and patient and assumed control of the consultation. If Juana became too noisy or came too close to Clarita, Alma would hold her off with a gesture or tell her to wait.

Alma encouraged Clarita to stand up on her own by telling her repeatedly that she would not fall. She got her on her feet and held her arms over her head. Every time she released them, however, Clarita would begin to fall forward. Alma seated the patient again, and the mediums offered her black coffee. They encouraged her to hold the cup herself and to finish the contents. When she did so, they were very appreciative and remarked on how well she had done and how much she had drunk. During the consultation Clarita trembled periodically. so the mediums tucked a covering around her legs. They told her to keep herself warm when she sat in the day room.

Anna then began repeatedly asking Clarita her name and requested her to open her eyes. When she did not stimulate a response with these instructions, she returned to exhortations to stand and walk. She helped Clarita to a standing position, repeating "Walk! Walk! You can walk by yourself. Three steps, just three steps!" All this time Juana made noises characteristic of a *congo* spirit. Together they succeeded in getting Clarita to take one step unaided, but had to support her for the rest. Occasionally Alma would rap the patient three times on the forehead.

Suddenly Juana threw a glass of water to the floor and shouted, "*¡Coño!*" A spirit bothering Clarita was presumably manifesting itself, but Alma cautioned Juana to stop and she pulled out of it almost immediately. (Alma apparently did not think Clarita was ready for "working the spirit.")

Alma continued her quiet encouragement and renewed her efforts to get Clarita in control of herself. She told Clarita her name and got her to repeat it. She then placed some tissues dipped in coffee on the back of Clarita's neck—a procedure designed to "open the door" for the passage of spirits.

At this time Alma took her protective spirit, who continued working with Clarita in the same quiet fashion. She again got the patient to stand and turned her around several times to the right and left, telling her to open her eyes. Tapping her three times on the forehead, she told her there was nothing wrong with her that necessitated her being in a mental hospital. She needed "work," and they were there to help her. At this point, Alma's spirit left her.

After a quiet conference between Alma and Juana in which they discussed the patient's seriously regressed condition, Alma began a new dialogue with Clarita about the necessity for cooperation if she wanted to get better. She then asked Clarita her name, how many children she had, and other basic questions. This time the patient responded, and the mediums commented approvingly on her behavior. The rest of the consultation proceeded in this vein, with the mediums trying to get Clarita to respond either in words or action to questions and commands. The mediums' efforts focused on three themes: to get Clarita to know and remember Alma's name, to discover who Clarita's protection was by asking her if she "knew" various saints, and to encourage her to act normally so she could get out of the hospital ("this cage"). Alma told Clarita, "You don't want to stay in this cage. You are in this world for a purpose, and your purpose is to work with the spirits and help people. Return to the world, return to your mission!"

After the mediums had determined by their questioning that Clarita's protection was St. Martha and La Milagrosa, they provided her with a pad and pencil. Alma held the pencil in Clarita's hand and began drawing circular patterns on the paper with her. She then let go of the pencil and allowed Clarita's hand to roam over the paper at will. (This paper, called a *clave,* 'key', is used by mediums to provide clues to a client's spiritual problems.)

Alma then reminded Clarita that she had greeted a spirit at the last session and asker her if she wished to do so again. She refused, and the mediums asked if her *cerebro* (the back of the head where spirits enter) hurt. She replied that it did, and they prescribed a poultice of grape juice and beaten egg (foods associated with particular protectors) to be placed on the back of her neck every day at noon. They then fed her honey and holy water, which Clarita guzzled greedily. With that, Alma again asked Clarita if she knew her (the medium's) name, and when Clarita responded correctly, the session came to an end.

Commentary

This consultation produced no results as dramatic as the first. The mediums were concerned and somewhat disappointed over Clarita's unresponsiveness. They, particularly Juana, had planned to start "working" Clarita's offending spirits but found her too withdrawn and weak to profit from this mode of treatment. They therefore concentrated instead on preparing her body and *cerebro* for treatment another time. They did this by feeding her honey and holy water (to attract protective spirits) and by prescribing the poultice for her *cerebro*. This latter form of treatment, called a *chofo*, is designed to attract protective spirits and to "loosen up" this crucial area of the anatomy for the passage of spirits.

In discussing this second session with Juana, I gained an interesting insight into a technique of spiritist diagnosis. During our conversation Juana admitted feeling somewhat ashamed that she had let herself go into trance in front of the psychiatrists. She said that she had been thinking about this at home after the session and realized that she had put her hand up over her face while reviewing her behavior in her mind. She equated her own gesture with Clarita's characteristic pose of putting one arm over her eyes and suggested that perhaps Clarita was ashamed of something, just as she herself had felt ashamed when she made the gesture. Juana said that mediums are attentive to their client's gestures and often tell them what they think particular gestures mean. She claimed that her own "ESP" was founded mainly on such sensitivity to gestures.

The contrast between Alma's and Juana's ways of approaching Clarita suggests a number of things about the treatment process in spiritism. In spiritist terms, the two mediums were simply acting in accord with the personalities of their respective protectors, who come from different spiritual cadres. Juana's major protection is St. Barbara; Alma's is La Mercedes. In psychoanalytic terms, however, these spirits might be said to stand for id and ego functions respectively. Juana's *congo* punctuated the session with animal noises and displayed poor impulse control by throwing the glass to the floor and constantly pushing to bring on a spirit. Alma, in contrast, approached Clarita rationally, assuring her that she was capable of simple activities and encouraging her to act in ways that would get her out of her "cage." Notably she also controlled Juana's tendency toward unrestrained behavior. If, to push the psychoanalytic interpretation of the situation further, Clarita's problem were a conversion reaction (that is, if her bodily symptoms resulted from unacceptable, unconscious sexual or other id impulses), then Alma was demonstrating ego control over similar impulses as they pressed for release in Juana. If treatment had proceeded (that is, if Clarita had been ready), Juana might have acted out some of the patient's unacceptable impulses and led Clarita to do so as well. (Note that Juana did attempt to get Clarita into trance at the beginning of the session by hyperventilating and snapping her fingers rhythmically.) Meanwhile Alma, as ego, would have exercised control over the situation. Successful treatment in such a case would have consisted in Alma's ultimately handing over her protective spirit (ego control) to Clarita, so that she could then master these impulses herself.

A major difference between spiritist therapy and psychoanalytic therapy becomes particularly apparent in this example. Both id and ego functions in spiritist therapy are invested in entities outside the client (that is, in spirits) which the client then learns to control and internalize. In contrast, a major psychoanalytic goal is for clients first to acknowledge impulses as their own and then to exert internal controls on them through rational choice. This important, recurrently observable contrast between spiritst therapy and mainstream psychiatry is discussed more fully in the concluding chapter of this book.

A final observaion about this session concerns the syncretic character of the procedure. Although both Alma and Juana considered themselves to be Mesa Blanca mediums, St. Barbara, La Mercedes, and Juana's *congos* are all part of Santería practice, as are the use of the *chofo* and honey to attract protective spirits. Use of the *clave,* however, is a Mesa Blanca procedure. Almost all spiritist sessions which I witnessed, regardless of the name of the tradition the practitioners went by, melded Mesa Blanca and Santería traditions in similar fashion.

CASE CONFERENCE

Following the session, the mediums again met with the chief psychiatrist on the ward, several social workers, and some of the attendants. The tone of this conference was not nearly so hopeful as the last, and the psychiatrist seemed more skeptical of the mediums' technique.

Juana began by clarifying a few matters for herself with the doctor. She first asked what the effect of shock treatment was. The doctor began by admitting that medical people do not know specifically what its effect is, but a nurse interrupted him to suggest that it causes greater activity in the brain, and he then agreed that there is some evidence for this. Juana then checked to make sure that Clarita's medication had been eliminated as promised, and the doctor assured her that it had.

The doctor then asked Juana and Alma what they thought Clarita's chances were. Less cautious than Juana had been at the last conference, they jointly stated that at this point her chances for recovery looked good. The doctor said that improvement might be expected in anyone who had received so much attention. He also expressed fear that Clarita would become too dependent on the mediums and ward staff who were providing the care recommended by the spiritists. He urged the staff to make sure that the patient did not become too dependent on any one of them. A Black ward worker mentioned that Clarita knew some English and that therefore non-Spanish-speaking staff could also talk to her. Juana reinforced this, although she discreetly disagreed with the doctor about Clarita's dependence. She said that during treatment this seemed necessary but that after treatment she would not expect Clarita to be any more dependent than she had been before becoming ill. The psychiatrist urged the staff to notice how many people were being "tied up" in treating this one patient. Juana said that as a medium Clarita had helped other people in the past and suggested that the staff look upon their work with her as repayment for this prior service.

The doctor then commented on the mediums' approach, likening it to "a school of psychiatry" which advocated returning a patient to an infantile state by having the therapist feed and hold the patient on his or her lap. He claimed that this kind of therapy had been shown not to work very well, and he felt that the staff should not infantilize Clarita. They should require adult behavior of her and give her recognition when she displayed it. He asked if they were doing this and was answered affirmatively.

Discussion of why prayers had not been said as ordered was initiated by Fernanda. She seemed angry that someone had not covered for her in this regard during her weekend off. Another Spanish-speaking staff member was delegated to attend to this duty in Fernanda's absence.

Quite unexpectedly the doctor mentioned that if Clarita seemed reasonably well, he would give her a day pass to go home for the next treatment session. Juana was very happy about this.

STAFF PERCEPTION OF CLARITA'S REACTION TO THE CONSULTATION

Ward Staff's Perception

The day following this consultation. I spoke with the head ward attendant about Clarita's reaction to the consultation. He reported that after the treatment Clarita had walked into the dining room herself, something which she had done only rarely. Later in the afternoon she urinated on the floor and, without prompting, got up and asked for a mop to clean it up. This was the first time she had voluntarily cleaned up after herself since she had been readmitted to the hospital three months earlier. The ward staff, he said, took this as a good sign.

A week after the consultation I spoke with the same attendant, who reported that Clarita was now much more angry than she used to be. Her resistance to getting out of bed, eating, or sitting in the day room had changed from passive inactivity to an active hitting out at the attendants. Another worker noted that Clarita's tremors had stopped, and others had seen her walking erectly and unaided as she sneaked down a rear corridor back to her bed from the day room.

Two staff members remarked on the gamelike quality of Clarita's interaction with them. For example, she would hide under her sheet and peak out to see if an attendant was watching her when he or she came into the room. She also groaned only when people were around. In short, she seemed to want to provoke their attention by her behavior.

Fernanda's Perception

Following the second session, Fernanda saw to it that the prayer was recited with Clarita for the required nine days. She reported that on the first day Clarita tried to read the words herself, but on the following days she simply stood by while an attendant read them for her. Fernanda expressed concern over Clarita's failure to make any overt effort to improve. In fact she reported that Clarita had told her. "Don't bother me. Let me die. Leave me alone. I want to die." Fernanda told Clarita that it was entirely up to her, that she had to put forth some effort on her own behalf. Fernanda also felt that Clarita functioned better when left alone. Whenever people were around, according to her, Clarita would moan and complain about aches and pains, but she seemed to get along well on her own. Fernanda mentioned the presence of "unbelievers" among the ward staff, who she felt were undermining the efficacy of the treatment.

Psychiatrist's Perception

In discussing the case with the head psychiatrist on the ward, I learned that he judged the mediums' technique as appropriate for treating "hysteria" but that he did not see Clarita's behavior as hysterical. If she were really hysterical, he observed, she would be far more interested in people's reactions to her behavior. At this stage of her illness, however, he (in contrast to Fernanda and other attendants) saw no evidence that this was so.

The physician also observed that Fernanda had become "very attached" to Clarita during her first admission to the hospital and had then become "frightened" by the relationship and so backed off. He saw Clarita's present regression as related to Fernanda's withdrawal.

Commentary

The above observations of Clarita's behavior as reported by various staff members have been included here to give some indication of the ambiance on the ward during her treatment as well as the situation which prompted the head psychiatrist to allow her release for further therapy. My own assessment is that the staff was divided in their opinions over the form of treatment Clarita was receiving. Some were openly in favor of it and working to see that it was maintained; others were antithetical or at least indifferent and did not cooperate in the regimen. The head psychiatrist was, to my mind, ambivalent—willing to try anything in view of the patient's failure to respond to his own mode of therapy, but distrustful of the mediums' procedures. His dampened enthusiasm at the second case conference was also prompted by growing dissension among ward staff over the attention accorded Clarita. The problem to some extent reflected tensions between Black and Hispanic workers which had nothing to do with Clarita herself, although the special attention that Fernanda was showing the patient did lead to accusations that she was not bearing her part of the burden of general ward work. This situation on the ward, coupled with the psychiatrist's growing misgivings about the appropriateness of spiritist therapy for Clarita's condition, help make his decision to discharge her for further treatment more understandable.

My own view of the psychiatrist's belief that Fernanda's withdrawal from Clarita had contributed to her regression is that his conclusion was based on an impression that had been carefully managed by Fernanda. As I saw it, Fernanda was very much involved with Clarita and her treatment during the period I followed the case, although of course I had no opportunity to observe the relationship between the two during Clarita's earlier hospitalization and thus compare it with their more recent behavior. I know that she was in almost daily telephone contact with Juana and acted as her emissary with Clarita. The staff's gossip about the amount of time Fernanda devoted to the patient also seems to corroborate their continued attachment. The doctor's warnings to staff not to allow Clarita to become too dependent on any one worker may well have influenced the impression that Fernanda sought to foster in his presence, and thus led to his belief that she had indeed withdrawn from Clarita.

OBSERVATIONS ON SPIRITIST TREATMENT IN A HOSPITAL SETTING

Although obviously no conclusive statements about the possible utility of spiritist psychotherapy for hospitalized patients can be drawn from this one case, the experience was nevertheless instructive. A number of factors must be considered in attempting this form of therapy. First, in spite of the commendable willingness of the hospital administration to try this form of therapy, and the sincere efforts of many staff members to carry out the therapeutic regimen, certain social structural conditions on the ward clearly militated against a favorable outcome. Work schedules, the needs of other patients, and social tensions among ward workers hampered the staff, however well-meaning they were, in carrying out the regimen. The resultant noncompliance with the procedures that Clarita had heard her therapist prescribe and that she, as a medium, knew to be therapeutically "proper" for her condition as she conceived it (*castigo*) must have influenced her response to treatment. Indeed her increasing anger toward the staff, as reported by the head ward attendant, may well be seen as a reaction to their failure to follow through on her care.

To use this mode of treatment for a hospitalized patient therefore implies a formal reallocation of duties among the staff to permit some members to carry out the uncommon routines of a spiritist regimen at least part of the time. As long as ward workers must deal with all the patients all the time, and thus oversee normal patient routines as well as the special ones entailed in spiritism, friction among staff members is likely to develop and the special routines neglected. Some formally sanctioned assignment of responsibility for the management of the spiritist patient would thus seem necessary.

A second factor that almost certainly influenced the outcome of this attempt at spiritist treatment was its experimental nature. As a demonstration, it produced an expectation of quick results among a staff already somewhat exercised by the patient's behavior. In spite of Juana's and the psychiatrist's modest predictions for improvement, staff members understandably became impatient and disappointed with Clarita's halting efforts at recovery and were perhaps too soon disillusioned with the form of treatment. This disillusionment was of course sustained by Clarita's own behavior, which suggests the third lesson to be drawn from this instance of treatment. If one is trying a form of therapy as a demonstration, it is advisable at the beginning to choose patients who are most likely to profit from that therapy. In this way the staff can gain some appreciation not only of what the therapy can accomplish but also of their role in it before being confronted by its limitations. This conclusion suggests the need for criteria for differentiating patients most likely to profit from spiritist therapy. We return to this task at the conclusion of the chapter.

HOME TREATMENT OF THE PATIENT

Juana eagerly took up the doctor's suggestion that Clarita be allowed out on a day pass for further treatment and asked me to see whether a longer leave might be arranged. She was willing to keep Clarita at her apartment if she could be reimbursed for the patient's board. Through the auspices of the Medical Director of the Health Center, which took medical responsibility for the patient's care, and with the permission of the family, the hospital agreed to give Clarita a two-week pass to stay with Juana. Arrangements were also made with the Department of Social Services to pay for her board.

Unfortunately, in all the planning and permission-getting, no one (including Juana) secured Clarita's cooperation and approval for the arrangement, although she was certainly told what was in store for her. As a result, Clarita became violent when the attendants tried to dress her on the day of the move. The patient had to be carried into Juana's apartment.

The following summary of Clarita's home treatment is based on a daily log kept by Juana.[1] It is divided into three sections, each focusing on a different aspect of the treatment (the spiritual regimen, independence training, and the client's reactions). Although Juana lived alone and the major responsibility for Clarita's care thus fell on her, she was assisted in some of the daily routines by an aunt and a friend, who stopped by every few days. Before Clarita's arrival, Juana gave her apartment a spiritual cleaning.

SPIRITUAL REGIMEN

Every morning, noon, and evening Juana prayed with Clarita and encouraged her to "elevate her thoughts to God" and to renew the faith that had supported her in the past. In an effort to rouse the patient to participate in the ongoing treatment, she repeatedly reminded her of the maxim, "God helps those who help themselves." The medium also impressed upon Clarita that she would owe Juana neither gratitude nor money if she got better—that Juana was treating her as part of her own calling.

In addition to these verbal attempts to get Clarita into a frame of mind for spiritist treatment, Juana administered daily baths and massages designed to prepare her body as well. She also exorcised the patient

[1] The log was kept in Spanish, and the passages quoted below were translated by me.

at least once a day with *agua florida* and encouraged Clarita to apply the cologne herself. Glasses of water were kept in every room to catch and hold malicious spiritual influences, and when Clarita began getting out of bed, Juana played *santero* records to her in the living room. In short, Juana provided Clarita with an environment replete with spiritist symbols.

These measures were designed to prepare Clarita for four spiritist meetings, which were held on Tuesdays and Fridays during her stay. For these meetings Juana enlisted the help of Alma and another medium. The mediums hoped that by the final Friday Clarita might be well enough for them to "work her cause," but, as will become apparent in reviewing her behavior below, she at no time displayed sufficient interest in the treatment to participate in the cure.

INDEPENDENCE TRAINING

Partly in response to the psychiatrist's concern about Clarita's independence, Juana let her know from the start that she expected her to take care of her own bodily needs. For the first three days, during which Clarita stayed in bed, Juana provided her with a chamber pot. As she became more mobile, however, Juana encouraged her to walk to the bathroom and to wash and bathe herself. She also left food for Clarita to eat but, except for the first days, did not attempt to feed her.

At first Juana's encouragement to Clarita took the form of positive suggestion and a display of confidence in her ability. She would say, for example, "You can walk, Clarita," or "You can take this cup and drink yourself." Juana would remain nearby to be of assistance, when necessary, but essentially let Clarita manage as best she could. By the fifth day, Juana began speaking to her angrily—at first spontaneously, but when she saw that it produced results, she continued in this vein: "*Coño, maricona,* do your part! I won't support you. If you fall, tough luck." She interspersed this approach with her encouraging tone.

CLIENT'S REACTIONS TO TREATMENT

For the first three days Clarita stayed in bed. At first her manner and facial expression were withdrawn, but gradually she began participating in the spiritual and ordinary routines of the household. She applied *agua florida* to herself and fed herself. During the first days she cried intermittently and at the first Tuesday session (her second day at Juana's) began sobbing as the mediums recited prayers for her. The following day she was more cooperative and opened her eyes a little, until her youngest daughter called on the telephone. During this call the daughter asked if she could visit and, when Juana told her to come on Sunday, replied that perhaps it would be better if she did not come after all, because Clarita "might change on seeing her." After the call Clarita again became less responsive.

On the fourth day Clarita got out of bed, once with assistance and once entirely on her own. She still did not communicate verbally with Juana and did not cooperate with the mediums when they held a meeting with her the following day. Although they prayed with her and exorcised her as before, this time Clarita did not respond at all. Around this time Juana began her angry approach to Clarita, interlarding her abuse with more kindly exhortations:

> How come you don't want to help me? You don't look at me. You don't talk to me. Why, since I want to help you? I know that you have feelings. Help me. Ask God; if you were a medium, you can elevate your thoughts to Him so that He helps you. Now, come on! Let's go to the living room. You can walk alone. I can't carry you. ¡*Coño*! Help me!

Interacting with Clarita in this manner, Juana got her into a routine of walking to the living room and sitting up straight in a chair for awhile, eating, listening to *santero* records, and washing herself. On hearing the records, Clarita would occasionally cry, although she would not tell Juana what she was crying about. She also rubbed her stomach periodically, as though in pain, which gave Juana increasing concern.

On the first Sunday, when Clarita was in this state of doing a few things for herself, her son and daughters visited. She became very emotional with her son, crying and complaining that Juana was beating her and that the other mediums were trying to kill her (accusations that she had regularly made about the hospital staff as well.) Ignoring her daughters completely, she tried in this way to get her son to take her home with him. While the family was there, Clarita walked to the bathroom herself, which surprised them since she used to urinate on the floor in her children's houses. Juana told the family that she and the other mediums planned to "work" Clarita's spirits the following Friday and asked them to attend the meeting.

During the first six to eight days of Clarita's stay with Juana, Juana's notes reveal her optimism about the treatment and Clarita's greater responsiveness.

> Her expression is growing more pleasant. She is cooperating. She walks without leaning against me. If I tell her, "Get up," she does it without my having to plead with her, as was necessary in the beginning. Her body seems lighter.

During this period Clarita also spoke to Juana for the first time. It was simply to refuse an egg that Juana had offered her, but Juana considered it significant.

On the second Tuesday of Clarita's stay, however, she was still rubbing her stomach periodically and had not evacuated since her arrival. Juana therefore gave her a patent medicine, which she thought would relieve her. Instead, Clarita vomited the medicine, and Juana called the hospital to see if she should bring her in for an examination. The doctor told her to do so if she continued vomiting. In the meantime Juana gave Clarita oregano tea (a folk remedy for settling the stomach) and "blessed" (*santiguó*) her abdomen (see Chapter 1 for a discussion of *santiguo* in the treatment of intestinal problems.) Clarita soon stopped vomiting but remained lethargic, slumped on the bed in her typical hospital attitude, with one arm over her eyes.

After several hours of periodically trying to get Clarita out of this attitude, Juana completely lost her temper with the patient.

> Impulsively I let out a loud "*¡Coño!*" and said to her, "Look at me. We are going to talk. It isn't that you can't cooperate. It's that you don't want to." Clarita opened her eyes and began to tremble and cry. I said, "Cooperate, because you can! Who do you think you are? If you don't pull yourself together, I'll throw you out the window." Clarita's legs began to tremble, and I said, "Here you don't pull that shit! Don't be an ass." Finally I said to her, "If you want to die, it won't be [by lying around] this way. You'll die when God wills it."
>
> Five or ten minutes later Clarita said, "I want to go." I asked her where, and she said, "Home." She got up and told me clearly, "I want to go home." She took off her nightgown and began heading for the door in her panties. I told her she couldn't go into the street in panties, and she told me to look for her bathrobe and shoes. I answered, "If you want to go, dress yourself"—which she did! She even put on her shoes perfectly. I said, "Let me comb your hair," and she raised her arms and began fixing her hair herself. Afterward she began walking toward the door, and I asked her, "Where is home? The hospital?"

Clarita said no and asked Juana to call her eldest daughter on the telephone. She then complained to the daughter about the treatment she was getting and asked her to come get her. The daughter said it was raining very hard, but she would try to come. The rest of the day Clarita spent trying periodically to open the front door of Juana's apartment and later, when her daughter failed to come, listlessly sitting on the hall floor. In the late afternoon Juana apologized to her for speaking so angrily, but the long-run effect of her outburst seems to have been to drive Clarita into withdrawal and passive resistance.

That night Alma and the other medium arrived for their Tuesday meeting. Alma told Clarita that they had come to help her. Clarita responded by getting up and walking to the table but did not participate actively in the session. The mediums prayed and exorcised her, and one of them again blessed her abdomen.

For the remainder of her stay Clarita cooperated minimally, ate little, and spent much of the time in bed. Although Juana continued trying to cajole her out of her withdrawal, the only things she would do regularly were to walk to the bathroom and take a daily bath. On Thursday Clarita announced that she wanted to go back to the hospital and spent the day in the hall by the door. Since Juana wanted to try one more session with her, she left her there, giving her food and periodically sitting and talking with her.

On the night of the last session Clarita had to be coaxed out of bed to the table, where she sat with eyes closed. Of her three children in the city, only the younger daughter appeared for the session—and only after a last-minute phone call urging her to come and promising that she could leave early. Alma assumed direction of the meeting and spent a great deal of time trying to no avail to get Clarita to take a spirit. Alma then took her main spirit guide and announced that someone in the family had died tragically and that there were in fact many tragedies in Clarita's family. Speaking to Clarita's daughter, she said, "Your father, dead! Your grandmother, dead! Someone else, also dead in the hospital." Clarita's daughter responded that her grandfather (Clarita's father) had died in a hospital for the insane. She also said that two of Clarita's sisters were also "crazy" (*loca*) even though they could take care of themselves.

The mediums then reviewed the series of *causas* that were responsible for Clarita's condition. The situation was, in their words, "gigantic." First, there were physical causes: insanity in the family, which the mediums felt had some congenital basis, plus the shock treatments and drugs she had received over the years. Second, there were environmental determinants of her condition: her years in mental institutions and the suffering she experienced in her family. Finally, there were three spiritual causes: sorcery on the part of the woman who had long ago taken Clarita's husband away from her (a woman whom the mediums identified as a friend Clarita had helped in the past); a *castigo,* brought on by Clarita's renunciation of her protectors after being deceived by her husband and friend; and a *cadena* which had plagued the family through generations. (The last *causa* had been revealed by Clarita's own protector at the first consultation at the hospital.) The most important factor among these, according to the mediums, was Clarita's continued renunciation of her protection and fundamental unwillingness to make the effort to resume her faith.

The mediums decided that it was useless to try "working" the spiritual causes of Clarita's condition because she was too regressed to participate. After a few additional prayers, they therefore closed the session.

During the remaining two days of her stay with Juana, Clarita continued performing only basic necessities for herself and returned to the hospital behaving much as she had before her release.

OBSERVATIONS ON CLARITA'S HOME TREATMENT

In reviewing the procedure and the outcome of Clarita's home treatment, a number of factors in the situation stand out as worthy of special note. Prime among these, of course, was the state of the patient herself. Since, however, I shall have more to say on this subject in my concluding remarks to this chapter, I shall focus here on the three major social influences in Clarita's life: the hospital staff, Juana, and her family.

THE ROLE OF THE HOSPITAL IN ARRANGING FOR HOME TREATMENT

Clarita's opposition to being moved, which contrasted vividly with her cooperativeness on the day of the first hospital consultation, indicates to me that she did not really approve the transfer to Juana's apartment for treatment. Whereas she had initiated the quest for spiritist help and received it willingly at first, she seemed to be in a different frame of mind after treatment in the hospital. She communicated her current emotional state to Fernanda in the words, "Leave me alone. I want to die." Whether this hopelessness and depression could have been overcome in the hospital before removal to Juana's seems moot, but without some change in attitude the therapy, it seems to me, was almost doomed to failure. That Juana succeeded at all in bringing about small changes in Clarita's behavior seems significant, given the patient's opposition to continued treatment.

JUANA'S ROLE IN THE TREATMENT

Juana had used anger to provoke her client to action successfully at her first consultation. It appears, however, that what started as a salutary therapeutic device, largely under the therapist's conscious control, turned, on daily contact with Clarita, into a rage which was difficult for Juana to use productively. Clarita's resistance to therapy was only partly responsible for this rage; in part it was also due to Juana's own investment in the success of the demonstration. Although her predictions for success were modest after the first consultation, they became more optimistic at the second case conference. Furthermore, since she attributed much of the failure of the hospital treatment to the staff and the hospital environment, her expectation for success at home was high, and its frustration was all the more difficult to accept. In intimate and almost constant contact with Clarita, she ceased being satisfied with small but measurable gains.

CLARITA'S PERCEPTION OF HER FAMILY'S ROLE IN THE TREATMENT

Clarita may well have perceived her family's failure to take her into their own homes as a rejection. By the second Thursday of her stay with Juana, when she expressed the desire to return to the hospital, she had apparently realized that her rather impassioned requests to both her son and older daughter to live with them would not be met. This realization, I suggest, contributed to her general despair and hopelessness.

Another family-related factor that may also have contributed to Clarita's depressed state were the deaths of her son-in-law (José Cruz) and her estranged husband. Although the family claimed that they had not told her about these misfortunes, they talked about the death of Cruz while their mother was in the room on the Sunday that they visited her in Juana's apartment. My observations of other Puerto Rican families in the course of this study indicate that adults often speak in front of children and "*locos*" as though they do not understand. Although we cannot establish how much the family might offhandedly have communicated to Clarita about these deaths, we also cannot rule out some knowledge of these tragedies in assessing the causes of Clarita's despair and withdrawal.

SUMMARY AND GENERAL ASSESSMENT OF CLARITA'S TREATMENT

Juana's contact with Clarita extended over a period of three months; Clarita's illness, according to her family and hospital records, had extended over 20 years. To have expected significant gains from a patient diagnosed as either a chronic schizophrenic or a long-term sufferer of *castigo* would have been unrealistic, and in fact no marked changes in the patient occurred. What, then, can we conclude from this demonstration? I think that two important items of information can be drawn from the experience with Clarita. First, we can state more clearly some of the goals and methods of spiritist psychotherapy as these were manifest in this case. And second, we can say something about the kind of patient who is unlikely to respond perceptibly to this form of treatment and, on this basis, suggest the kind of patient who might well profit from it.

this?

THE GOALS AND METHODS OF SPIRITIST PSYCHOTHERAPY

Although this demonstration did not provide much information on spiritist treatment methods (specifically "working the cause"), since the client never reached a level of functioning where they could appropriately be applied, a number of observations can nevertheless be made about some of these methods and particularly about preparation of the client for therapy. This preparation basically involved establishing a therapeutic relationship with the client. We can isolate several features of Juana's efforts in this regard.

1. The patient was never viewed as a hopeless case. At no time (even during her anger) did Juana treat Clarita as though she did not have the resources to get better. Indeed, before Clarita returned to the hospital, Juana sat her down and told her, "You have a very heavy burden, and you can help yourself if you wish. . . . From time to time you have moments in which you are okay, but you do not do your part. You prefer your bed; yet you know that God says, 'Help yourself that I may help you.'" According to spiritist belief, all Clarita had to do was to pray to God for the will to get better, and the therapy could commence. She was repeatedly reminded that this resource was open to her; her case was not hopeless, and Juana was ready to help whenever Clarita herself was ready.

2. The medium, through demonstrating her skills and knowledge of spiritism, established herself as someone who could indeed help the patient. Contrary to most psychiatric therapies, in which the criteria for judging the therapist's skill are usually unknown or even unknowable to the patient and may rest solely on the inferential evidence of diplomas hanging on the wall, a spiritist must demonstrate by concrete acts for the patient that he or she is skilled in the therapeutic technique. Juana demonstrated her skill not only by using the jargon and manipulating the paraphernalia of the therapy but also by taking spirits herself. Furthermore, both she and the patient shared knowledge of the therapeutic jargon as well as the criteria for evaluating a good therapist—a feature lacking in most instances of psychiatric therapy.

3. The therapist showed that she cared about the patient both by the attention she accorded her and by her emotional reactions to her behavior. Furthermore, Juana's attention to Clarita went beyond what is usual in most psychiatric psychotherapy by including body massage and of course coresidence. As part of the process of establishing her relationship with Clarita, Juana also expressed her genuine reactions, both positive and negative, to Clarita's behavior, and attempted to use them

in accordance with her therapeutic goal of getting the patient into a frame of mind where she could receive spiritist therapy.

4. The therapist consistently controlled the definition of the situation as a treatment situation, refusing to accept Clarita's withdrawal and reminding her constantly to do her part in their joint effort.

We have described the use of some treatment methods specific to spiritist therapy in this case and speculated about possible therapeutic developments that might have occurred had the patient been more receptive. One additional feature of the therapeutic technique is evident from Juana's attempt at home treatment—namely, her creation of an environment different from the patient's ordinary surroundings. In burning candles, keeping glasses of water in every room, and playing *santero* records, Juana created an ambiance suffused with objects considered helpful to the therapy. Juana, in short, transformed her apartment into a place of healing, an apparently universal therapeutic technique (Torrey, 1972:45ff.).

DIFFERENTIAL DIAGNOSIS OF THE PATIENT AND SPIRITISM AS THE TREATMENT OF CHOICE

The reader at this point may well have become impatient and justly ask, "Well, if all these positive features of psychotherapy were present, why didn't Clarita improve?" To respond we must raise the issue of differential diagnosis and evaluate the evidence concerning Clarita's suitability for this form of treatment.

Although Clarita, as a believer in spiritism and a former medium, seemed a likely candidate for spiritist therapy, her demoralized state ultimately prevented her from ever formally undergoing treatment—that is, "having the cause worked." In spite of Juana's efforts to prepare her for "working the cause," the mediums were never able to put the therapy into effect. Whether Clarita's demoralization was caused by the advancing disease process of schizophrenia (the psychiatrist's view), or by years of institutionalization coupled with drug and shock therapy (Juana's view), or by a reactive depression brought on by the deaths of close relatives, feelings of being rejected by her family, and anger over the hospital staff's handling of her therapy (my own view), the point remains that Clarita, after her initial response to the therapy, ceased participating in it. Indeed, Clarita's past failure both to maintain her ties with the spiritist community and to continue practicing as a medium indicate a history of only desultory attempts on her part to control her illness.

The major factor that might have helped to predict the outcome of

Clarita's therapy therefore seems to be the chronicity of her condition. If, on the one hand, we accept the psychiatrist's diagnosis of schizophrenia, then chronicity is always evidence of a poor prognosis. For, as the symptoms linger on, "the problem is no longer schizophrenia alone but is also one of bringing hope and motivation to a human being sunk in a quagmire of hopelessness and despair" (Will, 1967:655). In the spiritist conception of the illness, renunciation and years of neglect of one's protective spirits similarly betoken a poor prognosis, as Juana's early assessment of her client indicates. Clarita, in short, had over the years settled into a way of behaving which she apparently could not (if schizophrenia be taken as the cause) or would not (if *castigo* and renunciation of her protection be the cause) give up.

I suggest, therefore, that spiritist therapy may be more effectively attempted with patients who not only believe in spiritism but also either are experiencing early, acute symptoms or have a history of continued use of spiritist therapy to control their symptoms. Another anthropologist, Dr. Vivian Garrison, has been working on the problem of the kind of patient who is most likely to respond to spiritist therapy (personal communication). Her findings (based on a larger sample of intensive case histories of hospitalized patients) will undoubtedly take us beyond this first effort at a detailed observation of spiritist treatment to a deeper understanding of its specific methods and successes.

SIX

Spiritism and Social Relations in the Family and Neighborhood

In this chapter we switch focus from the formal organization and ritual of spiritism to the ordinary settings of daily life so that we can examine the use of spiritist beliefs and practices in the context of family and neighborhood social relations. Our data for this analysis derive from participant observation in the 79 study households by the five Puerto Rican researchers, four of them spiritist believers or practitioners. The researchers' field notes detail the happenings witnessed and things spoken about during crisis periods in these households and in the ordinary circumstances of life. These data, though not amenable to statistical analysis, derive validity from their emergence out of the natural flow of events.

SPIRITIST BELIEFS AND PRACTICES IN THE HOME AND FAMILY

THE WIFE AND MOTHER AS CARETAKER OF THE FAMILY'S SPIRITUAL PROTECTION

In keeping with the Puerto Rican woman's traditional role as caretaker of the household (Landy, 1959:79; Padilla, 1958:149; Stycos, 1955:124) the wife/mother in spiritist families tends to the spiritual welfare of the household members just as she tends to their material needs. To do this, she periodically cleans the house "spiritually" and maintains an altar for the family's protection.

Since Tuesdays and Fridays are considered days on which unenlightened spirits, directed by sorcerers, do most of their malevolent work, the woman of the house regularly performs a spiritual cleanup (*una limpieza espiritual*) on these days. In this process she fumigates the apartment and washes the floors and sometimes the walls with various combinations of substances, supposedly noxious to malevolent spirits. We have already discussed some of the substances in Chapter 3 and will simply comment here that many of them, such as ammonia, creosote, and various commercially manufactured antiseptics, have material as well as spiritual effects, since they are germicides.[1] After dispersing evil influences, the wife/mother sprinkles perfumes or burns sweet-smelling incense around the house to attract protective spirits.

In addition to keeping the home environment attractive to favorable spiritual influences in this way, the wife/mother maintains an altar in the house containing the statues of the major protectors of its members. The altar is usually located in a closet or unused room of the

[1] Regular home use of these germicides by spiritists suggests an interesting hypothesis concerning the relationship between biological survival and the espousal of this belief system. Particularly in the tropical environment of Puerto Rico (or even, perhaps, the environment of substandard housing in urban America) the semiweekly removal of microorganisms from the home might well lead to a higher survival rate of the children of devout spiritists than of members of other religions. One might even suggest that the pervasiveness of spiritist beliefs in rural Puerto Rico is the cumulative result of the higher survival rate of its practitioners. Stated this way in unqualified form, the proposition is of course overly simplistic. Its virtue, however, is that, with appropriate qualification, it is testable and would provide a fascinating demonstration of the interrelation between culture and biology.

apartment, where it is not generally visible, although a woman will proudly display her altar to visitors whom she knows to be believers. Most home altars contain goblets of water and candles in addition to statues of saints and likenesses of lower-order protectors (Madama dolls, plaster effigies of an Indian, Arab, or *congo,* or pictures of John Kennedy or Martin Luther King, Jr.). In tending the household altar, the wife/mother regularly replaces the ever-present water, dusts and sometimes dresses the figures, and lights candles or places flowers beside the figures of saints on appropriate occasions. It is she, too, who usually prays to these protectors on behalf of the entire family.

Besides the altar, the wife/mother tends to several additional spiritist objects usually kept around the house. To stop evil influences from entering the premises, for example, a glass of water or scissors may be placed over the entrance lintel, or a likeness of Elegua may be set up facing the door. Glasses of water to entrap intranquil spirits may routinely be placed under the beds at night and carefully emptied every morning.

These home rituals give the devout woman confidence and pride in maintaining a spiritually orderly household, just as she takes similar pride in keeping the physical premises neat and clean. Indeed the wife/mother's role as spiritual caretaker of the family, particularly in families of strong belief, may contribute markedly to her influence over family members. Although ultimate temporal authority is traditionally vested in the husband/father, the woman may use her spiritual powers to exert control over family members, as we see in the following discussion of spiritist practices in familial relationships.

Since, as mentioned earlier, spiritists sometimes conceive physical illness or discomfort as spiritually caused, part of the wife/mother's role as spiritual caretaker of the home involves being the vehicle for messsages from spirits concerning the health of the family. Unless the woman is a medium, these messages derive most often from dreams in which a protective spirit informs the wife/mother of a remedy for a health problem which a family member is having. Our data include reports of spiritually-inspired cures for asthma, menstrual cramps, and fever, for example. We discuss the effect of such spiritually-inspired health practices on medical usage patterns in greater detail in the concluding chapter.

SPIRITIST BELIEF IN MOTHER-CHILD RELATIONS

As attested by the large literature concerning the Puerto Rican family on the island (Fernández-Marina et al., 1958; Landy, 1959; Maldonado-Sierra et al., 1960; Rogler and Hollingshead, 1965; Steward et al., 1956; Stycos, 1955; Wolf, 1952) and the mainland (Berle, 1958; Glazer and

Moynihan, 1970; Lewis, 1965; Minuchin et al., 1967; Opler, 1967; Padilla, 1958), mother-child relations are strongly conditioned by the allocation of authority between husband and wife. According to traditional standards, the husband has authority over his wife and children, but de facto the wife/mother, because of her responsibility for actually raising the children, often becomes the disciplinarian of the family (Landy, 1959:81ff.; Mintz, 1973:63–64). Although she may use the father's authority as an ultimate threat over the children and may on occasion report misbehavior to him for punishment, she exercises a great deal of direction over the children herself. This situation creates a dilemma for the wife/mother, which has been summarized succinctly by Stycos: "Unfortunately . . . the wife appears to have responsibility and accountability *without authority*, and she must always operate in the name and as executrix of her husband" (1955:134, emphasis in the original). In family relations the mother may also mitigate the power of the father in her affective role as comforter of the children after he has disciplined them. Indeed she may come to be seen by the children as their protector against the father (Padilla, 1958:170–171).

Among long-standing migrants to New York and New York-raised Puerto Ricans, this general pattern of family relations may be altered somewhat by three factors. First, greater opportunities for women to work in New York have contributed toward undermining the husband/father's economic position in the family and hence his absolute authority (Berle, 1958; Lewis, 1965:xlii; Padilla, 1958:65). Even in families where women do not work, accommodation to the American pattern has led fathers to become less authoritarian and more flexible with their children than would have been traditionally acceptable (Padilla, 1958:150). Finally, the more rapid Americanization of children than parents has led youngsters to question parental ways of doing things and contributed toward undermining the authority of both the father and mother (Glazer and Moynihan, 1970:123–125; Padilla, 1958:165).

These multiple factors, all contributing to undermine the authority of the parents, cause particular difficulty to the mother, since it is she who regularly and directly disciplines the children. In response to this difficulty, some women use spiritual power to bolster their influence over the children. This may be done in various ways, the most direct of which is for the mother to send or threaten to send a spirit to discipline the child. For example, when Cruz's 13-year-old niece went out without her mother's permission and had not returned by 9 P.M., her mother frantically called Cruz and both women went looking for her. They found the girl at a friend's house, drunk. When they returned home, the mother cuffed the child a few times, and Cruz threatened that if she ever drank or went out without permission again, she would send the Madama after her.

Examples of mothers taking responsibility for sending spirits to frighten their children also occur from time to time at *centro* meetings. At one such meeting I witnessed, a teenage girl, the daughter of one of the members of the *centro*, had come to a session with a number of friends. During the proceedings the girl suddenly fell to the floor and began bouncing around the room and hitting herself against chairs. Several of the *mediunidad* rushed forward to restrain her, and the head medium worked with the girl for about 10 minutes, trying several techniques to restore her to normal behavior. After she finally brought the girl around, she explained to her that she had been seized by a spirit, sent with her mother's permission by the medium herself. The spirit was a punishment for the girl's wild behavior "in the streets" and would be sent against her again unless she desisted from this behavior.

As these examples suggest, direct threats of spiritual invocation are mostly used with teenage girls. Since the two traditionally valued qualities of a young woman, virginity and innocence, are perceived as keenly threatened in New York, and the mother is held responsible for maintaining her daughter's purity, the motives that prompt a mother to use these threats with a teenage daughter are understandable. Moreover, the young teenage years seem to be a time in the life cycle of Puerto Rican females when seizures are prevalent (Rendon, 1974). Occurrences of seizures thus serve to verify the effectiveness of spirit invocation against girls in this age range. We might also point out that threats of spiritual punishment may be felt beyond the girl immediately warned, since dramatic scenes, like the one at the *centro* described above, are witnessed by other teenagers and younger girls in the congregation.

Most instances in which spiritist beliefs function to enhance the authority of the mother are more subtle than the bald threats discussed above. In one of the families in the study, for example, the mother, who was a medium, had a very stormy relationship with her 14-year-old daughter. The daughter, by means of several precognitional experiences, had already established that she, too, had faculties. She was very rebellious, however, and frequently flew into a rage against her mother. The mother interpreted this behavior as a *prueba* which the child was undergoing in the course of developing her faculties. She therefore persuaded the daughter to join her in going to a *centro*, where the girl would have to learn to control her rebelliousness as part of the process of development.

A mother need not be a medium to enhance her authority over her children by spiritual means, however. Some mothers acquire a reputation for correctly foretelling events in their children's lives and then use their premonitions to dissuade the children from behaving in ways they disapprove. These premonitions may come to the women in dreams, precognitional feelings, or visions. In one of the families visited in this study, for example, the mother had a vision in which her 18-year-old son was beaten up in the street by four men. As a result, she warned the son not to go out. He did so nevertheless and returned home late that night bruised, reporting sheepishly that his mother's premonition had come true. A similar situation occurred in another family when the mother warned her daughter not to visit her cousin, who lived in a housing project in another part of the city. The girl went anyway and was mugged in the building elevator. In both these cases the incident was only one of a series of validated premonitions that were attributed to the mother and recounted whenever she advised her children against doing something. Once a woman has established a reputation for precognition, she can exert considerable influence on her children's actions—even into adulthood.

To someone outside the spiritist subculture the previous accounts of mothers using their spiritual powers to influence their children's behavior may appear to be an indirect and manipulative mode of dealing with children. From the viewpoint of the subculture, however, these actions are sincere attempts by mothers to provide their children with important and, in some cases, life-saving information. To a believer in the reality of spirits, these mothers are being no more manipulative than a mother who warns her children of the hazards of crossing the street against the traffic light, since the effects of spirits are as palpable as the effects of cars. This exposition should therefore not be construed as impugning the motives of the mothers who employ spiritist concepts in interaction with their children. I am simply pointing out that whatever the motivation of these women, the consequence of their behavior is greater maternal influence.

Indeed, as mentioned above, this maternal influence may extend into adulthood, as the following case illustrates.

Elena, a 20-year old, reported to the researcher that her infant had recently been ill. The baby had had a high fever and would not eat, so she took him to the doctor. Because the doctor said that nothing was wrong and yet an *azabache* shattered every time she put one on the baby,[1] Elena called her mother who was a medium and *santiguadora* (someone who knows how to

[2] *Azabache* (jet) is used to protect children against the evil eye (*mal de ojo*). The *azabache* is believed to shatter when the child receives the evil eye.

> *santiguar,* see p. 20). Her mother came and blessed the child, dressed him in a red gown, and put a red ribbon around his wrist to protect him. Afterward the child was better.
>
> Elena's mother also told her, however, that her *comadre* (the child's godmother, who in this case was also his mother's brother's wife) had done a "job" (*trabajo*) on her, and this job had "caught" the child instead. Elena said that she used to visit her *comadre* a lot. Her mother had been warning her not to go because the woman had practiced sorcery to turn her into a tramp. For Elena the child's illness confirmed this revelation, and she told her *comadre* that she would never visit her again. To prove that she had kept her promise, she told the researcher that she had recently refused to go to her *comadre* in response to a message she had received that the woman was ill.[3]

In addition to demonstrating the continued influence a mother can exert on her adult child's behavior through spiritist beliefs, this case exemplifies other features of the spiritist subculture. First, Elena turned to spiritism only after she had consulted a physician about her son's condition and failed to receive a satisfactory diagnosis. We have already called attention to this general tendency in patterns of spiritist consultation in Chapter 4. Second, a child's illness may be taken as a sign that his or her parents (or other adults in the household) have a problem which is spiritually caused. Since children are generally believed to have weaker protection than adults, the problem may be deflected onto the child, causing him or her to become ill. In treating this kind of problem, the therapist increases the child's protection (as done by Elena's mother in the previous example), but the major effort is centered on the adults involved. In other words, the child receives supportive attention but is removed from implication in the adults' interpersonal problems. We shall have more to say on the effects of spiritual harm to children below.

SPIRITIST BELIEF AND PRACTICE IN HUSBAND-WIFE RELATIONS

In the traditional role allocation between spouses, Puerto Rican husbands are dominant over their wives (Fernández-Marina, 1958:180; Padilla, 1958:149; Stycos, 1955:155), have a great deal more freedom to come and go as they please (Padilla, 1958:151; Stycos, 1955:58), and have primary responsibility for supporting the family (Padilla, 1958:152; Stycos, 1955:39, 125). Complementarily, "the ideal wife is seen as submissive (obedient, respectful, compliant, and helpful) and faithful, and

[3] This case and others cited in this chapter are abstracted and summarized by me from the field notes of community researchers.

as a good housekeeper and mother" (Stycos, 1955:124). Furthermore, continuance of inordinate parental influence over children into adulthood (whether spiritual or otherwise) has been noted to produce a strain among lower-income Puerto Ricans in the performance of spouse roles (Mintz, 1973:64; Stycos, 1955:especially 132–134). This strain holds true particularly for males, whose role-defined dominance may be undermined by viewing wives as mother-replacements (Stycos, 1955:80–83, 103–105; Wolf, 1952).

One implication of the Puerto Rican definition of spouse roles (specifically in the relegation of the female to the home and the freedom of the male to come and go as he wishes) is that couples rarely socialize together or undertake much activity in common (Mintz, 1973:63; Padilla, 1958:151–152; Stycos, 1955:148–149). Stycos further documents "a high degree of mutual suspicion" between spouses (1955:149–153, 156) and little communication between husband and wife, except on matters concerning the children and family finances (Stycos, 1955:149; see also Mintz, 1973:63–64, 80–81). This pattern of mutual suspicion and limited communication, added to the difference in status between males and females and the limited number of common activities in which couples engage, all contribute to make "the husband-wife bond in the [Puerto Rican] lower class relatively weak, perhaps the weakest of immediate family relationships" (Stycos, 1955:133).

Padilla (1958:106, 160) reports that Puerto Rican women raised in New York express a desire for a more equal relationship with their husbands, where responsibilities for child care and housekeeping are shared more equitably and the pair do more things together. In New York, she reports, women also seek more time for themselves outside the house, and men evidence greater willingness for their wives to work. Padilla does not indicate the degree to which these expressed wishes are put into practice, however, and my own data suggest that, with the exception of the greater freedom of women to work and the greater sharing and equality in the relationships of New York-born Hispanos now marrying, role allocation between husbands and wives still tends to follow the traditional pattern.

As might be expected, spiritist practices (particularly sorcery) come into play in this already suspicion-laden and brittle marital relationship at its most vulnerable points: the greater sexual freedom of the husband, and the spouses' (particularly the husband's) strong ties to their families of orientation. Thus in our data both sorcery accusations and actual attempts at sorcery occur most frequently within two classic triads: among the wronged wife, the philandering husband, and his paramour; and among the domineering mother, the dependent son, and his wife.

The specific instances of sorcery in conjugal relationships on which the following remarks are based were collected as they arose in conversation with families in the study. Some instances derive from gossip about acquaintances who lived in the building or neighborhood; other instances involve acts of sorcery reportedly committed by a member of one of the study families. In some cases acts of sorcery were directly witnessed by the researchers. Since our sample of cases thus comprises such a variety of data from different sources (third-party reports, protagonists' reports, and eyewitness accounts), no statistical treatment of the material is warranted. The following remarks are intended to document the use of sorcery between spouses and to indicate some of the problems in understanding its effect on conjugal relationships.

Spiritism and Extramarital Affairs

Should another woman threaten a marital relationship, the wife who believes in spiritism may undertake sorcery against the woman to destroy the extramarital affair or against her husband to recapture his love. Should the other woman succeed in taking the husband away from his wife, however, the latter may offer the post hoc explanation that the paramour used sorcery to destroy the marriage. Spells and charms for these purposes are widely known among women in the subculture and may therefore be put into effect even without consultation of a medium.

The outcome and function of such attempts at sorcery without benefit of a medium are difficult to assess, since they are usually spoken about only when they are unsuccessful in preserving the marriage—namely, when the husband leaves or when he discovers the spell and becomes enraged with his wife for perpetrating it. Since our observations are thus biased toward instances of sorcery correlated with marital breakup or disharmony, the impression one gets is that sorcery activities by and large fail in their intended purpose of restoring marital concord. The prevailing gossip among women, however, does not support these observations and attaches considerable efficacy to the use of sorcery in holding a husband. One might speculate therefore that many more acts of sorcery without the assistance of mediums are performed than ever come to light.

The following case describes one such "successful" use of sorcery in a marital relationship (in this instance undiscovered by the husband) and provides an eyewitness account of additional acts of sorcery that seem to have performed an entirely different function in the marriage. The couple in this case are extreme in our data both for the amount of infidelity reported in their marriage and for the violence of their relationship. The case is included nevertheless because the wife's self-reported, successful use of sorcery is representative of other cases in our material and because the directly witnessed instance of sorcery reveals another aspect of its role in relations between husbands and wives.

Victor and Delores had been married for 12 stormy years and had three children, aged 11, 9, and 6. Their marriage had been characterized by physical fighting and several extramarital affairs on the part of each of them. Delores was known to have spiritual faculties, although she had never developed as a medium.

When the researcher began visiting the family, Delores and Victor's relationship was in a quiescent phase, undoubtedly caused by Delores's recent hysterectomy for cancer of the uterus. About six months later, however, the couple began quarreling about a number of issues, among which was their eldest daughter, Mona, who had been sent to live with Delores's widowed aunt. Victor wanted the child back home, because, he complained, she no longer respected him and listened to the aunt instead. Another issue of contention was Delores's continued denial of Victor's demands for sexual intercourse on the ground of her operation.

At about this time, Victor's family in Puerto Rico called upon him to come home and settle a problem they were having with his younger brother. In Victor's absence, Delores began attending parties and [in the words of the researcher] "looking like a teenager." Delores claimed that her cousin in Puerto Rico wrote her that Victor was "playing her dirty" there, and in retribution she began having an affair with one of Victor's friends.

When Victor returned about a month later, Delores continued rejecting his sexual advances, and they fought almost constantly. Victor may well have heard about his wife's behavior during his absence, but he apparently did not discover the identity of her paramour, since he confided his marital troubles to his cuckolding friend, who reported everything back to Delores. During one of their fights, Victor threatened Delores with a rifle, and she called the police but refused to have him arrested.

At this point Delores decided that she had to get Victor out of the house. She confided to the researcher that she had summoned her spirit guides to discover a spell to get rid of her husband. She claimed that the spirits had told her to buy a toad and sew up its mouth, eyes, and rectum and then leave it in a corner of the apartment. The spirits told her that the toad would die slowly and so would Victor. Delores rejected the spirits' advice because she didn't want to harm her husband, only to get him out of the house. She then called upon St. Martin, her protector, to give her some way of getting him to leave, but St. Martin told her he only works to cure the sick and not to do harm.

Delores told the researcher that in the past the spirits had given her spells that worked. She related how when Victor was having an affair with a woman down the street several years ago, she asked the spirits to tell her what to do so he would leave the woman. They advised her to buy seven lemons for her husband and seven for the woman and to cut crosses on them. She was then to squeeze the lemons while saying, "As sour as these lemons are, so let Victor become with that woman." Afterward she was to throw away the juice and peels at an intersection. Very soon after she did this, her husband had a fight with the woman and ended the affair.

Through her paramour, Delores learned that Victor had consulted a spiritist in the neighborhood and had given her money to prepare something to make Delores fall in love with him again. To check the story, Delores went to the spiritist to ask her to make something to get rid of Victor. When the medium said she was too busy to do so, Delores suspected that the story was true, since ethical spiritists will not accept work directed against their own clients.

Although in the following weeks Victor began professing greater love for Delores than ever before, he also began drinking heavily and continued fighting with both Delores and her aunt. One night, acclaiming his great love for his wife, Victor tried unsuccessfully to force her to have sexual relations with him. This incident seems to have been the breaking point for both of them.

A few days later Victor bought a car and began coming home less regularly. The first time he did not come home for over 24 hours, Delores became worried because she knew he was not an experienced driver. Consequently, she phoned several of his relatives to ask if they had seen him. When they reported that they had not, she took the opportunity to inform them of Victor's recent behavior.

Following Victor's attempted assault, Delores consulted a spiritist who gave her a spell to make Victor quit the house entirely. The procedure involved burning an animal horn in the house and sprinkling various essences around the premises with a wand made of the *pasote* plant. Victor and his brother saw her returning home with the *pasote*, and his brother joked that Delores was bewitching Victor. Delores replied that she was like their grandmother [a woman reputed to have ensorcelled her husband].

During the next week Victor's absences from the house increased until 10 days after the *pasote* incident, he phoned Delores to pack his things because he was leaving. He continued visiting the children periodically over the following month but had a brawl with Delores during one of the visits. She went to Family Court over the case and secured a court order barring him from the apartment.

The instance of sorcery with lemons is typical of the secret use of spiritist practices in marital relations, not only because it involves the wife as sorcerer but also because it entails an extramarital affair of the husband as the occasion for the act. To account for the reported efficacy of such acts without recourse to a supernatural explanation, I suggest that the act may have a psychological effect on the wife/sorcerer which alters her behavior in the marriage (for example, by reducing her feelings of inadequacy and helplessness in the situation or by serving as an alternative, symbolic means of expressing anger in a situation where its overt expression might well be counterproductive). Alternatively, extramarital affairs may commonly be only temporary and soon disintegrate from causes entirely unrelated to the wife's behavior.

The use of sorcery by Victor and Delores against each other in this case suggests another function that such acts perform in husband-wife relationships—communication. Whatever the psychological motives behind Delores's and Victor's perpetration of acts of sorcery, sociologically they served to communicate each party's wishes concerning the relationship to the other. Thus, in spite of his drunkenness and abusive behavior, Victor not only told Delores that he loved her more than ever but, by going to a spiritist to have a charm prepared for regaining her love, he also let it be known how strongly he desired the relationship. (Going to a neighborhood spiritist and talking about it to friends guaranteed that Delores would find out about his action. Indeed Delores's visit to the same spiritist to procure a spell to get rid of Victor also clearly announced her wishes in the matter and gave the spiritist the opportunity to convey Delores's sentiments to Victor.) Delores's own act of sorcery, which she virtually let Victor witness, was an additional message to him of her desire to end the marriage.

Although to the outsider acts of sorcery may seem an indirect and inefficient way for spouses to make their desires known, one must recall the limited amount of communication between husbands and wives that has been reported among lower-class Puerto Ricans. As this case demonstrates, of course, spouses do not rely solely on this means of communication. Nevertheless, acts of sorcery appear to be a culturally understood and particularly forceful way of expressing a spouse's wishes with regard to the marital relationship. Delores's act of sorcery seems to have precipitated Victor's actual departure, and she did not take definitive legal action against her husband until she had performed the act of sorcery. (Although she had had numerous provocations, she simply complained to the police before ensorcelling Victor; afterward she brought him to court.) It would thus seem that acts of sorcery can serve both to communicate and to precipitate action with regard to a disrupted marital relationship.

Up to now our discussion of sorcery in marital relationships has focused on instances where spells were actually cast by one or both spouses. In such cases, when a medium is consulted to perform the sorcery, the medium may comply with the request but does not attempt to call in the other spouse for joint spiritist consultation. In contrast to these cases, one or both spouses may consult a medium with no specific request for a spell. In such circumstances the medium may still utilize the concept of sorcery in interpreting the situation but would do so in a very different way—namely, by imputing sorcery to someone outside the marriage and drawing the couple into joint treatment against the external threat.

Rita and Berto were having difficulty in their marriage. Berto was unsuccessful in finding a decent job and would come home in a rage and fight with her. Rita consulted a [male] spiritist who told her that her husband would sometimes come home fighting and yelling "like a devil." The spiritist said that Berto was also occasionally impotent, and if things continued that way, he would soon "be no good at all." He told Rita that someone had done something to Berto and that when he yelled or fought with her, it was not he but the spirit which had been sent against him. He recommended that she bring him in so that he could dispel the spirit and deactivate the sorcery. The couple went and were still going to *centro* sessions together when the research ended seven months later. The fighting had decreased, and their relationship had improved.

Unlike Victor and Delores's situation, both parties in this case were sufficiently committed to the marriage to attend the *centro* together. Treatment consisted of first preparing Berto for "working the cause" and then performing an exorcism similar to those described earlier. Berto was also informed that he had an Amerindian warrior as protector and was encouraged to take on the combative spirit of this warrior during *centro* meetings. In addition, the couple was counseled about the importance of harmony in the home, and rites were performed to help Berto get a better job.

Instances of sorcery like Berto's, in which the sorcerer is not one of the spouses, typically bring husband and wife into joint treatment with a spiritist. As we have seen from the case of Carmelo in Chapter 4, a diagnosis of *mala influencia* may also have this effect and indeed is a more common spiritist diagnosis for marital problems than is sorcery.[4] These diagnoses share the important feature of attributing interpersonal friction to a source outside the marriage—in the one case to an envious sorcerer and in the other to the spirit of a spouse from a previous existence of one of the partners. Spiritist intervention into marital problems produces reconciliation more frequently when the problem is defined

[4] See also an example of *mala influencia,* cited in Minuchin et al. (1967:241), in which a medium interprets a wife's infidelity as possession by the spirit of a prostitute and institutes treatment for both husband and wife to rid the woman of this spirit.

according to either of these diagnoses than when the spiritist cooperates with one of the spouses in perpetrating an act of sorcery against the other. In short, one type of intervention by a spiritist (a diagnosis in terms of either *mala influencia* or sorcery from an outside party) tends to hold marriages together. Another type (cooperating with one of the spouses in an act of sorcery) promotes separation.

Spiritism and In-Laws

In our data every case of in-law problems that eventuated in sorcery accusations involved dissension between a mother-in-law and daughter-in-law, although these women were not necessarily the ones incapacitated by the purported acts of sorcery. The following example illustrates a case of a mother-in-law's sorcery deflected onto one of her grandchildren.

When the researcher entered the Vs' apartment, she found Perfecta and her mother hovering over Perfecta's 4-year-old daughter Mimi. The child had suddenly come down with a fever, something which the women claimed often happened to her. They had taken her to doctors many times in the past but had never received an acceptable diagnosis. Recently, therefore, Perfecta had taken the child to a spiritist. The spiritist had said that Perfecta's mother-in-law had performed sorcery against Perfecta and that the child had "caught" it instead. She claimed that the mother-in-law was very envious of the good relationship that her son Miguel had with his wife.

Relations between mother-in-law and daughter-in-law had never been particularly good, but about a year before, when Miguel had given a surprise birthday party for Perfecta, his mother had refused to come. Since that time Miguel spoke to his mother infrequently and only visited her when she was sick.

To treat Mimi's condition, the medium had given the child an herb bath and prepared a special candle which Perfecta was to burn every day for a month. She had also recommended that certain prayers be said along with the treatment. She advised that if this procedure did not work, she would do something to turn the spell back on the mother-in-law.

Like the case of Elena and her child (pp. 148–49), this case demonstrates that sorcery is believed capable of striking any household member whose protection is weak, regardless of the specific person against whom the spell has been worked. This belief can thus unite a household against a presumed threat from outside—just as external sorcery against one of a conjugal pair may draw them together, as illustrated in the previous section. Obviously, however, the husband's mother is not conceived as a sorcerer or hostile outsider unless there has been a history of animosity between her and either her son or her son's wife. In the above case, for example, Miguel's mother had never fully recognized Perfecta as her daughter-in-law, since she was still fond of Miguel's first wife, whom he had abandoned for Perfecta.

Contrary to the situation in Miguel's case, a son's loyalty to his mother may sometimes prevail over his attachment to his wife, and the latter may become the "outsider," accused of ensorcelling the mother. The following case illustrates this situation but also reveals something about the etiquette of sorcery accusations and some of their psychological consequences.

Hortensia married Tito, who was an only son and very attached to his mother, Maria. Both times Hortensia became pregnant during their marriage, Tito moved back to live with his mother. Four years ago, after the birth of their last child, he did not return to the house to live, although he visited the children several times a week. He confessed to Hortensia that Maria had told him that his wife had "hired" (*alquilar*) La Milagrosa to bind him to her forever. Hortensia admitted having made a *promesa* to La Milagrosa but said that Tito was free to come and go as he pleased. She later heard that her mother-in-law had loosely accused her of sorcery to other family members. Hortensia sent a message to Maria through Tito, telling her that if her mother-in-law continued accusing her of sorcery, she would indeed use it to "take care" of her. On several other occasions she again told Tito that she would "see to" Maria.

At the time of our research, Maria, who was diabetic, became hospitalized with gangrene and had to have a leg amputated. Tito begged Hortensia to visit his mother in the hospital, but she refused on the ground that she did not want Maria to think that after several years of neither seeing nor speaking to her she would now go to witness her suffering. Hortensia freely admitted that she was furious with Maria and blamed her for coming between Tito and herself, but quickly added that the woman was "in God's hands" (that is, that she had done nothing to harm her).

About a month later Maria died, a fact which Hortensia only learned through her mother, who lived near some of Maria's relatives in Puerto Rico. That Hortensia was not informed directly of the death by one of Maria's relatives in New York indicated that the family considered her responsible. Hortensia confided to the researcher that although she thought her mother-in-law deserved her fate, she had never done anything to harm her. She regretted having sent Maria threatening messages and asked the researcher, a believer in spiritism, what she thought of the situation. The researcher diplomatically replied that it was none of her business to venture an opinion. She did say, however, that since God sees all, He would know whether or not Hortensia did anything wrong.

In subsequent visits to Hortensia, the researcher noticed that she was burning an inordinate number of candles in the house. She did not think it politic to ask her directly about the significance of the candles, but as a member of the spiritist subculture offered the following alternative explanations of Hortensia's actions: (1) Hortensia might be repaying a promise to a spirit with whom she had contracted to cause Maria's death, (2) she might be seeking expiation for the threats she had made to Maria in the past, or (3) she might be calling on all her protection to defend herself against possible countersorcery from Maria's family.

After Maria's burial, Tito resumed visiting the children and, so far as the researcher could learn, never mentioned his mother to Hortensia again.

Among affines sorcery accusations would seem, in sum, to help define the solidary pair (mother-son or husband-wife) against the outsider (the wife or mother, respectively) and precipitate a break with the outsider. The two cases cited above exemplify these two logical possibilities: in the first, the husband-son chose his wife over his mother; in the second, the son opted for his mother. More commonly, however, the husband-son vacillates in his allegiances, and gossip of sorcery between the two women persists while he tries to maintain a measure of both inner and outer peace with the two significant females in his life.

FAMILY REACTIONS TO SPIRITUAL PROBLEMS

In the previous sections on spiritism in the home, we have focused on specific social relationships in the family and demonstrated the use of spiritist beliefs and rituals in these relationships. In this section we shift focus to the family as a whole and examine the operation of spiritist beliefs within the whole set of familial relationships, and the contrasting ways in which different families deal with problems defined in a spiritist idiom. To do this, we focus the analysis on two families, whom I call the Maldonados and the Cruzes. These families represent polar opposites on a continuum of effectiveness in using spiritist practices to help solve family problems. After a consideration of these families, I shall offer some comments and criteria for differentially evaluating spiritist believers who present themselves for care at health facilities.

The Maldonado Family

Carmen Maldonado was a 50-year-old woman living in a common-law relationship with Marco, a man considerably younger than herself. Pepe, her son, appeared on her doorstep one day from Puerto Rico. He had abandoned his wife there and run off to New York with another woman.

The couple stayed with Carmen several weeks and then decided to visit another relative in the Midwest. Pepe wanted to buy a car for the trip and asked his mother for $500 to finance it. When she denied having that much money, he said that he had found her bankbook and knew she was lying. She claimed that the money in the account belonged to Marco, and she therefore could not give it to him.

After this incident Carmen went to visit Socorro, a medium who performed consultations and gave advice to various neighbors in the building. Carmen explained the situation to Socorro and claimed that Pepe had no respect for her because she had not raised him. She feared that he might say something disrespectful to her in front of Marco, and the two men would get into a row. She also suspected Pepe's girl friend of having prevailed upon him to ask for the loan and thought it best for him to return to his wife. Socorro told Carmen to send her son down to talk with her but warned Carmen not to let the couple abscond with her money.

Although Pepe believed in spiritism and went to visit Socorro, he gave her a hard time during their conversation. Since this was not a formal consultation, he simply changed the subject every time she brought the matter around to his spiritual situation, which the medium implied was being influenced by a "job" done to him by his paramour's mother.

Two days later, while the Maldonados were sitting in the living room, Marco went into the kitchen for some beer and discovered a fire spreading from the window curtain down the molding onto the floor. After the family extinguished the flames, they sent for Socorro who interpreted the situation as a fire spirit sent by Pepe's girl friend's mother. The couple admitted that the mother practiced spiritism and had not approved of their liaison. The family claimed that several other strange things had been happening around the house—unaccountable knocking and doors opening. Socorro said she would have to hold consultations with Pepe and his girl friend separately. Although the researcher did not find out exactly what Socorro did at these sessions, in about a week Pepe left for Puerto Rico to return to his wife, and his girlfriend moved in with her aunt who lived in New York.

Several weeks later Carmen confided to the researcher that she suspected Marco of having an affair. The pair was not getting along well, and each had moved into a separate room in the apartment. A few days later Marco was late returning from work, and Carmen went to search for him. She found him drinking beer with his brother-in-law and complained carpingly about his tardiness. Not showing him proper respect as her husband, she snidely asked when she could expect him home. Marco ordered her to go home and returned there himself several hours later.

He told Carmen that although he loved her more than his mother, he could not live in the apartment with her anymore. He packed his bags and left.

Carmen went immediately to Socorro, who came up to the apartment. Socorro said that the evil current (*mala corriente*) that Pepe and his girl friend had brought into the house was still present and was causing the disturbance between Carmen and Marco. The current had to be removed by a thorough spiritual cleaning, the procedure for which she outlined to Carmen. She also counseled Carmen to calm herself and to take special herbal baths to attract her protection. During the course of the visit Socorro got Carmen to talk about the tension she still felt over her son's visit.

Several days later Marco called Carmen to arrange to pick up a set of tools he had left behind. When he came to the house, Carmen played the role of the dutiful wife. She professed her love and told him it was bad to live in someone else's house (*en casa ajena*) instead of his own, where there was someone who would willingly do his bidding. Marco returned that night but, according to Carmen, acted like a young beast ("*muy cachorro*"). Consequently she made a *promesa* to St. Barbara to make him more agreeable. About 10 days later she reported that things were going better between them and showed the researcher the service (*servicio*) she had prepared to repay the saint.

The Cruz Family

Isabel Cruz was a woman of about 30 with 3-year-old twins and two other children, ages 5 and 1. She had lived with a series of men and was now with a merchant marine, who was soon to leave for overseas. About a year before the research had begun, Isabel was sent to the city hospital for psychiatric observation, and the children temporarily placed in homes. Although the researcher was never able to get a clear account from Isabel about what had precipitated her hospitalization, she had apparently become enraged at one of the twins and almost choked him. She admitted being unable to control herself when angry and claimed to have "beaten" landlords, doctors, welfare workers, and lovers.

Isabel had remained in the hospital only a short time and was provided with homemaker service when discharged. She ran through six homemakers in about nine months, ending each one's services in high dudgeon. Thereafter she spent most of her time in the apartment, claiming that caring for the children kept her from going out. (The children were frequently ill, and one of the twins suffered from asthma.) Isabel also refused to take the medication she had been given on discharge from the hospital, saying that it made her even more contentious. She also periodically sought out private physicians "for her nerves," but never followed through on any course of chemotherapy they prescribed.

Isabel claimed that she possessed faculties but had never developed them. She attributed her inability to find a permanent mate to a *castigo* laid upon her by her protectors for not developing. She blamed the children for keeping her too busy in the house to attend a *centro,* although she also claimed that all mediums were thieves and would only cheat her anyway. Isabel's faculties were manifested in dreams and visions in which her protectors advised her on the proper candles to burn in order to find a better apartment or a more cooperative welfare worker. She faithfully cleaned her apartment spiritually on Tuesdays and Fridays and took periodic herbal baths designed to maintain her protection. On occasion she vaguely talked of sorcery directed against her but was never clear about its source and never did anything about it.

The Maldonados and the Cruzes: Spiritism in Familial Relationships

These two households contrast markedly. Spiritist beliefs and practices seem to be integrated into the interpersonal relations of the Maldonado family, but almost isolated from whatever limited interpersonal life Isabel Cruz maintained. The Maldonados viewed their interpersonal life as conditioned by spirits and acted accordingly. In contrast, even Mrs. Cruz's most intense relationships, those with her children, were not ordered by spiritist convictions. At no time did she interpret any of her children's illnesses in a spiritist framework, even though the asthmatic problem of one of the twins commonly receives spiritual as well as medical attention in this subculture. Isabel's relationship with the remote bureaucracy of the Welfare Department was her only social contact tinged with an element of spiritism. Beyond that, her involvement in the spiritist subculture consisted of performing protective rituals, using wish-fulfilling magic (such as lighting candles to get a better apartment but never going out to look for one), and maintaining a spiritual self-image (victim of a *castigo*) that provided a rationalization for her inability to establish a satisfactory relationship with a man.

The Maldonados, in contrast, interpreted social relationships (and certain unusual material phenomena, such as the fire) in a spiritist framework with some consistency. Such interpretations seemed, moreover, to enable them to deal with social situations effectively. Phrasing Pepe's relationship with his new girl friend as one fraught with sorcery (instead of just maternal disapproval) helped him to withdraw from the relationship. Carmen, furthermore, seemed better able to deal with her relationships with both Pepe and Marco when difficulties with them were couched in spiritist language. In the course of dealing with the particular spiritual problems entailed in these relationships (possible sorcery and *mala corriente* respectively), she managed the interpersonal problem as well.

The two families also differed in their reliance on mediums to intervene and help in interpersonal or intrapsychic problems. Both Mrs. Maldonado and Pepe were willing to speak to a spiritist for what they conceived might be a spiritual problem in their lives; their behavior was therefore both consistent with their view of the situation and oriented toward a solution of the problem as they conceived it. Although Mrs. Cruz interpreted some of her problems in spiritual terms, unlike the Maldonados she made no effort to seek out the solution provided by these terms. In other words, she defined and labeled her problem within a spiritist framework (as a *castigo* for failure to develop her faculties) but did not take advantage of the solution provided by the subcultural framework—development as a medium. In this sense her behavior was irresponsible or, in the words of the researcher who was visiting her, "What she talks is nonsense to me. She doesn't look like a woman that has four children. She acts like another child." Isabel's vague innuendos about sorcery, her profession of faculties, and talk of a *castigo*—all without appropriate action—were evidence to the researcher, who was herself a participant in the spiritist subculture, that Isabel was "disturbed."

Differential Evaluation of Spiritist Believers and Their Relationships with Mediums

The lack of consistency between Isabel's professed beliefs about spirits and her behavior with regard to them led the researcher to judge the woman as "disturbed" and childlike. Awareness of such subcultural standards seems particularly important for lay and professional mental health workers who must make judgments about clients with different cultures or subcultures from their own. With particular reference to evaluating the psychological state of a Puerto Rican who is a spiritist, knowledge of the standards of the spiritist subculture would enable the worker to diagnose and treat differently a person who uses spiritist beliefs and practices consistently with the standards of the subculture, and one who uses these concepts and rituals in a disturbed or disorganized fashion. In this evaluation process it would seem appropriate to solicit the opinions of participants in the subculture about the behavior of an individual under examination.

The Maldonado case permits an additional important observation about spiritist therapy. A believer in spiritism need not necessarily attend a *centro* (that is, turn to the formal institution of the subculture) to receive the psychological and social help that the subculture can give. Establishing a relationship with a medium who consults with neighbors informally in her apartment, as did Mrs. Maldonado, seems to provide some of the same kind of personal support available at *centros*. The informal relationship with a medium, as opposed to membership in the *centro*, does not, of course, entail participation in an ongoing formal group. The following section provides additional information about informal relationships with mediums and compares them with the more formal relationships with heads of *centros*.

SPIRITISM AND NEIGHBORS

For purposes of this discussion, "neighbors" are defined as coresidents of the same building. The term thus emphasizes relations of people living in close propinquity and does not imply a clearly institutionalized status, although a few diffuse rights and obligations are conventionally recognized among coresidents of the same building. (These include the injunction against interference in other households' affairs and the duty to assist in medical or other emergencies, if asked.) By emphasizing propinquity, our definition specifically encompasses not only the multiplex social relationships of those building coresidents who may simultaneously be extended family members, *compadres*, and/or friends, but also the simplex relationships of those who merely exchange pleasantries when passing one another on the stairs or when standing on the front stoop waiting for the mailman. Our contention is that propinquity has social significance both for multiplex relationships, by intensifying, specifying, or otherwise modifying the rights and obligations of the component statuses, and for simplex relationships, by necessitating relative strangers to accommodate to one another because they frequently share the same public places. As we shall see, spiritist notions may be invoked in both the multiplex and simplex relationships of building coresidents.

In the following discussion the reader will also note many more instances of women than men using spiritist concepts or practices in their relations with neighbors. We recorded 38 women (44% of the women in the sample families) who either discussed or dealt with neighbors in terms of spiritist concepts. Only two men (3%) did so. This difference is undoubtedly due partly to certain biases in our method of data collection (that is, focusing on the household, which is the woman's domain, as the unit of study, as well as employing only female researchers) but partly also to a real difference between males and females in the frequency with which the two sexes use spiritist concepts in defining relations with neighbors. For, in spite of its focus on women, our method yielded data on males which indicate that they commonly use spiritist beliefs and practices to structure other social relationships outside the household and family—specifically with people in authority, such as judges, parole officers, Workmen's Compensation physicians, and potential employers, and with co-workers. Thus, although the few instances in our data of males using spiritism in their relations with neighbors may in part arise from a bias in our method of data collection, I am inclined to think that it reflects a real difference between the two sexes.

The reason for this difference is, however, obscure. Our own observational data and Garrison's survey results from a similar and nearby geographical area of New York (1972:194) indicate that women depend on neighbors for services such as shopping and child care more than men do. Perhaps this greater interdependence is associated with the more frequent use of spiritist concepts in neighborly relations among females. We examine this association further after reviewing the nature of spiritism in neighborly relations.

SPIRITISM AND SOCIAL RELATIONS IN A REPRESENTATIVE BUILDING

We begin by examining in some detail neighborly relations in one of the buildings in our sample. Social relationships in this building were typical of those in similar buildings in the study with a high proportion of Hispanic tenants. A number of apartments in the building were occupied by kin or *compadres* with, consequently, a great deal of visiting and sharing among residents of these apartments. In addition, a number of women, not kin, spent a great deal of time with one another, gossiping and providing mutual assistance with child care, shopping, and the like. Beyond these close ties, marked by almost daily visiting, there were more casual ties among other residents which involved occasional visits in one another's apartments or long conversations on the stairs or in hallways. This social activity, as well as publicly observable events, ensured that a substantial fund of information and misinformation about the affairs of residents circulated among the women of the building.

A shared belief in spiritism affects this pattern of social relationships in buildings with a high proportion of Hispanic residents in two major ways. First, it provides a special set of statuses for defining social relationships (e.g., medium-client, sorcerer-ensorcelled) and, as a result, creates in the social network of building residents a subset of people who interact somewhat differently with one another than they do with the remaining residents. Second, the content of interactions among this subset differs. We discuss these differences more specifically after describing neighborly relations in the selected building.

The study building contained 18 apartments, most of which (72% to 89%) were inhabited by Hispanic families throughout the study. Of the Hispanic households, 42% contained at least one active practitioner of spiritism; others (17%) contained nonpracticing believers. A few of the residents have been introduced previously in case material included to illustrate other points.

At the start of our observations in the building two of the residents were mediums. One, Doña Carolina, a woman of about 55, had been part of the *mediunidad* at a *centro* that had folded about three years earlier. During the study she regularly performed rituals at her home altar and attended private consultations with El Indio, a well-known medium in another part of the city, whenever she perceived herself as suffering from a spiritual problem she could not handle herself. She never became involved in another *centro* as a regular member, however. The other medium in the building, Doña Julia, was considered somewhat manic and not highly "developed" by several spiritist researchers who were assigned to the building. Her preference for cartomancy as a form of divination supports this estimate of her expertise, although she frequently used spirit communication in her treatment of Nilda, another resident of the building. (See pp. 97–99 for more about this relationship and Nilda's background.)

In addition to these two mediums and Nilda, the lay practitioners and believers in the building included Doña Carolina's niece, Delores, whose stormy marriage with Victor has already been described above; Inez and Frank López, a couple in their early 30s who lived next door to Delores; Mira Rodríguez, a 55-year-old woman whose boyfriend's sister, Teresa Romero, also lived in the building with her husband. An elderly lady, Sra. Moscoso, was also a practitioner of spiritism, although her son and his wife, who lived in the building were not. Two devout Catholic families in the building were also not practitioners. These households constituted a stable core of residents, although both Julia's and Nilda's families moved out during the course of the study. The remaining seven apartments in the building had a high turnover rate during the study. Although a number of the inhabitants were spiritists, we shall not comment individually on their rather brief social relationships with the long-term residents, except for the case of Clara. We note, however, that in general spiritists who moved into the building were included into the information network of the building more rapidly than other newcomers.

A crucial feature of the social life of the building was ill feeling between Doña Julia and two other residents—Delores and Doña Carolina. Julia claimed that once when she went to Puerto Rico, she did not tell her Welfare investigator she was going and told only Delores, who was at that time her next door neighbor. According to Julia, Delores reported the trip to her investigator, so that she was cut off Welfare on her return. She also claimed that she had several times started working (selling artificial flowers or sewing at home) but her efforts came to nought because of the gossip and *envidia* of her neighbors.

When researchers began visiting the building, Julia still visited with Carolina and Delores, although relations were obviously strained. Neither Carolina nor Delores would invite Julia to lunch with them, an act that signals closeness and trust between neighbors. In addition, Doña Carolina would complain to Doña Julia that her work with spirits of the dead (Mesa Blanca) interfered with her own work with saints (Santería). Faced with the conflict between the two mediums, the other women in the building, spiritists and nonspiritists alike, tried nevertheless to maintain cordial relations with both.

About a month after the study began, Doña Carolina's husband Roberto suffered a stroke and after lingering in the hospital about a week, died. While he was in the hospital, Carolina confided to a researcher that she had felt spirits in the house recently and experienced something bad and "heavy" there (that is, someone had performed sorcery against her and her husband). She had planned to visit El Indio to increase her "strength" and then give the apartment a spiritual cleansing, but Roberto died before she could accomplish this. On the evening when one of the researchers visited Doña Carolina's family at the funeral parlor, Doña Julia was also present. As Julia approached the corpse to pay her respects, Carolina asked the researcher to watch and make sure that Julia did not put something in the casket—an act only a sorcerer would perform. A number of rumors were also circulating among the Hispanos in the building that Carolina's apartment smelled "bad" and that Carolina had discovered Roberto's photograph hanging upside down. The clear implication of all this gossip was that Carolina's husband had been ensorcelled.

For nine days after Roberto's death the family observed the novena by, among other things, keeping lighted candles and a glass of water in the apartment. During this time the spirit of the deceased is commonly believed to linger on the premises and finally to depart when he realizes he is incorporeal. On the tenth day Carolina fumigated her entire apartment and sprinkled holy water in all the corners but claimed not to have seen a medium to procure a special preparation for cleansing the premises.

During the novena for Roberto, Nilda came down with a severe asthma attack and was hospitalized. Directly after her discharge she went, along with Doña Julia, to her *comadre,* who was also a medium. The *comadre* divined that Nilda's illness had been due to the spirit of Carolina's husband, who was attached to her. Together with Julia, she performed an exorcism of the spirit. The next day Doña Julia went to Delores to report the diagnosis; Delores in turn went to Nilda to confirm Julia's gossip and learned from her that the medium had removed Roberto's spirit "*de mala manera*" (that is, by sending it to hell instead of giving it light). This infuriated Delores, and she and Doña Carolina began claiming that Roberto had been such a good person that his spirit would not have become attached to anyone and that therefore the whole divination was a lie. This statement was designed to scotch gossip, which had spread through the building, that Carolina had made a pact with Roberto's spirit and was therefore responsible for Nilda's illness.

Roberto's death and the spiritist meaning attached to it affected building residents in different ways. Sra. Rodríguez, for example, called upon her daughter, who was a medium, in an attempt to get confirmation (*comprobación*) of the etiology of Nilda's asthma attack. Her daughter maintained that Nilda's *comadre*'s divination had been a fabrication (*embuste*), thus vindicating Doña Carolina. However, Sra. Rodríguez still did not trust Doña Carolina because she had once told her that her boyfriend was being unfaithful, a divination which Sra. Rodríguez considered to be nothing but malicious gossip. As a result of these contradictory opinions, Sra. Rodríguez maintained friendly but reserved relations with both Carolina and Julia.

On the other hand, her boyfriend, a self-proclaimed nonbeliever, maintained that all talk about Roberto's spirit was nonsense. To prove this, one evening after having drunk several cans of beer, he began invoking Roberto's spirit. Quite suddenly he began to shiver and, as he put it later, "catch the *fluido* of the dead man." He began exorcising himself, and Sra. Rodríguez invoked her Madama to remove the spirit from the house. The boyfriend's shivery feeling passed, and he henceforward stopped making light of spirit manifestations. (Since he already knew how to invoke and exorcise spirits, he had clearly been enculturated in spiritism and was thus returning to a familiar pattern of interpreting death.)

For both Sra. Rodríguez and her boyfriend the spiritist view of Roberto's death, though obviously important to them psychologically, did not greatly influence their relations with neighbors. This was not so for Clara, Nilda, and Julia, however. Clara, a tenant who was considered crazy (*loca*) by most building residents, had intermittently spent time in mental institutions when her children were growing up. Amid the flurry of gossip, she accosted Carolina on the stairs and accused her of killing Roberto through sorcery. The women exchanged angry words and did not speak to each other again during the course of the study.

The social effect of the spiritist interpretation of Roberto's death was more complicated for Nilda and Julia, although the final outcome was similar to Clara's alienation from Carolina. After Nilda's exorcism Doña Julia continued treating her for *mala influencia* deriving from Roberto's spirit, and for *envidia* attributed to neighbors. (See pp. 97–99 for the description of a treatment session between them.) The two developed a close relationship—*como pan y manteca* (like bread and butter), as the neighbors put it. Nilda confided to a researcher, however, that although Doña Julia was really helping her, she missed her former friendly relations with Carolina and Delores. Julia had directly caused this alienation between the three women by warning Delores not to visit Nilda any more, since she was carrying *mala influencia* into the apartment. Delores informed Julia that if Julia needed Nilda's friendship, she herself did not.

To prevent further evil influence from entering their apartments, Julia and Nilda fumigated the hall and spiritually cleansed the doorways of both their apartments. Not to be outdone and to frighten the two women, Delores then set fire to alcohol in the hallway between her apartment and Julia's (an accepted way of getting rid of evil influences). According to Delores, moreover, her effort was worthwhile, because Nilda and Julia came to beg her pardon and renewed friendship. (Nilda told the researcher that Julia had confided to her that she was still terrified of Delores.) The three women thus returned to an amicable, if not close, social relationship.

Within two months, however, Nilda and then Julia moved from the building. Although both moves were multiply determined, relations with Carolina and Delores played a part in both decisions. Nilda, after an incident in which Julia had caused a fight between her and her boyfriend, began seeing Julia more and more as a troublemaker rather than as a friend. She could never recapture her old easy cooperative relations with Carolina and Delores and so felt isolated and friendless in the building. In addition, as plans to marry her boyfriend matured, the pair decided to bring Nilda's older children home to live with them and needed a larger apartment. Therefore, when Nilda's *comadre* found a suitable place in her building, the family moved immediately. Julia became an isolate in the building. Even the nonspiritists now mistrusted her for the way she had caused a rift between Nilda and her former friends. Since Julia's husband was ill and she felt she could no longer rely on anyone in the building for help, the couple decided to move near their married daughter.

A number of observations can be made about the use of spiritist concepts in neighborly relations that are exemplified by the data from this building, observations that also pertain to other buildings with a majority of Hispanic tenants in the sample. First, a shared belief in spiritism, like any shared ism, constitutes an initial basis for association between new tenants in a building and the previous residents. Participation in spiritist practice is usually evident from various paraphernalia around people's apartments and from the smell of biweekly fumigations around the premises of the most observant practitioners. As is clear from the above material, however, what follows from the initial association may vary considerably, although there is always a special bond (be it positive or negative) among spiritist neighbors that does not exist among others. The two Catholic families in the building, for example, did not become nearly so involved in the gossip about sorcery as the spiritist families, although both believed that sorcery might indeed have occurred.

Second, the use of concepts like sorcery and *envidia* is perfectly acceptable within the spiritist subculture. Sorcery and the harmful effects of envy are not aberrant fantasies of the insane but shared standards for explaining what is and what to do about it (that is, a culture) that lend a certain predictability to human interaction. This is not to say that the mentally disturbed do not also use concepts of sorcery and *envidia* in explaining social relationships, but, to return to an earlier point, they do so in a way that seems patently disturbed to bearers of the culture. Clara's sudden and vehement confrontation with Doña Carolina, like Isabel Cruz's concern but inaction about her spiritual problems, was identified by sharers of the subculture as an inappropriate way of behaving.

In addition to being considered acceptable ways to structure social relationships, the concepts of sorcery and *envidia* are contrasting ways. *Envidia,* as our initial discussion of this term in Chapter 4 indicates, is applied to relationships that are outwardly friendly but where there is underlying, unexpressed hostility. Before the incident over Roberto's death, while she was still outwardly friendly toward Carolina and Delores, Julia pointed to the *envidia* of her neighbors as the source of her various business failures. In addition, she treated Nilda, who wished to remain on friendly terms with Carolina and Delores, for *envidia* (although she herself was more concerned with the sorcerous implications of the situation). In contrast with *envidia,* sorcery among neighbors is likely to be overt and occurs when relations among the neighbors are openly hostile rather than reservedly amicable.[5] To understand the dynamics of these contrasting ways of defining and handling social relationships, let us examine several representative cases in detail. The question we seek to illuminate in these cases is what effect these contrasting ways of structuring social relationships have on the behavior of the individuals involved and on the social relationships themselves.

ENVIDIA AND SORCERY AMONG NEIGHBORS

The following case of *envidia* emerges from a situation that commonly leads to this mode of conceiving neighborly relations—when a person has excelled his neighbors in some way and senses or imagines that they are envious of his accomplishments.

José and Frani lived in a tenement building that was still in good, though deteriorating, condition. José was very handy and had renovated his apartment so that it was the envy of other tenants in the building. The landlord appreciated José's work (and recognized a good thing when he saw it), so offered him

[5] The use of sorcery in overtly antagonistic relationships has been documented for practitioners of other spiritist cults (e.g., in Brazilian Batuque by Leacock and Leacock, 1975:274–275).

a larger apartment in the building and several rooms in the basement for his tools and materials. José recouped $500 for his work on the first apartment from the new tenants and set to work remodeling his new quarters.

Around this time José and Frani's 4-year-old son Felipe started acting up around the house. He broke some furniture and built a small fire out of wood chips on the kitchen floor. Frani took him to a spiritist who said that the child's behavior was the result of *envidia,* which other tenants in the building felt toward the family. Felipe, because he had the weakest protection, was the recipient of the maleficent influence of the envy. The spiritist recommended certain herbs and essences for baths, which would increase the child's protection.

In the course of counseling Frani, it became apparent to the medium that José had been spending a great deal of time working on the apartment and constantly told Felipe to keep out of his way. The medium suggested that José allow the child to help him with simple things. Within days Felipe's behavior around the house had changed for the better. Furthermore, Frani and José's relations with some of their more gossipy neighbors became more distant.

As this case demonstrates, the notable result of conceiving a problem in terms of *envidia* is that it turns the family in on itself for the task of building up its spiritual resources. Relations with neighbors remain amicable but more distant, while the family's ability to deal with problems purportedly resulting from neighbors' envy is enhanced. In other words, the envy of neighbors is taken as a given but the family's capability for coping with it is worked on and intentionally improved.

In contrast with *envidia,* sorcery is an intentionally harmful act directed at a specific person, and involves the magical preparation of a material substance. As a result of this last characteristic of sorcery, suspicions concerning its use may be based not only on a hypothetical link between an experienced misfortune and a hostile social relationship, but also on direct material evidence. Thus, in the course of a year's observations in this study, four families in four different buildings reported that they had found such evidence on their doorsteps. In each instance the victims interpreted the evidence (powder or herbs) as an attempt on the part of a specific neighbor or neighbors with whom they were on bad terms to get them to move. In each case the cause of ill will was different, but a prior pattern of overt hostility among the neighbors was apparent. In two cases, for example, the neighbors who lived underneath the recipient of the sorcery had frequently complained about the noise and destructiveness of the latter's children. In another case the object of sorcery was a gossip who had caused trouble in the building by telling tales about various residents. The final example involved a tenant whom the superintendant's wife was trying to get out of the building.

An examination of the consequences of these four discoveries of sorcery, although admittedly a small sample, is nevertheless instructive for understanding two possible consequences of defining a social relationship in terms of this concept. Specifically, the four instances were handled in two contrasting fashions. In three of the four cases, the objects of sorcery publicly and loudly conducted a spiritual cleaning of their doorways and the halls in front of their apartments. (In the absence of direct evidence but with the suspicion that Doña Carolina had ensorcelled her and Nilda, we saw Doña Julia acting in precisely the same way.) In addition to cleansing activities, the woman who was purportedly being hounded by the superintendent's wife loudly announced to whoever was in earshot that if she had to leave the building, she would put a curse on it. These protective rituals, with their accompanying noise and aroma of incense, clearly announce to all neighbors in the building that the officiant's family can and will protect themselves against the sorcery of other residents. The one victim out of four who did not perform this type of ritual kept quiet about the evidence she had found and took it to a spiritist to have the "job" revoked—that is, sent back to the perpetrator.

These two methods of handling sorcery had different consequences in terms of social relations within the buildings in which they occurred. The public method alerted nearly all households in the building to the conflict among neighbors and afforded the opportunity for factions to coalesce around the combatants, who were known to residents through preexisting gossip networks. In two cases these factions brought about changes in the social situation. The tale-teller became more and more isolated from the interdining and mutual assistance ties among women in the building and within two months opted to move; one of the women with obstreperous children became subject to critical comment from other residents who had also been bothered, with the result that she began taking her children to a relative's apartment when she could not be at home with them. In the building described in detail above, factions also emerged through the introduction of the idiom of sorcery into neighbors' relationships, with the result that the members of one of the factions (Nilda and Julia) ultimately moved from the building. In this light Sra. Rodríguez's attempt to get a confirmatory divination from a medium may be understood as part of a process she was going through in deciding whether to join one of the factions; the medium's advice, coupled with Sra. Rodríguez's distrust of Carolina, led her to retain amicable relations with both factions.

In contrast with the public handling of sorcery or suspicions of sorcery, the covert way of dealing with the problem, by having the "job" revoked, may perhaps reduce the anxiety of the original victim but, on the basis of our data, does not seem to affect social relations among neighbors in any patterned way.

With the review of these cases of *envidia* and sorcery in mind, we can return to the question of the effects these contrasting ways of defining neighborly social relationships have for the individuals involved and for the social relationships themselves. *Envidia* leads people to turn to a spiritist or to private rituals to gain strength against the purportedly harmful effects of envy. In the course of consulting with a medium, familial problems that have been attributed to *envidia* may also be addressed and alleviated. Thus, the effect of *envidia* is a turning inward of a family to develop its resources in an effort to maintain amicable relations with neighbors in spite of the envy these outsiders are believed to feel.

Sorcery, on the other hand, leads people to assert their spiritual power either through public performance of rituals or through conducting a covert "war" with a neighbor by having a spell returned to the sender. In either case the result is a power struggle. If handled publicly, it may involve the crystalization of factions among neighbors and ultimately the expulsion of one of the factions. If handled covertly, the power struggle persists, but the individuals involved may become sufficiently convinced of their own power to enable them to continue living beside a hostile neighbor or neighbors.

A CASE OF SPIRITISM IN A SIMPLEX SOCIAL RELATIONSHIP

So far in this discussion of the use of spiritist beliefs among neighbors we have focused mainly on relationships that are multiplex—people who were friends, kinsmen, or medium and client to one another, as well as neighbors. The unique instance in our sample of one Puerto Rican household in a building where all other residents were Black provides an instructive case for examining the operation of spiritist beliefs among people who stand only in the relationship of neighbor to one another—a simplex relationship. Of course the fact that the neighbors in this case were in different ethnic categories affected their social relations considerably; since the household head of the Puerto Rican family almost never interacted with others in the building and thus did not develop anything but a categorical relationship with them, her behavior with respect to her neighbors was based solely on propinquity and ethnic categorization. Obviously not much evidential weight can be placed on this one instance; nevertheless the behavior parallels markedly what one would expect from our previous discussions.

Providencia lived in open fear of her neighbors, whom she viewed as violent and thievish. Except for casual greetings, she spoke to them only when necessary. Early in the study she told the researcher about her children's illnesses and school problems and attributed them to the *envidia* of her neighbors. To deal with this, she kept a statute of her major protector facing the front door of the apartment, constantly burned candles on her altar, and fumigated the premises almost every day. Whether these actions reduced the anxiety under which Providencia lived is moot; they did have an interesting social consequence for her, however. Although none of the building residents shared Providencia's specific subculture, many were familiar with some tradition of sorcery and viewed her fumigations, which were detectable throughout the building, as some form of voodoo. As a result, they approached her cautiously but in general treated her politely and distantly.

During the course of the study, however, a cat belonging to the woman who lived above Providencia got into her apartment through an open window and broke the statue of her major protector. Providencia viewed this happening as an act of sorcery, since cats are generally held to be potential agents of sorcery. Providencia confronted the owner of the cat and demanded the price of the statue. Although she did not accuse the woman of black magic, she nevertheless went to a medium to have the "job" revoked. Thereafter she repeatedly vilified the woman to the researcher and claimed she would "put her in hell" if she did anything to her again. Her social relationship with the woman became overtly hostile.

At the beginning of the study, Providencia, although she feared her neighbors, maintained an agreeable, though reserved manner toward them. Like the other spiritists we have discussed who sought to maintain courteous relations with their neighbors in spite of suspecting ill feelings from them, Providencia defined their relationship in terms of *envidia*. When open hostility erupted between her and the woman upstairs, however, the relationship became defined in terms of sorcery—again like the spiritists in other buildings who shared the same ethnic and religious subcultures. Furthermore, being of a different subculture from her neighbors and having no potential allies to support her faction, Providencia handled the suspected sorcery in a covert, rather than public, manner. Providencia thus behaved in her simplex relationship with neighbors exactly as her spiritist counterparts in other buildings behaved in their multiplex relationships.

TWO ISSUES IN THE USE OF SPIRITIST BELIEFS IN NEIGHBORLY RELATIONS

In concluding this section on spiritism and neighborly relations, I would like to return to two issues raised earlier in the discussion: the difference in the frequency with which females and males utilize spiritist concepts in defining their social relations with neighbors, and the contrast between the content and manner of interaction among spiritist and nonspiritist neighbors.

Our data indicate that both male and female spiritists use spiritist concepts to structure kin, affinal, and amorous relationships about equally. However, females tend to order relationships with neighbors in spiritist terms; males rarely do so, but do use them in relationships with co-workers and people in authority. We have suggested that the greater interdependence among female over male neighbors is associated with this difference in the use of spiritist concepts. The data we have just reviewed on *envidia* and sorcery shed further light on this association.

Envidia and sorcery seem to concern two different social-psychological phenomena. *Envidia* is a cultural means of defining ambivalence and doing something about it. Since one may depend upon neighbors for various things (from specific services like shopping or child care to more general activities like information sharing about suspicious goings-on in the vicinity or the whereabouts of one's children) yet not fully trust them, the social relationship is ambiguous, and the feelings one entertains toward neighbors are ambivalent. *Envidia* is a cultural concept that labels just such a situation in which outwardly the social relationship is amicable and mutually dependent but simultaneously fraught with feelings of distrust.

Sorcery deals with an entirely different social-psychological phenomenon: power in social relationships where the parties are open antagonists. Besides the cases detailed above of Julia and Carolina and of Providencia and her upstairs neighbor, a particularly telling demonstration of the association between sorcery and overt antagonistic relations derives from the behavior of Isabel Cruz. One of the aspects of Sra. Cruz's conduct that convinced researchers who knew the spiritist subculture that she was "crazy" was her inappropriate use of the concept of sorcery. Instead of thinking about or using sorcery with reference to a specific antagonistic relationship in which she was involved, she instead talked vaguely of sorcerers in her vicinity, a situation more appropriately conceptualized in terms of *envidia*.

With regard to the different use of spiritist concepts by males and females in neighborly relations, it would thus seem that males either do not experience the kinds of relations with neighbors that are conceptualized by *envidia* and sorcery, or that they handle these relations in another way. It is indeed doubtful that men feel the ambivalence toward neighbors that women do, since they do not depend upon them for concrete services to nearly the same extent. For males suspicious feelings toward neighbors can exist without the need of employing *envidia* as a culturally patterned means of handling these feelings, because for males neighborly relations do not also involve interdependence and they therefore do not sustain a relationship fraught with suspicion. Furthermore, instead of using sorcery to structure antagonistic relations with neighbors, males are more likely to fight it out openly on a one-to-one basis. In short, since men have much greater freedom of movement than women in Puerto Rican society, their involvement with neighbors is much less frequent to begin with, and their chances of becoming involved in intense, adversary relationships with them is correspondingly less. In relations with both co-workers and people in authority, however, ambivalence and antagonism arise for men, and spiritist concepts are used.

To turn to the contrast between spiritists and nonspiritists in style and content of interactions with neighbors, both categories participated in the information networks that carried news of sorcery, *envidia*, and evil spiritual influences in buildings. With the exception of the few college-educated people in the study, some young, more Americanized families, and some of the people who had been raised as evangelical Protestants, comprehension and acceptance of this kind of news was widespread—a further indication of the degree to which concepts about spirits and magic are part of the public culture of Puerto Ricans. Behavior following receipt of such news, however, differed for spiritists and nonspiritists. In situations of overt sorcery spiritists actively sought more information about events as they unfolded, in an effort to place themselves with respect to developing factions. Nonspiritists, however, maintained distance from these events, obtaining only such news as came to them through normal channels. In short, spiritist families involved themselves in the politics of overt sorcery (if only to keep abreast of developments and avoid association with a faction). Nonspiritists purposely did not do so. Privately, however, nonspiritists occasionally performed rituals within their own religious systems to ward off the effects of sorcery or *envidia*—Protestants with prayer, and Catholics with prayer and candle offerings. There is no indication that any nonspiritist in our sample, in spite of believing in the efficacy of sorcery, ever actively practiced it—an additional condition that kept them aloof from political struggles with neighbors. Nonspiritists thus seem to handle conflicts with neighbors differently from spiritists. They withdraw from association with the adversary and do not involve other neighbors in the dispute.

IMPLICATIONS OF THE SOCIAL AND PSYCHOLOGICAL DYNAMICS OF SPIRITIST CONCEPTS FOR PSYCHIATRIC PSYCHOTHERAPY

In comparing the material on neighborly relations with the data from families discussed earlier in this chapter, a common pattern in the use of spiritist concepts in interpersonal relations can be observed. In both neighborly and family relations sorcery is used to structure overt power struggles. In the family, triangular situations that involve the wife in a struggle with either her husband's mother or paramour for the affections, attention, or support of the husband are, as we observed, dealt with through sorcery. A similar phenomenon may be observed between spouses who have become antagonists, as exemplified in the case of Delores and Victor. (In that situation, Victor sought to exert power over Delores through sorcery in order to preserve the marriage, while Delores used sorcery to force Victor out.) The use of sorcery in family relations by Elena's mother (in her attempt to reduce the influence of her daughter's *comadre* over her) also falls into this pattern. The use of sorcery among neighbors similarly occurs among openly antagonistic parties, as the data from the two buildings with different ethnic compositions has shown.

The concepts of *envidia* and *mala influencia,* in contrast, are applied to ambivalent social relationships, in which disagreement or hostility exists but where a commitment to sustain overtly amicable relations also obtains. Conceptualizing these kinds of social situations as *envidia* or *mala influencia* focuses therapeutic attention on the individual or group (for example, the family) in an effort to deal with the ambivalence by either removing its presumed source (as in the exorcism of an intrusive spirit in *mala influencia*) or by enhancing the client's ability to deal with suspicions or hostility (as in the rites to increase spiritual protection provided in cases of *envidia*).

For professionally trained psychotherapists working with Puerto Rican spiritist believers and practitioners, the material presented in this chapter has a number of implications. First, an understanding of the differences between the social and psychological dynamics of *envidia* and *mala influencia,* on the one hand, and of sorcery, on the other, will enable the therapist to communicate more readily with patients or clients who utilize these two concepts in dealing with interpersonal relationships. Furthermore, as pointed out in the material on Isabel Cruz, this understanding can also help the therapist in differential diagnosis by enabling the therapist to distinguish whether a patient or client is operating with these concepts in a culturally appropriate fashion. Finally, the nuclear family, as we have seen, is regarded as a unit in which any member with weak spiritual protection may fall victim to sorcery or *envidia* directed against any other member by outsiders. Thus, a problem experienced by one family member, which is either diagnosed or even suspected as resulting from these two causes, mobilizes concern for the well-being of the whole unit. Of the various modalities of professional psychotherapy, family therapy thus shares an important assumption with spiritism—namely, that the problem of one family member is symptomatic of a problem with the whole. This common assumption would, I suggest, predispose spiritist families toward family therapy as a mode of professional treatment. Moreover, since children are most often defined as the family members with weakest spiritual protection, family therapy would probably be most acceptable when a child's behavior constitutes the presenting problem.

SEVEN

Practical and Theoretical Implications of Spiritist Beliefs and Practices

In the first chapter I outlined the practical and the theoretical concerns that motivated the research and writing of this book. The practical purpose, as I stated there, was to examine Puerto Rican spiritism as a mental health resource. The theoretical concern was to consider, on the basis of the spiritist data, the nature of psychotherapeutic healing in general. In this final chapter we return to these two themes. We shall first devote four sections to spiritism as a community mental health resource. The first of these sections focuses on preventive aspects of spiritist practice; the remaining three focus on spiritism as a form of psychotherapy for the treatment and rehabilitation of mental disorders. The concluding section of the chapter considers the second major theme, the nature of psychotherapeutic healing.

PREVENTIVE CONTRIBUTIONS OF SPIRITISM TO COMMUNITY MENTAL HEALTH

As we have noted throughout this book, spiritism is not solely a form of psychotherapy. Like many social institutions, it is multifunctional, contributing to the social and psychological well-being of its adherents by serving as a voluntary organization, a way of ordering social relationships, a religion, and an identity. In the following sections we examine each of these functions in turn.

SPIRITIST *Centros* AS VOLUNTARY ORGANIZATIONS

For many Puerto Ricans living in the midst of a large, alien city like New York, the *centro* becomes an important primary group outside the family and assumes many of the functions voluntary organizations perform for urban migrants the world over. For example, the *centro* operates as a job-referral network and offers assistance to members during life crises. It also serves as an agent of social control through informal gossip among its members, through the more formal rules of the organization, and, during séances, through the ritual authority of mediums. (See p. 109 for one example of a medium's use of her authority.)

Most importantly, the *centro* and its head medium serve to socialize members to new urban ways in the context of a group and subculture that combines both traditional and new foci of interest. (Witness for example, the head medium, described in Chapter 3, telling her congregation how to deal with landlords and where to get the best buys in religious statuary in New York City, or the common practice of requiring clients to secure the bath essences, herbs, and other materia medica themselves—an activity that frequently necessitates trips to different parts of the city.) The combination of traditional and new elements and activities in spiritist cults has sometimes led students of these groups to conclude that they are either conservative or progressive forces in acculturating adherents to new life styles.[1] In my experience, however, *centro* membership may affect different people in different ways: the same cult can encapsulate certain members in a familiar, traditional setting while at the same time it facilitates the participation of other members in new urban roles and situations (for example, through job referrals and activities related to the management of the *centro* and its rituals).

In addition to these major services which spiritist *centros* perform for members, they offer benefits to the Puerto Rican community at large. The rituals, for example, are looked upon by some as a form of entertainment, and a number of teenagers reported going to spiritist meetings from time to time instead of a movie. Besides their rituals, many *centros* sponsor summer picnics to parks outside the city and dinners on important ceremonial occasions. These activities are open to nonmembers and thus furnish recreational opportunities that may otherwise be unavailable to low-income urbanites.

Among the indigenous mental health resources of the Puerto Rican community, the *centro,* in short, serves as a preventive agency that furnishes material and social services to members and, to some extent, nonmembers as well. By providing job referrals, assistance in life crises, recreational opportunities, acculturative experiences within a traditional ethnic setting, and stable social contacts outside the family, it fills needs that contribute importantly to mental health.

SPIRITISM AS A SET OF STANDARDS FOR ORDERING SOCIAL RELATIONSHIPS

As we saw in the preceding chapter, the concepts of *envidia* and sorcery provide ways for people to deal respectively with ambivalent social relationships (in which outward amicability is combined with inner distrust) and with overtly antagonistic relationships, usually prompted by a power struggle.

Weidman's theory of the psychological function of witchcraft beliefs sheds considerable light on the phenomenon of *envidia* and its social usage among Puerto Ricans in New York. In an ingenious attempt to

[1] For the conservative judgment see, for example, Seda, 1973:148–149 on a rural community in Puerto Rico, or Macklin, 1974:417 on spiritism among Chicanos in Texas and California. For the progressive position, see Halifax and Weidman, 1973:319–320 on Cuban Santería in Mami. Brown (referred to in Pressel, 1974:212) has even observed the use of related spiritist groups, the Umbandists, as a basis of support for politicians in Rio de Janeiro. Although it seems unlikely that spiritist groups would ever come to serve that function in this society, the example illustrates another way in which such groups can involve its members in wider urban participation.

relate social and psychological phenomena, Weidman (1968) has suggested that ambiguously defined social expectations may lead psychologically to feelings of ambivalence and ultimately to a sense of unreality and powerlessness in interpersonal relations. People "may believe they perceive a situation clearly, but then they begin to doubt. An individual may actually not have intended harm. . . . One never knows, and one is afraid to act until one is sure. . . . With this kind of ambiguity in social situations, anxiety, doubt, and distrust must become an integral part of the whole social process. Ambivalence . . . becomes in this formulation the psychological counterpart to social ambiguity" (1968:29–30). Witchcraft beliefs, according to Wiedman, operate in such situations to establish greater certainty by reifying feelings of distrust through labeling certain people as clearly malevolent. Interaction with these individuals can then proceed in a more predictable and thus less anxiety-provoking fashion.

Although Weidman (1968:28) in her formulation attributes social ambiguity to cultural standards that define human nature as inherently evil, I think the social ambiguity among Puerto Ricans in New York is attributable more to the absence of clear normative rules for social interaction among neighbors who are neither real nor fictive kin (*compadres*).[2] Her formulation, nevertheless, seems to fit the facts of these relationships. First, although *envidia* may, according to cultural standards, be attributed to both neighbors and extended family members, my data indicate that neighbors are the most frequently cited source. Second, after diagnosis and treatment of *envidia*, people do seem to act with less ambivalance toward suspected neighbors. Witness, for example, Julia's distant and circumspect relations with Delores and Doña Carolina after attributing various misfortunes in her life to their *envidia*, or Frani and José's decreased involvement with some of their more gossipy neighbors, as recounted in the previous chapter.

Sorcery beliefs also allow people to structure their relationships with others in a more predictable fashion. In the conflict between Doña Carolina and Doña Julia, for example, building residents who did not wish to become involved were alerted to the two women's mutual antagonism by their accusations of sorcery and took appropriate action to disengage themselves. In strained relations between mothers-in-law and daughters-in-law, sorcery may provide a rationale for decreased interaction between

[2] In a later article, written jointly with a psychiatrist (Wittkower & Weidman, 1960: 182–83), Weidman also discusses "modernization" and "change" as possible sources of the social ambiguity required for her theory of witchcraft and sorcery accusations, a position closer to the one I am suggesting in the Puerto Rican situation.

the antagonists as well as a partial removal of the power struggle to a supernatural plane.

An additional effect of structuring social relationships in terms of witchcraft and sorcery is that it allows people to avoid full responsibility for the outcomes of their relationships. Conceiving a mother-in-law's sorcery as the cause of a marital breakup, or a neighbor's *envidia* as the source of a child's misbehavior, for example, deflects attention from familial relationships to one outside the nuclear unit. These displaced explanations of interpersonal problems and the whole issue of individual responsibility in spiritist therapy will be explored more fully in a later section.

SPIRITISM AS A RELIGION

If we accept Geertz's now famous definition of religion as "a system of symbols which acts to establish powerful, pervasive, and long-lasting moods and motivations in men by formulating conceptions of a general order of existence and clothing these conceptions with such an aura of factuality that the moods and motivations seem uniquely realistic" (1966:4), then spiritism clearly falls within this institutional category. As such, it fulfills many of the general social and psychological functions commonly attributed to religion [for example, resolving contradictions among cultural standards, explaining "the strange opacity of certain empirical events, the dumb senselessness of intense or inexorable pain, and the enigmatic unaccountability of gross iniquity (Geertz, 1966:23).] In addition to these general functions, however, spiritism contributes to the social and psychological health of Puerto Ricans in New York (and probably also on the island) in certain special ways.

One of these ways it shares with other possession cults throughout the world. That is, it allows for what Bourguignon (1973:329) has called "therapeutic status transformation." A common feature of religions in which possession occupies a significant place is the bestowal of high status on individuals who attain acceptable standards of possession performance. Thus, as various writers have pointed out (I. M. Lewis, 1971; Mischel and Mischel, 1958), a person of low status, who may enter a possession cult as a form of therapy for uncontrolled possession, may emerge as a priest or shaman of the cult with higher social standing. As Lewis observes (1971:189–190),

> In both peripheral and main morality possession cults . . . an enhancement of status accrues to the shamanistic candidate who succeeds in mastering the grounds of affliction and thus proves to the world his claim to be considered a

healer. The temporary rise in status of the possessed woman or downtrodden man in peripheral possession cults is itself an intimation of the fuller and more permanent rewards which lie in store if the acolyte perseveres to later become a fully-fledged shaman.

In Puerto Rican spiritism the path from spirit-ridden client to head medium of a *centro* is precisely this form of status transformation, a transformation apparently more characteristic of Puerto Rican women than men. Although data are conflicting on this point,[3] my own observations, as well as those of Bram (1958) and Seda (1973:141–142) on the island, indicate that mediums are more frequently women than men. Given the lower status and minimal power granted women in Puerto Rican society, at least traditionally, their attraction to the medium role as a way of achieving special status in the community seems understandable. It is particularly interesting to note, furthermore, that the voluntary organizations of most Hispanic churches in New York, both Roman Catholic and Pentecostal, even today are sex-segregated (Garrison, 1972: 260, 263), so that spirit mediumship provides one of the few opportunities for a Puerto Rican woman to achieve formal leadership in a group composed of males and females. If Puerto Rican women progressively achieve higher status positions in the occupational sphere, I would predict that the importance of mediumship as an avenue to prestige will decline.[4]

SPIRITISM AS AN IDENTITY

Being a spiritist can constitute a social identity that provides the basis for relationships with strangers when moving into a new situation. Thus, in the buildings under study, new residents who were spiritists quickly made contact with other spiritists on the basis of this common identity. Because of the widespread belief in spirits among Puerto Ricans, furthermore, spiritism (as mentioned in the first chapter) has somewhat the same standing as "soul" among Blacks as a basis for ethnic identity.

[3] Garrison (1972:281) claims that the two sexes were about equally represented among mediums in the South Bronx *centros* she studied, while males predominated among *Presidentes de la Mesa*. The *centros* she studied seem to have been more purely Kardecist than any I observed, which may relate to the sex difference in some way, although I cannot say how.

[4] Rogler's perceptive account of the history of a Puerto Rican community organization in a meduim-sized Eastern seaboard city indicates that a woman of unusual energy and intelligence can achieve leadership in a civic organization composed of both sexes. In doing so, however, she must persistently buck the prevailing sentiment that "women do not take a front seat" (Rogler, 1972:21, 114).

Although some devout Catholics and most Pentecostals are avowedly antispiritist, the shared belief in the participation of spirits in human affairs nevertheless constitutes a commonality among Puerto Ricans which acts as a latent definer of the Puerto Rican ethnic identity.

SPIRITISM AS A FORM OF PSYCHOTHERAPY

Besides the preventive contributions of spiritism to community mental health, its contributions as a form of treatment and rehabilitation of psychological disorders must be considered. As mentioned earlier, this aspect of spiritism has usually been the focus of earlier writers on this cult. The following discussion therefore depends on their work as well as my own research. We begin by summarizing the nature of spiritist psychotherapy briefly, and then indicate some of the similarities and differences between it and psychotherapy as practiced by mental health professionals in this society.

A SUMMARY OF SHORT-TERM THERAPY OR CRISIS INTERVENTION

As noted, the vast majority of people who consult spiritists do so on a short-term basis during crisis or transitional periods in their lives. These clients' problems most often involve relationships with spouse, in-laws, other kin, or people on the job; the death of a close relative; life transitions (puberty, menopause, and terminal illness); vague anxiety manifested in *manía,* nightmares, and the like; and physical complaints for which the person has not received satisfactory medical attention. For these sorts of problems therapy typically involves three elements: diagnosis of the problem in sociospiritual terms (that is, in terms of both the client's social relationships and spirit intervention); acts to improve the client's relationships with the client's spiritual protectors; and direct counseling. These activities may take place in private sessions between the medium and client, in family groups, or in larger groups at *centro* meetings. Most commonly treatment occurs in a combination of individual and group contacts. The most common spiritual diagnoses of these short-term problems are *envidia, mala influencia,* and *brujería.*

Envidia *and Social Ambiguity*

Envidia, as we have seen, often entails the illness or misbehavior of a child as the presenting "symptom." Because of the belief that envy directed toward parents may redound on children because of their weaker spiritual protection, this diagnosis often draws the whole family into a therapeutic regimen which involves both counseling and steps to enhance the family's spiritual protection. (Since, as we have noted, the behavior of children is primarily the mother's responsibility in Puerto Rican society, it is usually she who consults the medium in cases of problems with children. Therefore the husband-father may not attend sessions with the medium, although his behavior comes under scrutiny in the diagnosis of the problem and his protection also receives attention in treatment. The case of Felipe, recounted in Chapter 6, is typical of this regimen.) Adults, too, may be diagnosed as suffering from *envidia,* sometimes followed by the same type of family-focused treatment. In short, the treatment for *envidia* may bring the whole family under spiritual scrutiny through the influence of the mother as spiritual leader, and treatment operates to restore structured relations within that primary group.

These therapeutic effects exemplify the cybernetic action of healing cults, as described by Prince (1968:157–65) and Turner (1968), among others. According to this view, disturbed relations among members of a group bring about suspicions of witchcraft or some other mystical intervention, which lead in turn to consultation of diviners. The diviners recommend rituals that bring group members together in highly structured settings to perform activities heavily freighted with symbolic meaning. Performance of these rituals operates ultimately to restore some form of social integration among the members.

In addition to restoring social equilibrium to the family, diagnoses of *envidia* by mediums may produce the same results as the self-diagnoses which we discussed above in relation to Weidman's theories of witchcraft. That is, the medium's diagnosis serves as a "reality test" to confirm and reify feelings of distrust toward neighbors or more distant kin. Once these feelings have been confirmed, the client can then develop social defenses—for example, avoidance—against the supposed source of the envy.

Mala Influencia *and Uncovering the Unconscious*

In contrast with *envidia,* a diagnosis of *mala influencia* often occurs in connection with marital problems. [See, for example, the cases of Carmelo in Chapter 4; Rita and Berto in Chapter 6; Minuchin et al.'s unfaithful wife (1967:241); or Purdy et al.'s Case II (1972:73).] However, any behavior or circumstance (such as the death of a loved one) that seems to get in the way of satisfactory social relationships may be diagnosed and treated under this rubric. Treatment ("working the cause") involves attributing disturbing behavior to an intrusive spirit (usually a kinsman, spouse, or lover from a previous incarnation); and, after interrogation of the spirit by mediums, removing it from the client. Following removal, various measures are taken to improve the client's relationship with his or her protective spirits to prevent recurrent spirit intrusion. In addition, direct counseling concerning the disturbed social relationship occurs.

This treatment procedure clearly resembles abreaction in psychoanalytic theory, in which unconscious conflicts or resistances are brought to a level of consciousness and defined as ego-dystonic, with the result that associated behaviors are then presumably abandoned. [See, Lévi-Strauss (1963:186–205) on the central importance of abreaction in shamanistic cures.] Seda (1973:117–119) and Garrison (1973:14) have also drawn a parallel between this form of therapy and psychodrama. According to this view, the medium enacts the psychodramatic role of the auxiliary ego by expressing and dramatizing clients' unconscious conflicts, and in doing so helps clients to externalize and separate themselves from the conflicts.

Brujería *and Hostility*

The third diagnostic category that usually initiates a short-term relationship between client and therapist is *brujería* or sorcery. Treatment of this kind of problem parallels the "abreactive" or "psychodramatic" treatment of *mala influencia,* since both conditions are attributed to the interference of a malicious spirit. But because sorcery also entails a malevolent perpetrator (a person, as we have seen, with whom the client already has an openly hostile relationship), additional attention may be given in treatment to enhancing the spiritual protection both of the client and of the clent's family to prevent further harm befalling them at the hands of the malefactor. As noted in the previous chapter, diagnoses or acts of sorcery may also precipitate the severance of a social relationship, so that therapeutically the treatment may be seen to have two effects: abreaction of repressed conflicts, and preparation of the client to abandon or restructure hostile social relationships.

Attendance at Centro *Meetings*

Koss (1970:277) has suggested that *centros* perform a very important therapeutic function for those who attend sessions only irregularly and do not receive treatment directly. Because the problems of clients in treatment are discussed publicly at spiritist meetings and the medium openly offers advice about these problems, she claims that members of the audience benefit both by seeing that they share the same kind of problems with other people and by utilizing the medium's counsel to others for coping with problems in their own lives. Attendance at *centro* meetings thus provides some of the same supportive measures available in psychiatric group therapy.

LONG-TERM THERAPY: A SUMMARY

Long-term therapy is undertaken for clients diagnosed as having faculties or its possible sequela, *castigo*. Clients who are treated for faculties usually present serious and persistent psychological symptoms such as fugue states, suicidal feelings or attempts, and seizures. (See Chapter 4 for a more complete description of these symptoms.) These symptoms are attributed to the periodic intrusion of low-ranking spirits into the client's body. Treatment, as we have seen, involves the client in a long-term relationship with a mediumistic group, during which the client learns to control spirit intrusions (that is, the symptoms). In the course of treatment the client is encouraged to allow these spirits entrance (to go into trance) during spiritist meetings but to limit this behavior to such contexts. Early in treatment these spiritual visitations are fairly violent, and the client demonstrates little control over his or her behavior. During the process of development, however, the client enters into a special relationship with one spirit (the *predilecto* or *guía principal*), who is seen as assisting the client to limit the entry and exit of spirits to appropriate times and circumstances. With the help of this spirit and under the guidance of the medium, the client gradually gains control over the trance behavior, until it is sufficiently socialized to permit a dialogue with purported intrusive spirits. In time, the spirits that the client manifests relate to the context of the *centro* and speak as *causas* (spiritual causes) of others' problems, and the client thus emerges from treatment as a medium. To the extent that the client actually succeeds in eliminating self-destructive or dissociative behaviors from his or her life outside the *centro*, the treatment accomplishes a therapeutic status transformation and a therapeutic personality transformation for the client (Bourguignon, 1973:329).

According to spiritist belief, moreover, this form of treatment entails a lifelong commitment on the part of the medium to his or her *predilecto*, a commitment usually fulfilled by remaining a member of the mediumistic group that performed the cure and continuing to use one's powers to help others. Failing to retain a good relationship with one's *guía principal* is believed to precipitate a return of the original symptoms (*castigo*).

Castigo is treated by relearning the controls previously developed. Had Clarita (Chapter 5) responded to the initial attempts to "work the causes" that were besetting her, this therapy would have been instituted.

A second but less common diagnosis that initiates long-term treatment is *cadena*. Since, as we pointed out in Chapter 4, *cadena* involves familial influences from the past, its treatment focuses on the client's early social relationships (either directly or in more remotely symbolic form—that is, by attributing the problem to an ancestor several generations back). In both theory and practice the treatment of *cadena* closely resembles psychoanalysis. Since my data on this diagnostic category consist of only one diagnosed instance and one case in treatment (apart from cases in which this diagnosis was combined with a diagnosis of faculties), I cannot be more detailed about the procedures and goals of the therapy involved.

SIMILARITIES AND DIFFERENCES BETWEEN SPIRITIST AND MAINSTREAM PSYCHIATRIC THERAPIES

In using the term "mainstream psychiatric therapies" in the following discussion, I refer jointly to the major psychodynamic schools of therapy (psychoanalysis and derived therapies), behavior therapy, and more recent "systems" approaches to therapy (as represented, for example, by the theories of Don Jackson, Jay Haley, and others). Although it is difficult to characterize all these psychiatric therapies in any unitary fashion, it is nevertheless possible to indicate how they differ as a class from spiritist psychotherapy in terms of therapeutic goals and techniques.

THERAPEUTIC GOALS: SIMILARITIES AND DIFFERENCES

In discussing ways of measuring the extent to which psychiatric treatment accomplishes its reputed goals, Frank (1967:1306–1307) has differentiated two notions that he calls "face validity" and "construct validity." The former type of validity involves psychotherapeutic goals so widely shared by both laypersons and therapists that improvement with respect to any of these goals is "universally" accepted as a measure of therapeutic success. Frank specifies these goals as "subjective comfort; the capacity to establish mutually rewarding relationships with other individuals within and outside the family; the ability to do one's job adequately and to derive some satisfaction from working; and the possession of certain social skills" (1967:1306). In contrast to this form of validity, construct validity involves goals specific to certain techniques and theories of therapy. For example, "the congruence between the patient's actual and ideal self would be the crucial measure of improvement for the client-centered therapies; the psychoanalytically oriented therapies would be evaluated on the basis of the patient's awareness of his inner needs, conflicts, etc." (loc. cit.). Ultimately, as Frank points out, construct validity rests on face validity, since the goals of specific therapeutic schools must, to be credible, produce behavioral results that are generally accepted as desirable.

Spiritist psychotherapy shares with psychiatric therapies the goals embodied in the concept of face validity. With regard to construct validity, however, the specific goals of spiritist and psychiatric therapies present notable differences. Before discussing these differences, I shall first restate the construct goals of spiritist therapy, although I shall not do the same for all psychiatric therapies before indicating divergences between the two. (For summary statements of the goals and techniques of the major psychiatric therapies, however, the reader may wish to consult Ford and Urban, 1963; Freedman and Kaplan, 1967; Harper, 1959; Masserman, 1967; Redlich and Freedman, 1966; or Stein, 1966.)

It seems fair to say that the principal "construct" goal of spiritism is to relate clients to a transcendental, spiritual order in the universe from which they can derive the power and skill to attain the "face-validity" goals catalogued above. This construct goal obviously rests on a cultural assumption of the existence of such a spiritual order. As we have seen, in short-term spiritist therapies efforts are directed toward removing malevolent influences deriving from the spiritual order and toward enhancing the client's relationship with beneficent representatives of that order. In long-term therapy, efforts center on creating a special relationship between the client and at least one protective spirit so that the client becomes able to communicate directly with other beings of the transcendent order. The latter therapy involves a lifelong commitment to this special spiritual relationship and usually also to groups in which spirit communication occurs.

Stated in this fashion, the construct goals of spiritism seem to differ from the goals of psychiatric therapies in two major ways: (1) by including spirits within the therapeutic framework or paradigm; and (2) by seeing permanent involvement in a therapeutic relationship within the *centro* as a goal for some clients.

1. Spirits as Part of the Therapeutic Paradigm

Of the two differences between spiritist and psychiatric therapies, perhaps the most striking is the effort in spiritism to enhance the client's ability to form not only human but also spiritual relationships. In spiritist therapy the client is thus placed within a broader metaphysical framework than in any psychiatric therapy (with the possible exception of Jungian analysis). For clients whose culture already places them within a larger spiritual order, however, this therapeutic goal seems entirely appropriate. Yet including a client's relationship to spiritual beings within a psychotherapeutic system does suggest some additional divergences between spiritist and psychiatric therapies which require discussion.

One of the most obvious of these divergencies, which has repeatedly become apparent in our exposition of spiritist theory and practice, concerns the locus of responsibility for behavior. By attributing clients' symptoms to maleficent spiritual influences and implicating benevolent protective spirits in their cure, the spiritist system of therapy appears to deny the client's responsibility for either the problem or its cure. Such a system contrasts sharply with mainstream psychiatric therapies, which tend to stress the individual's responsibility for self and condition. To understand this apparent contrast more fully, however, one needs to analyze two different aspects of the problem of responsibility. First, one must distinguish between responsibility for the problem and responsibility for the cure. Second, one must examine ideas about proximate and ultimate responsibility in the two therapeutic systems. These two aspects of the issue of responsibility must be examined in turn, in the light of basic metaphysical differences between the two therapeutic systems.

Simply stated, the metaphysics of psychiatry (particularly as practiced in this country) derives from Protestantism; the metaphysics of spiritism stems from folk-Catholicism. Years ago Davis (1938) called attention to the clear correspondence between the values of Protestantism and the American mental hygiene movement. Among the assumptions that underpin both institutions he noted the importance of individualism, self-reliance, and rationalism. More recently Kiev (1973), in contrasting psychiatric and other forms of psychotherapy, has underscored some of these same characteristics of the psychiatric therapies. He has noted "our own [Western psychiatric] emphasis on *the patient's* responsibility for his difficulty" (p. 227; emphasis in the original), the related belief in man's "destiny to master the environment" (p. 230), and "too much emphasis on cognitive changes and intellectual comprehension" (pp. 231–232). In short, "the psychotherapeutic search for the patient's errors and the encouragement to work through problems provide a treatment technique consonant with our value system—one which places great weight on autonomy, self-reliance, and individual responsibility" (Kiev, 1973:

229). Both this metaphysical system and its parallel therapy thus view the individual as responsible in some measure for both problem and cure. It is important to note, however, that although psychiatric therapies thus place proximate responsibility on the client, they tend to place ultimate responsibility on society in general (as the growth of community psychiatry attests) and/or on more specific social relationships (for example, early experiences with parents).[5]

In contrast to the psychiatric therapies, spiritism is more closely related to the metaphysics of folk-Catholicism and other folk religions in attributing ultimate responsibility to the powers of the supernatural world—a view which Macklin (1974:415) neatly epitomizes in the phrase, *si Dios quiere* (if God wills). Proximate responsibility in this metaphysical system clearly rests, however, with the individual, whose duty is to act according to an accepted code of conduct and to solicit the help of supernatural powers in doing so. Applied to spiritist therapy, this view dictates that if one is beset by maleficent spirits, one is personally responsible not only for seeing that they are removed (by enlisting a medium to secure the aid of beneficent spirits in this task), but also for following the medium's instructions about preparing oneself for their removal. The ultimate disposition of the problem is, however, in the hands of the spirits.[6] The case of Clarita (Chapter 5) provides an appropriate empirical demonstration of this allocation of proximate responsibility to the afflicted person and ultimate responsibility to spirits. Thus among the various causes cited by Clarita's healers for the unsuccessful outcome of their treatment, a most important one was the client's failure to make the effort to resume a relationship with her protective spirits. Since protective spirits do only good, they would have been ultimately responsible for curing her, but Clarita's refusal to enlist their aid demonstrates her own responsibility in the cure as well.

In sum, both psychiatric and spiritist therapies attribute the proximate responsibility for cure to the individual, but ultimate causal responsibility to an agency outside the individual. In psychiatric therapies cause is attributed to social factors; in spiritism, to supernatural powers. These conceptions seem to function in both therapies as a way of distancing the client from and thus objectifying certain emotions or patterns of be-

[5] Another "ultimate cause" entertained in contemporary psychiatry is of course physiochemical. But since this book focuses on methods of instituting behavior change that depend on the social relationship between a healer and sufferer (see Frank's definition of psychotherapy cited in Chapter 4), I intentionally omit organic theories and therapies from consideration.

[6] Koss (1970:275) discusses the notion of responsibility in a similar fashion in developing her ideas about the "therapeutic paradoxes" of spiritist therapy.

havior for treatment purposes—in psychiatric parlance, for changing behavior from ego-syntonic to ego-alien.[7]

In psychiatric therapies distancing is accomplished by ascribing unwanted behaviors to social causes remote in time from the client's immediate situation. Thus in psychodynamic therapies current feelings and behaviors may be assigned to unresolved conflicts deriving from early social relationships. In behavior therapy distancing entails focusing on behaviors learned in past social situations, which the client inappropriately generalizes to present situations. In systems and family therapies distancing involves labeling certain behaviors as faulty or inappropriate methods of communication, also developed in past social situations. The basic formula of all these therapies is, in sum: *There is a residue of past social experience that intrudes into the client's behavior at the moment. It is this residue that is causing the person's problems in life. The client currently has no control over the intrusion of these persistent behavior patterns into present situations, and the goal of therapy will be either to teach the client how to deal with the behaviors or to eliminate the behaviors entirely.* Specific psychiatric therapies tend to favor one or the other of these goals, although the nature of the behavior often determines which approach will be followed.

It seems clear that spiritist therapy follows the same formula but objectifies the client's problematic behavior in terms of spiritual influence rather than as a residue of previous social interactions.[8] The basic formula of the psychiatric therapies, as stated above, can therefore be transformed into the formula of spiritist therapy by substituting the word "spirit" for every reference to past social interactions. Even the therapeutic goals of spiritism are identical to the psychiatric goals: either to teach the client to live with the spirit or spirits or to eliminate (exorcise) them. In short, I suggest that the idea of ultimate social causation in psychiatric therapies serves the same therapeutic function as the idea of ultimate spiritual causation in spiritist therapy—namely, to bracket off or separate the client from some aspects of his or her behavior in order to change them.

It is interesting to note, furthermore, that while the psychiatric therapies rely on the time dimension to conceptualize distance in dealing with unwanted behaviors, spiritist therapy relies on space for the same pur-

[7] This general point was first suggested to me by my colleague, Professor Barbara Ayres.

[8] In fact, of course, spiritism also includes etiological conceptions that attribute present behaviors to prior social relationships. Both *mala influencia* and *cadena* do this, although the prior relationships may be assigned to previous incarnations.

pose. Thus, psychiatric theory attributes unwanted behavior to past (temporally distant) events, and spiritist theory attributes such behavior to a spirit which has intruded into the bodily space of the afflicted, with distancing accomplished by removing and consigning the spirit to a remote spatial location.

2. *Integration into the* Centro

As noted previously, the more seriously disturbed clients in spiritist therapy undergo a form of treatment called "development" (*desarollo*), from which they may emerge as mediums with special, long-term relationships with a particular protective spirit (the *guía principal*). This special relationship with the *guía*, who assists the medium in communicating with other spirits, is best maintained within the social setting of the *centro,* where mediums use their powers to assist others. Although membership in a *centro* is not an essential consequence of this form of treatment (so long as mediums sustain a relationship with their principal guide by means of the required rituals), it is nevertheless strongly encouraged both by verbal directives and by the example of the *mediunidad* who have trained the novice. Although some of the peripheral psychiatric therapies today (for example, the Langian and Sullivanian schools) as well as certain treatment programs for the addictions (like Synanon and Alcoholics Anonymous) also encourage long-term, if not permanent, incorporation of the sufferer into a therapeutic group, none of the major psychiatric therapies has traditionally done so (at least in theory). The expectation that certain clients will maintain a long involvement in a therapeutic relationship, partly as client and partly as healer, thus constitutes the second major contrast between the construct goals of spiritist therapy and those of most psychiatric therapies.

Before commenting on the merits of this particular feature of spiritist therapy for the population studied, it is well to note that incorporation of the healed into a curing society is a common phenomenon cross-culturally. Indeed, on the basis of its frequency in human societies as well as its recent recrudescence in this society in the form of self-help groups of amputees and other rehabilitated victims of various illnesses, one must begin to question why psychiatric therapy has tended to stress independence from the therapeutic relationship as a goal rather than the cross-culturally more common practice of rehabilitating and socializing the sufferer into a long-term mutual aid group. One can speculate that certain dominant values of this culture (for example, the stigma of mental illness and the individualistic ethic mentioned previously) have played a role in promoting the goal of independence, although the relatively recent development of self-help groups for former mental patients, supported by psychiatrists, argues for a growing change in attitude among mental health professionals.

The merits of prolonged *centro* membership and participation in the *mediunidad* as a treatment goal clearly require further investigation. It is my observation that *centro* leaders, whatever mental anguish they may have gone through in the course of their lives, are fairly stable individuals, most with a good grasp of the techniques of living in New York City and the psychological subtleties of interpersonal life. [See Lubchansky et al.'s supportive findings on the psychological attitudes of spiritists (1970:315–317).] Members of the *mediunidad,* however, seem less stable and continue to experience periods of upset and unusual difficulty in coping with their lives. During these periods they receive the support and therapeutic assistance of the *centro,* which in my observation carries them through. Although this apparent therapeutic benefit of long-term incorporation into a *centro* requires quantitative documentation, involvement in a *centro* does have the clearly demonstrable merit of warding off a permanently damaging public diagnosis of insanity (*locura*), as Rogler and Hollingshead (1965) have pointed out. Furthermore, *centro* membership clearly provides additional benefits in affording people the opportunity to socialize outside the family and to learn values and social skills applicable in the wider urban society.

THERAPEUTIC TECHNIQUES: SIMILARITIES AND DIFFERENCES

Although the construct goals of all psychotherapies are embedded in the values and cognitive schemata of particular cultural systems and are therefore quite varied, the techniques used by different psychotherapies reveal considerable similarity. Since comparative studies by Frank (1961), Sargant (1957), Kiev (1973), and Torrey (1972) have already summarized the commonalities between techniques of psychiatric and religious or "primitive" psychotherapies, I shall concentrate in this section on the outstanding points of similarity and difference between psychiatric and specifically spiritist therapeutic techniques.

Assigning Meaning to Behavior

The importance of placing the client's behavior into a cognitive framework that provides a label or meaning for the behavior is, according to the above writers, characteristic of all psychotherapies. As we have seen, spiritist cosmology provides a framework that permits the organization of nightmares, fugues, suicidal urges, envy, feelings of anxiety and restlessness, and interpersonal conflicts into a culturally and personally meaningful structure. The fact that each client creates a personal understanding (myth, interpretation) of his or her behavior out of a culturally accepted framework has the important effect of enabling the individual to communicate his psychological state to those around him.

Confession and review of past history are also techniques common to both psychiatric and spiritist therapies. They occur in spiritism during the process of diagnosis and more extensively in treatment of certain problems like *cadena*. These techniques ensure that most of the client's anxiety-provoking feelings and unresolved interpersonal conflicts will be evoked and thus subjected to labeling within the explanatory system of the therapy.

Emotional Arousal

Common to all psychotherapies is the elicitation of certain emotions from the client in relation to the therapist. Indeed some commentators on Western psychotherapy (for example, Ackerknecht, 1959:84; Lederer, 1973:250; Weiss, 1962:473), as well as research findings comparing the effects of different psychiatric therapies (for example, Fiedler, 1950; Frank, 1961:130ff.), suggest that the relationship with the therapist is far more important in healing than the particular cognitive framework by which the client's behavior is understood.

The emotions most commonly aroused in psychotherapeutic relationships are said to be hope, self-confidence, and trust in the therapist (Frank, 1961; Kiev, 1973; Torrey, 1972). Although some of the techniques for eliciting these emotions from clients are specific to certain therapeutic traditions, both the personal characteristics of the therapist and the presence of culturally accepted symbols of the therapist's competence seem universally to aid in this emotion-arousing process. Research with psychiatric healers indicates that the personal characteristics of therapists that correlate most strongly with behavioral change in clients are nonpossessive warmth, concern, optimism, genuineness, and accurate empathy (Betz, 1962; Rogers, 1957; Truax and Carkhuff, 1967; Yalom, 1970). Although I have no direct measures of these traits for the spiritists studied, my observation is that they conveyed these qualities in their interactions with clients. [See Juana's activities in Chapter 5 as well as Lubchansky et al.'s similar observation concerning the trait of empathy in spiritist healers (1970:320).] With regard to communication of the therapist's competence, in spiritist therapy this is done not only symbolically through the paraphernalia of the *centro*, but also manifestly through proofs (*comprobaciones*) of the medium's diagnostic and prognostic skill. (It will be remembered that in the diagnostic procedure of spiritism the medium tells clients what their problems are and can therefore be judged on the accuracy of these statements.

The positions of psychiatric and spiritist therapies concerning the anxiety level to be maintained in the client during psychotherapy seem to me to contrast. While it is generally accepted that one of the empirical effects of all psychotherapeutic intervention is to reduce the client's initial anxiety, most psychiatric therapies consider a certain "optimal" level of anxiety to be necessary for therapeutic change to occur (Luborsky, 1962; Rogers, 1957; Schofield, 1964; Weiss, 1962), most notably in the treatment of neurotics. Frank (1961) has even argued that the effects of Western psychotherapy, like other forms of thought reform, may well be due to a heightened suggestibility of clients which is produced in part by the attendant anxiety of the usual psychiatrist-patient relationship.

It is my observation that spiritist therapy is predicated neither on the maintenance of a certain level of anxiety in the client nor, as Frank maintains for psychiatry, on the use of ambiguity to promote anxiety. On the contrary, spiritist therapy explicitly aims at curtailing the most anxiety-associated aspect of clients' behavior, uncontrolled spirit possession, by demonstrating very early in therapy the healer's ability to control this behavior. In every spiritist session I witnessed, the medium extricated at least one person from violent or torpid trance and thus clearly illustrated to the entire congregation his or her ability to control these sources of anxiety. Indeed, I would agree with Koss (1970:274) that it is this demonstrated ability of the medium to control the client's trance behavior that constitutes the basis for the medium's influence in effecting change in other aspects of the client's behavior.

Apart from anxiety, both spiritists and psychiatrists may foster the expression of other emotions in particular clients for therapeutic reasons. I have particularly noted this technique among *santeros* in the choice of their clients' protective spirits. Since, as mentioned earlier, each saint and his or her lower-order assistants express different ranges of emotion, the medium, in deciding who a client's protective spirits are and encouraging the client to serve as a vehicle for the manifestation of these spirits, is in effect encouraging the client to express specific emotions. We return to this aspect of spiritist treatment in relation to trance induction below.

Trance Induction

Although hypnosis and drug-induced altered states of consciousness are part of the armamentarium of psychiatry, they do not occupy the central importance which the related technique of trance induction plays in spiritist therapy. Although little is known about the physiology of trance (Hilgard, 1975; Prince, 1968), it has been compared with hypnosis to illuminate many of its fundamental social and behavioral characteristics (Aaronson, 1973; van der Walde, 1968; Wittkower, 1970). Bourguignon, however, has observed that so little is in fact understood about the dynamics of hypnosis that using it to elucidate possession trance "is tantamount to attempting to explain one 'unknown' by reference to another" (1974:xv). While I share Bourguignon's skepticism, I think the analogy nevertheless has heuristic value for an understanding of spiritism.

Hypnosis, according to van der Walde, is a "ritual" relationship between hypnotist and subject in which the hypnotist acts the role of an omnipotent figure who takes responsibility for the subject's action, and the subject abdicates ordinary reality-testing in order to obtain some desired end. In studies of the motivations of hypnotic subjects, van der Walde has observed that "most often, it is unacceptable wishes that are gratified in the hypnotic situation" (1968:61). He notes that the wishes may be either socially unacceptable or idiosyncratically unacceptable to the individual. If we accept van der Walde's observation and assume, as he does, that hypnosis and other forms of trance are psychologically the same, then it seems that trance in spiritist therapy provides an opportunity for the client to express otherwise unacceptable wishes and to share responsibility for this action with both the intruding spirit and the medium in charge of the session. Following this line of reasoning, we would further expect, in the *santero* form of spiritist therapy, that the protective saints whom the therapist bestows on a client would necessarily manifest personality traits that are unacceptable to the client under normal circumstances. Additional research to test the validity of this understanding of the dynamics of spiritist therapy is discussed below.

The psychologist Jay Haley has asserted that the cause of change in all psychotherapeutic systems is the universal presence of "therapeutic paradoxes," benign "double-bind" messages in which the therapist issues directives that are further qualified by additional conflicting directives. Koss (1970:268–269, 274–275), following Haley, cites trance induction as a prime example of this kind of paradox. For, on the one hand, spiritist theory attributes trance to an individual's own powers to manifest spirits; on the other hand, the trancer's behavior is obviously molded by the directives of the head medium. Koss calls attention to many similar paradoxes inherent in the theory of mediumistic development and argues cogently for their importance in effectuating therapeutic change. Thus, although spiritist and psychiatric therapies share the use of "therapeutic paradoxes" to bring about change, spiritism makes use of a form of paradox (trance) that is employed only infrequently in most psychiatric therapy.

not at R H

Transfer of Therapeutic Learning

Apart from behavior therapists and communication theorists like Bateson and Ruesch (for example, Ruesch, 1957; also Lennard and Bernstein, 1960), traditionally few psychotherapists have given careful attention to the important matter of techniques that would enhance the transfer of behavior and attitudes learned in the therapy situation to extratherapy circumstances. An important exception to this generalization is the work of Goldstein, Heller, and Sechcrest (1966), who advance a number of hypotheses concerning therapeutic modifications of psychiatric psychotherapies that would be likely, on the basis of learning theory, to increase the carry-over of clients' responses from therapy to other circumstances. Although Goldstein et al. do not subject their hypotheses to empirical test, the hypotheses themselves derive from empirical studies of factors that influence transfer of learning. Since several of the modifications in psychiatric therapy that these writers propose are integral to spiritist therapy, it is appropriate to review them here as part of this general comparison between spiritist and psychiatric techniques.

An experimental finding about learning that has implications for psychotherapeutic behavior change in general is that training stimuli must be similar to natural stimuli to which learned responses are to be transferred for carry-over of learning to occur. On the basis of this finding, Goldstein et al. propose that "transfer of learning from psychotherapy to extra-therapy situations will be greater when the therapy stimuli are representative of extra-therapy stimuli" (1966:226). "Therapy stimuli" in this formulation include the therapist, the therapeutic locale, and therapeutic messages (pp. 226–234, 240–250). In all three of these respects the stimuli of spiritist therapy resemble extratherapeutic stimuli for the population under consideration far more than would the stimuli of traditional psychiatric therapy. Thus, not only the medium but also the "co-therapists" (assistant mediums) share the subculture and often live in the neighborhood of the client; the *centro* is usually located in an area of the city frequented by the client; and the general framework and theory of spiritist therapy are already known to the client as part of the subculture.

A second hypothesis presented by Goldstein et al. is based on evidence that practice in emitting a response increases its availability in other situations. They therefore propose that "greater effectiveness of psychotherapy will be achieved if very strong emphasis is placed in therapy on emitting of [*sic*] responses considered desirable in other circumstances" (1966:236). Spiritist therapy, as Goldstein et al.'s hypothesis suggests, focuses heavily on clients' emitting behavior desirable outside therapy. For example, one of the strongest emphases in spiritist therapy is for the client to evidence control over the manifestation of low-ranking spirits (in other words, of symptoms). Spiritist therapy does not assume, however, that all symptoms will be entirely extinguished and allows and trains for their manifestation in appropriate circumstances (*centro* sessions).

Physical Contact between Therapist and Client

Psychiatric therapies have by and large tabooed any physical contact between healer and client within the therapeutic relationship. As we saw in the treatment of Clarita and other clients, however, massage, hugging, and occasionally feeding may be incorporated into spiritist therapy. Use of these techniques seems consistent with the general tenor of this type of therapy, which allows the therapist to fulfill some real and fantasied needs (for example, for a father or mother figure) in the client's life. Thus, spiritism employs techniques of physical contact that have only recently been accepted into the psychiatric armamentarium by a few of its practitioners (such as encounter, Gestalt, and bioenergetics therapists).

PRACTICAL IMPLICATIONS: THE ROLE OF SPIRITIST PSYCHOTHERAPY IN COMMUNITY HEALTH

As mentioned in the introductory chapter, the research that constitutes the basis for this book was undertaken with a view toward exploring how spiritists and spiritist groups might relate to a comprehensive health care program serving a Puerto Rican clientele. Now that we have examined the nature of spiritist psychotherapy and compared it to psychiatric forms, we are ready to present some observations and practical suggestions on its role in comprehensive public health care. A number of these suggestions incorporate material from the works of others who have written on spiritism among Puerto Ricans as a psychotherapeutic institution (Bram, 1958; Fisch, 1968; Garrison, 1968, 1973; Koss, 1967, 1970; Lubchansky et al., 1970; Rogler and Hollingshead, 1961, 1965).

THE CASE FOR SPIRITISM AS A THERAPY OF CHOICE

Viewing a system of psychotherapy as a set of techniques and symbols used by a healer to realign a client's subjective attitudes and behavior with a socially accepted pattern of symbols and activities (Frank, 1964: xii) enhances the observer's appreciation of how closely such a system relates to a particular sociocultural milieu and derives its symbols from that milieu. We have already called attention to certain parallels between psychiatric and spiritist therapies and the dominant metaphysical ideas of the subcultures of which they are a part. We have also observed that although the various techniques of psychotherapeutic systems (such as arousal of hope and trust, enhancement of self-esteem, and detailed review of the patient's past) are readily transferable cross-culturally, their particular symbolic systems are not. Thus, spiritist therapy is consonant with a more inclusive belief system in Puerto Rican culture—namely that spirits influence human behavior. Furthermore, the symbols of spiritism are, as we have seen, common currency for both Puerto Rican healer and sufferer; both can manipulate them to produce the desired realignment in the latter's attitudes and behavior. In short, since non-pharmacological psychotherapy depends heavily for its efficacy on the words, acts, and rituals of the participants, spiritist therapy has the particular merit of allowing both healer and sufferer to deal with the latter's problems within a shared symbolic framework.

Furthermore, because of this shared symbolic framework, potential clients are aware of criteria for evaluating therapists. Standards for differentiating skilled mediums from novices or charlatans are widely shared within the Puerto Rican subculture and equip potential clients with the ability to make an informed choice of therapist. In contrast, no clear criteria for evaluating psychiatric counselors exist among the Puerto Ricans studied, so that an informed choice among these kinds of therapists is impossible. Furthermore, the shortage of psychiatric therapists and the impossibility of "shopping" for a good one within the structure of the hospital outpatient clinics or community mental health centers, where most Puerto Ricans receive psychiatric care, preclude the possibility of a client's exercising choice in securing a therapist in those systems of care. Thus, both the opportunity for individuals to choose their therapist in the spiritist system and the presence of criteria for doing so favor spiritism as a treatment of choice.

In addition, because of the widespread acceptance among Puerto Ricans of the idea that spirits are active in the world, clients in spiritist therapy are not stigmatized (Rogler and Hollingshead, 1965). Consulting a spiritist is a culturally acceptable method for coping with spiritually caused problems. Undergoing psychiatric treatment implies that the client is *loco* and requires restraint and removal from society. This fact in itself strongly recommends spiritism as a form of psychotherapy.

An additional advantage of spiritist therapy is that mediums share the subculture of their clients. Although I have considered the importance of this earlier in relation to the transfer of learning, it has particular importance for the counseling and problem-solving aspects of therapy. As we saw in reviewing the kinds of advice given by mediums in Chapter 4, their counseling tends to be reality-oriented and designed to build the client's self-confidence. In addition, the spiritist may clarify problems for the client by summarizing alternative modes of action and then leave the ultimate choice to the client. The spiritist's participation in the client's subculture serves to ensure that the advice and alternatives offered in direct counseling are realistic in terms of the standards of the culture and the opportunities available to a low-income Puerto Rican in New York City.

In sum, spiritist psychotherapy recommends itself for Puerto Rican spiritist believers because it is consonant with certain basic premises of the culture, does not stigmatize the sufferer, and deals with clients' problems by direct counseling and by symbolic reeducation. Our research has also indicated certain subcategories of believers who seem to profit most from it. In view of the numbers of people who seek out spiritists during periods of transition in their lives, it seems plausible to assume that spiritism must be offering them some perceptible assistance in readjustment (or that no other source of comparable help for these problems exists for this population). On the other hand, our detailed case of a seriously disturbed person (Clarita) suggests that chronicity of symptoms and intermittent involvement in mediumistic activity are indicators of poor prognosis for this form of treatment. The implication of this observation, that people who have only recently begun demonstrating evidence of "faculties" are better candidates for treatment, is born out by our data from *centro* clients.

IMPLICATIONS OF SPIRITIST THERAPY FOR PROFESSIONAL PSYCHIATRIC TREATMENT

Both Prince (1968) and Parsons (1969:295–334) have stressed the importance of fitting the form of psychiatric therapy to the client's expectations and style of acting and thinking, and certain expectations among Puerto Rican clients concerning spiritist therapy carry implications about the types of psychiatric therapy most adaptable to spiritist clients. First of all, although the initial interview and diagnosis in the spiritist tradition may take place privately between client and healer, treatment itself always takes place in a group, since (as pointed out in Chapters 3 and 4) a medium must have assistants in attendance when he or she goes into trance. Thus, among spiritist believers there is an expectation that psychotherapy will occur in a group, often one including members of the sufferer's family along with the assistant mediums. Related to this expectation is the notion that group members are co-healers because they have gone through similar experiences in the process of their spiritual development (Garrison, 1968:21). The head medium and *mediunidad* can help the sufferer because "they have been there before." (The relation of this aspect of spiritist therapy to R. D. Laing's philosophy of treatment is almost too obvious to mention.)

A second important expectation about therapeutic situations that spiritists carry over into other forms of therapy is that the therapist must take an active role in diagnosis and treatment. Good healers in the Puerto Rican spiritist tradition cannot sit back and have their clients provide facts, feelings, interpretations, while they simply register understanding, acceptance, feedback, and so on. Instead they must actively participate in providing statements about clients' social and psychological states and even, perhaps, risk educated guesses about clients' unarticulated problems. Such behavior is expected of therapists, who are seen as experts and must therefore demonstrate and validate their expertise.

In short, behavioral expectations intrinsic to spiritist therapy imply that a community health worker, faced with choosing a mode of professional psychiatric treatment for a Puerto Rican client, might first consider group or family therapy and a therapeutic style in which the therapist plays an active role, since these modalities most closely fit the client's expectations of therapeutic procedure. Indeed one notes the apparent success of Minuchin in applying this very style of therapy to Puerto Rican delinquent boys and their families (Minuchin et al., 1967).

Besides indicating appropriate styles of treatment, our data can assist psychiatric therapists in differentially evaluating participants in the spiritist subculture who may come before them for professional assessment. Since many of the concepts and behaviors accepted by spiritists would be considered abnormal in terms of the American middle-class subculture, I have advocated the appreciation by psychiatrists of the standards by which spiritists themselves judge the competence of their peers' thinking and behavior. One of these standards, as pointed out in Chapter 6, is consistency between a person's professed beliefs about spirits and that person's behavior with respect to them. To evaluate difficult cases, however, I have recommended consultation with participants of the subculture. This form of consultation has been carried even further in the triage relationships that have been developed between psychiatrists and "witch doctors" in Nigeria (Lambo, 1961).

INTERRELATIONS BETWEEN SPIRITISTS AND COMMUNITY HEALTH PROGRAMS

Relations between spiritists and other health workers in the United States seem most likely to arise in two contexts: when a client is simultaneously receiving treatment from a spiritist and a health service for either a psychiatric or somatic problem, and when a community health service considers establishing a formal relationship with local healers.

Clients in Dual Psychotherapy

When a patient under psychiatric care undergoes treatment by a medium, the medium usually questions the client closely about any medication the client may be taking. Spiritists see mediumistic development as directed toward sharpening the client's mental faculties and therefore requiring a great deal of concentration. For this reason they are concerned about clients taking drugs and usually prohibit them from doing so during the process of development. Juana's request to the chief psychiatrist on the ward that Clarita's medicine be discontinued exemplifies this treatment practice.

Occasionally mediums advise clients to stop nonpsychotropic medication as well during the process of development. In the most extreme case of this phenomenon uncovered in our research, a medium had convinced a diabetic to discontinue orinase, because he interpreted the client's symptoms as a *prueba*.[9] In my experience advice to discontinue medication for physical conditions is uncommon, but tranquilizers and other psychotropic drugs are so routinely interdicted by spiritists that the staff of a psychiatric service may think that patients are taking prescribed medication when they are not.

Should the staff discover that a patient is receiving spiritist treatment, I suggest that a productive therapeutic arrangement would result from informal consultations between psychiatric personnel and the spiritist. Mutual instruction concerning the general goals and methods of the other therapy might constitute a useful component of such consultations, in addition of course to an evaluation of the problems and needs of the specific client. Lauer (1973:266), moreover, would carry this type of

[9] Since orinase has since been judged ineffective by the FDC and withdrawn from the market, the adverse effect of the medium's advice was probably nil in this case. (I would like to thank Dr. Gordon Harper for this information on the current status of orinase in the pharmacopoeia.)

relationship even further, so that the mental health worker and indigenous healer would also act formally as consultant, teacher, supervisor, or therapist with the other. Another treatment model, conjoint therapy, has been suggested by Pattison (1973:286ff.). In this model each therapist works with the patient in the way his or her own therapeutic system dictates, but the therapists support and complement one another's activities.

Spiritists and Somatic Problems

In cases involving somatic problems, our data have shown that mediums do not generally object to their clients' use of physicians and that indeed they may prepare clients for medical treatment by allaying some of their fears. (See Chapter 4 for examples.) Spiritually interpreted dreams or events may also persuade believers to undergo medical care, even without the intervention of mediums. The following example describes the experience of an elderly woman in one of our sample families. Mrs. G served as guardian of her daughter's child and prior to the event described had lain bedridden for several days with what was later diagnosed as pneumonia.

> Mrs. G said she was very restless that night and could not sleep. When she looked at the foot of her bed, she saw [the spirit of] her son there, and he was very angry with her. He told her to get up early in the morning and go to the hospital. Her son asked her, "Who is going to take care of the child if you die?" [Mrs. G explained that she and her son had adopted the little girl, and now that he was dead, he continued to look after the child.] After he had asked her the question, he disappeared. When she looked again to see if her son was sitting at the foot of the bed, he was gone. Next day when she went to the hospital, she had to stay.

Our data contain numerous examples of similar "medical referrals" by spirits and also of spiritual inspirations for herbal and pharmaceutical cures.

Although this example and others provide instances in which mediums or spiritual inspiration influenced people to seek medical care, some spiritist clients undoubtedly suffer from medically curable conditions that are treated exclusively by mediums. Without performing physical examinations on all clients, however, it is difficult to assess the proportion who receive only spiritual treatment for conditions that can be controlled medically. My impression, nevertheless, is that this proportion is low.

Three lines of evidence support this impression. The first was mentioned in Chapter 4—namely, that with the exception of those symptoms generally recognized as spiritually caused, spiritist believers tend to seek medical care for physical complaints and go only secondarily to spiritists if they are dissatisfied with medical treatment or if they suffer from a chronic or terminal illness.

The second line of evidence is that only very rarely in my experience did mediums actively discourage their clients from seeking medical help. (This does not rule out, of course, the passive discouragement that might occur because clients think that all their ills are being taken care of by the medium.) My data contain only one instance in which a medium actively discouraged a client from seeing a physician. The client had already gone to several sources of medical care without any relief, and the medium proclaimed categorically that the problem did not "belong to the doctors." Since this client was discouraged from consulting doctors only after he had already done so, the condition in question may indeed not have been medically treatable, at least by the medical services available to the population under study. The only negative effect of spiritist treatment on a client's medical regimen that I observed was the aforementioned advice to discontinue orinase, which in hindsight was apparently not damaging after all.

The final piece of evidence that supports my impression that only a small proportion of spiritist clients have medically treatable illnesses that are being treated spiritually is quantitative. It entails a comparison of the medical usage patterns of the families of spiritist believers and nonbelievers in our sample. The logic behind this comparison is as follows: if spiritist believers have medically treatable illnesses seen by spiritists instead of medical practitioners, then one would expect them, in comparison with nonbelievers, to have a lower percentage of illnesses treated at a medical facility over a given period of time. Data on the sources of treatment for all illnesses, both acute and chronic, that occurred in the families in our study over the course of a year's observation allow us to make this comparison. Before doing so, however, I must caution the reader about the reliability of these data, given the small number of nonbelieving families in the sample (N=10); furthermore, since two of these families experienced no illnesses at all during the period they were under observation, for purposes of this comparison the number is therefore reduced to 8. This limitation notwithstanding, the data indicate that, if anything, spiritists use medical facilities (private physicians, hospital outpatient facilities, pharmacists) for acute and for chronic illnesses more than do nonbelievers. Thus 67% of all believing families and 63% of nonbelieving families treated more than half the episodes of acute illness medically during the period of observation; for chronic illnesses 93% of the believing families referred more than half of the instances for medical attention, while only 63% of the nonbelieving families did so.

Although none of the aforementioned evidence is direct, it nevertheless supports the impression inferentially that few spiritist clients have medically treatable illnesses that are being handled exclusively by spiritists. Furthermore, since spiritist cosmology admits of joint spiritual and material causation of problems, and it is clear from direct evidence that spiritists often recommend medical consultation to their clients, it seems advisable for a community health facility to encourage local spiritists to continue making such recommendations simultaneously with their anxiety-reducing therapeutic measures, particularly for clients whom they judge to be avoiding medical attention because of fear. A health facility might also provide local spiritists with information on the early signs and symptoms of somatic illnesses that provoke anxiety for their target population and have a high probability of cure if detected early.

Formal Relations Between Spiritists and Community Health Programs

Establishing a formal relationship between a community health service and a spiritist, as has been done with folk healers in Nigeria (Lambo, 1964, 1966), involves several considerations. The first of these, as noted in relation to Clarita's treatment, is that spiritists are loath to work inside mental hospitals. Because they view many patients as suffering from harmful spiritual influences of various sorts, they fear that on going into trance in such an atmosphere they might be overwhelmed by these malevolent spirits. Spiritist treatment for the seriously disturbed, except by a few intrepid mediums, would thus be available only outside a hospital.

A second and very important factor in contemplating a formal relationship between a community health facility and spiritists is that, although a belief in spirits is common to many Puerto Rican subcultures, several competing social institutions exist for dealing with spiritual influences. Thus the Roman Catholic and Pentecostal churches, the largest formal religious organizations among Puerto Ricans, both have rituals for treating spiritual afflictions and consider spiritists as being in league with the Devil. Indeed it is a mortal sin for a Catholic to consult a spiritist, although in my experience this injunction is honored only by the most devout. Pentecostals condemn spiritists on the basis of a belief that the power to heal is a gift of God to the pure of heart (Acts 8:9–24), a characteristic which in their view spiritists do not exhibit, since liquor and tobacco are used in their religious rites.

For devout members of both these religious groups any formal relationship between a health facility and a spiritist would thus be in the nature of a compact with the Devil. Any discussion of such a relationship that I had with pious Catholics or Pentecostals met with disapproval. Some even said they would stop going to a health center should mediums be allowed to practice on the premises or should patients be routinely referred to them. In light of this opposition, any formal relationship with spiritist healers would seem to be out of the question for any truly community-oriented health program in a Puerto Rican neighborhood. Nevertheless, informal associations based on the needs and beliefs of particular patients would be possible, a suggestion that did not meet with disapproval from those Catholics and Pentecostals with whom I discussed the matter. Discussion with members of the local community should clearly be undertaken by any health program before adopting such referral procedures.

Should a health program decide to enlist the help of spiritists either formally or informally, identification of possible consultants would become an important consideration. For a patient who is already involved with a particular spiritist, working with the existing healer would doubtless be the best course of action. However, choosing a spiritist to receive referrals from a health facility on a regular basis presents a number of problems. For, as mentioned in Chapter 2, spiritist ideology allows believers to evaluate the activities of the same spiritist differently: some may see them as sorcery, others as work with good spirits. Thus different people may have varying opinions about the behavior of a single spiritist, and selection of a consultant who is universally recognized as beneficent is practically impossible. In addition, there is widespread opinion that although spiritists in Puerto Rico are almost all "real" mediums, many who practice on the mainland are charlatans. In view of all these conditions, the preferable course of action would seem to be to let patients choose their own therapists.

Yet there is still something to be said for selecting one or a few consultants who would be associated informally with a health facility on a long-term basis, since such an arrangement would permit mutual adjustment between psychiatric staff and spiritists, greater understanding of one another's methods, and the possibility of training the mediums to recognize those psychological or physical conditions that the health facility can treat successfully. Should a long-term relationship seem desirable, I suggest that it be developed with spiritists whom the medical staff has observed to be helpful to health center patients who have self-selected the healer.

IMPLICATIONS OF SPIRITIST PRACTICES FOR PSYCHOTHERAPEUTIC HEALING IN GENERAL

In our discussion of the times in life when people turn to spiritists, we observed that periods of transition (such as puberty, marriage, menopause, terminal illness, and mourning) were often represented. We also noted that the form of treatment for the most disturbed spiritist clients involves a social transition from a state of development (*desarollo*) or testing (*prueba*) to the status of medium. In this chapter we have also called attention to another kind of transition with which spiritist cults deal—namely, the transition between Puerto Rican and urban American society. All these forms of transition involve the separation of persons or groups from certain statuses and roles and their subsequent movement into new ones. From an anthropological perspective the activities and symbols that mark such transitions may be viewed as rites of passage. Examination of spiritist and psychiatric therapies as exemplars of such rites will, I think, illumine certain aspects of healing in general.

CLARIFICATION OF CONCEPTS AND TERMS

Before examining psychotherapy as a rite of passage, it is necessary first to clarify several concepts used in the analysis.

Rites and Rituals

The terms "rite" and "ritual" are used synonymously in the following discussion. In adopting these terms, however, I do not wish to imply that the activities involved in healing are necessarily directed toward supernatural entities (a common usage of these terms in anthropology, as exemplified by Turner's definition cited in Chapter 3 above). Nor do I wish to imply that healing rituals enact unconscious conflicts, as Freudian usage would suggest (Freud, 1959). Instead, I am using the term "ritual" as employed in more recent anthropological and ethological discussions of communication (for example, by Leach, 1954, 1966, 1968; and Rappaport, 1971, among others). According to this view, ritual refers to "conventional acts of display through which one or more participants transmit information concerning their physiological, psychological, or sociological states" (Rappaport, 1971:25). By using the term "ritual," we are thus emphasizing the conventionalized and communicative features of the therapeutic process.

Rites of Passage

According to Van Gennep's classic analysis of *rites de passage*, there are three subcategories or phases of these rites (1960:10–11): (1) separation, or the symbolic detachment of an individual or group from certain positions in the social structure; (2) transition or liminality, the socially ambiguous period during which the people or groups who have separated from former statuses prepare for new ones; and (3) incorporation or reentry into the social structure. An additional and less frequently cited point which Van Gennep also makes is that "in certain ceremonial patterns where the transitional period is sufficiently elaborated to constitute an independent state, the arrangement [of stages] is reduplicated" (1960:11, also 191–192). Thus, as Van Gennep himself shows for betrothal and parturition rites, certain transition states themselves may be viewed as comprised of separation, transition, and incorporation phases.

In applying this analysis to the healing process, it seems justified to view the "sick" role in any particular culture as a transition phase and the patterned activities that are specifically designed to prepare the patient for reentry into normal social life as transition or liminal rites. In other words, "sickness," like life cycle changes, will be viewed here as a liminal state "outside society," to use a phrase of Van Gennep's (1960: 114), and healing will be used to refer to the activities directed toward enabling the sufferer to pass out of this phase and once more enact a normal complement of roles and even, perhaps, entirely new roles.[10] To clarify this formulation, two of its key terms, "liminal state" and "healing," require further explication.

The Liminal State

In the discussion so far I have consistently tried to avoid the word "sick" as a label for the liminal state I am talking about; when forced to use it, I have placed it in quotation marks. I have done so to indicate that the liminal state to which I am referring need not necessarily be marked by the same distinctive features as "sickness" in this culture. Clients in spiritist therapy, for example, are not necessarily considered "sick" (*enfermo*), a term that is more properly reserved in Puerto Rican Spanish for malfunctions attributed to material causes. Yet I would include most

[10] Although Turner (1968, 1969) has used Van Gennep's framework to great advantage in analyzing healing cults, his application of the concept of phases in rites of passage is different from my own.

spiritist clients, along with those who are *enfermo* and receive treatment elsewhere, within a single liminal condition. I shall therefore (following Parsons) define the liminal state I am discussing in terms of social rather than cultural features: to wit, a state in which an actor is either exempted from performance of normal role obligations or excused for unacceptably executing such role obligations on the ground that the actor is not fully responsible for his or her actions. The person so exempted or so excused is expected to seek help from a specialist in order to return to normal role performance. I shall term this liminal condition "status remission."

Although my dependence on Parsons (1951, 1953, 1958) in this formulation is considerable, it differs from his conceptualization of the sick role in not making legitimation of status remission contingent upon consultation of a professional. This change takes account of one of Freidson's (1961–1962) most trenchant criticisms of Parsons's formulation and makes it consistent with observations among spiritists that self-diagnosis and self-treatment may constitute sufficient legitimation of the role. Furthermore, the proposed definition is broad enough to include the liminal states of mourning, menopause, puberty, and other life transitions that are also commonly brought to spiritists and other psychotherapists for treatment.

It is important to recognize at the outset of this analysis that persons who undergo healing rites in our own society are usually not completely segregated physically and socially, as they might be during rites of passage in a small-scale society. Since they are not completely removed from the necessity for ordinary social interaction, clients must continue during the course of therapy to interact in the statuses from which they have received temporary remission. The condition of status remission in this society thus generally entails only partial relaxation of both the obligations and the sanctions that are ordinarily applied to role performance rather than complete segregation from the social field.

In relation to this definition, it is also important to stress once more the multifunctional nature of spiritist cults and other healing institutions. Thus, not all clients who consult a spiritist or psychiatric healer are in a state of status remission. For example, clients who seek a spiritist's assistance in influencing the outcome of a trial or a romance are not, strictly speaking, in this state since they are considered responsible for their actions. Clients who seek psychiatric help because they are unhappy, depressed, anxious, and the like but who fulfill their normal role obligations are not in this state either. Our general approach, then, suggests the possibility of categorizing clients according to whether or not they enter therapy in a state of status remission. Obviously, to be useful, such a categorization would have to imply differential therapy and outcomes. Before dealing with this notion in greater detail, however, we must first explore the idea of variant therapeutic processes.

Healing and Curing as Therapeutic Processes

Earlier in this section I discussed healing as patterned activities directed toward enabling a sufferer to pass out of the liminal state and reenter full social life. To elucidate this notion of healing further and to emphasize its focus on social transition, I would like to propose an analytic distinction between those acts performed for a person during the liminal state that are specifically directed toward altering that person's physiological functioning to permit the resumption of normal activity, and those acts that have specifically to do with reeducating a person so that the person acceptably enacts normal social roles. I shall designate these two separate processes as "curing" and "healing" respectively. Thus, I define "curing" as a biomedical process that refers to procedures specifically directed toward repairing physiological malfunctions. "Healing" is a sociological process and refers to those procedures that transform a person socially from a state of liminality to one in which he or she begins to enact a normal complement of roles once more and also, perhaps, entirely new ones (see also Kleinman, 1973).

In terms of this distinction, the spiritist and psychiatric therapies that we have been discussing clearly constitute examples of healing. In contrast, most Western medical treatment emphasizes curing with relatively little explicit attention devoted to healing (except for certain conditions for which "rehabilitative" measures are routinely prescribed). This distinction between healing and curing is introduced to further emphasize the sociological aspect of therapy in keeping with our use of the analytic framework of rites of passage.

HEALING AS A TRANSITION RITE OF PASSAGE

With these preliminary considerations in mind, we can turn to the implications suggested by viewing healing as a rite of passage or, more specifically, as a transition rite of passage. This framework implies that the aim of healing is to prepare people who are in a liminal state for reincorporation into the social structure. One might therefore suppose that there would be healing rites appropriate to different kinds of status transition and consequently that clients entering therapy might be differentially diagnosed according to the kind of status transition they were undergoing in order to institute an appropriate form of therapy. I am not claiming, of course, that status transition should be the only factor considered in the diagnostic process; it is nevertheless one that should be consciously weighed in designing the content of therapeutic activities.

Although status transitions may be classified in different ways, one which seems to correlate with different healing activities in spiritism at any rate concerns the novelty for the client of the status(es) into which he or she is to be incorporated at the termination of therapy. Thus, some clients pass into an entirely new status or statuses, while others return to fulfilling in a socially more acceptable manner the obligations entailed in statuses held before the rite. Assumption of a new status or statuses does not of course mean that the client abandons all old statuses. This is true even for those rituals that have traditionally been considered rites of passage. Thus, for example, the child who emerges from an initiation rite as a young man or woman still remains a son or daughter to his or her parent. Because of the attainment of the new status, however, some of the rights and obligations pertaining to the old status relationship may change. In short, I am suggesting two forms of status transition which people in the condition of status remission might undergo: to an entirely new status or statuses, or to full performance of former statuses. Which of these two forms of transition the client will undergo may be apparent at the start of the therapeutic ritual or may only become apparent after it has begun.

Spiritist data provide evidence that these two kinds of transition are accompanied by different healing activities, as one might expect. Thus, "development" constitutes the treatment for assumption of a new status (that of medium). The tripartite treatment of removing harmful spiritual influences, counseling, and strengthening spiritual protection constitutes the preparation for reincorporation into full participation in former statuses. Discussion of these two treatment procedures as rites of passage may be aided by dividing the procedures into separation, transition, and incorporation phases, as suggested by Van Gennep's observation that ritual phases are reduplicated in elaborate transition rites.

Development: Transition Ritual to a New Status

As suggested earlier in this chapter, part of all psychotherapy entails separating the client from unwanted behavior patterns. In spiritist therapy this process, as we observed, begins during diagnosis by attributing those patterns to spirits. In the initial phases of development the healer is responsible for separating the client from spirits by either exorcism (*despojo*) or "working the cause." (See Chapter 4 for detailed descriptions of these procedures.) Gradually, however, as the client moves into the transition phase, three things occur. First, the client is expected to exert some internal control over the manifestation of these spirits and not simply to rely on the healer for their removal. This process in part entails development of the client's relationship with his or her principal spirit guide. Second, the spirits that the client manifests as development proceeds are increasingly attributed to other clients and not to himself—that is, the spirits are seen not as attached to and thus plaguing him but as attached to others at the séance. Third, the behavior of these spirits becomes increasingly socialized; unlike the early manifestations of spirits, later manifestations speak coherently, can carry on a dialogue with the head medium, and utter culturally standardized phrases of forgiveness, remorse, and the like. In short, the transition phase during development involves socializing disruptive impulses so that they appear as spirits only at culturally appropriate times and places, and so that the client can be seen as a person with what Goffman would call "good demeanor" —that is, as an entity "who can be relied upon to maintain himself as an interactant, poised for communication, and to act so that others do not endanger themselves by presenting themselves as interactants to him" (1967:77).

The incorporation phase of the healing ritual begins with tentative efforts on the part of the client to participate in the *mediunidad.* Early efforts in this direction are carefully controlled by other mediums, however, who may ignore or reinterpret the statements of a new recruit through the voices of their own spirit visitors. Because of the greater experience and proven powers of veteran mediums, their revelations usually prevail. The head medium also plays an important part in shaping the novice's behavior to fit the expectations of the medium role by the way he or she interrogates spirits which the novice manifests and, on some occasions, by directly censuring the novice's behavior by exorcising or "working" a spirit which the novice evinces—that is, by treating the neophyte's behavior as appropriate to a client rather than a medium. These learning activities culminate in an incorporation ritual in which the new medium in the Mesa Blanca tradition of spiritism is installed at the table or in Santería ceremonially receives the accoutrements of his protective saint or saints.

This description of spiritist healing rites for clients who are assuming a new social position suggests that such treatment strongly emphasizes separation from behaviors that have alienated the client from social interaction in the past. It also emphasizes role play and gradual socialization into the role requirements of the new status both by example and by reward and punishment. Conceptually the rite alters the meaning and evaluation of what was formerly adjudged antisocial behavior.

Transition Ritual to Full Status Enactment

The three phases of this transition rite, although conceptually distinguishable, do not necessarily follow in strict sequence but may occur throughout the client-healer interaction. The failure to enact the phases in strict sequence may be related to the absence in this society of physical isolation for clients during the rite and the consequent necessity for them to perform some of the obligations of remitted statuses during the course of treatment. In spite of the absence of strict sequencing, one can nevertheless distinguish three foci of the rite: an effort to remove spirits, counseling, and strengthening the client's spiritual protection.

As in the case of development, exorcism and "working the cause" serve in the first phase to separate the client from unwanted behavior. As we have seen from examples cited in Chapters 4 and 5, these two treatment procedures are used most commonly for the following causes: spirits sent through the malevolent activities of an enemy (sorcery); spiritual attachments from a former life (a spouse or parent from a previous incarnation, for example); or a spirit's need for "light" (that is, ritual attention from the living to effect the spirit's ascent in the spiritual hierarchy). We have seen, too, that these "causes" may be evinced in spiritist treatment to account for difficulties in marital and family relationships. In such cases, where the goal is to alter yet preserve these preexisting relationships, two treatment techniques are most used. First, suggestion plays an important part; the medium repeatedly tells clients that the unwanted behaviors removed through exorcism or "working the cause" will not return to interfere in their social relationships (see examples in Chapter 4). Second, direct counseling suggests appropriate behavior to clients and often, in cases where the relationshsip is to be sustained, involves both spouses or other family members in treatment (as case material in Chapter 6 illustrates).

Strengthening the client's spiritual protection may be seen as part of the incorporation phase of this transition rite. Consistent with the premise of spiritist cosmology that spirits are active forces in the corporeal world, enhancement of spiritual protection more fully incorporates the client into the cosmos, particularly in relation to its benevolent forces. By enlisting these forces to prevent the reappearance of behaviors that formerly impeded the client from full enactment of a marital or other status in the corporeal world, the treatment prepares the client for full participation in that world.

IMPLICATIONS OF HEALING AS A TRANSITION RITE: SUMMARY AND DISCUSSION

The point of examining healing as a rite of passage is to focus on the sociological aspect of the process of individual change. In this analysis we have, with a heavy reliance on Parsons, considered clients in therapy as being in a liminal state that I have called status remission. People in this state are excused for unacceptably executing normal role obligations on the ground that they are not fully responsible for their actions. Healing is then a rite that equips clients either for admission to a new status or statuses or for returning to the acceptable performance of roles associated with remitted status (es). Spiritist therapy in the former instance stresses separation of the client from unwanted behavior in addition to role play and socialization into the role requirements of the new status; in the latter instance spiritist therapy involves not only separation but direct counseling that often includes occupants of the complementary status or statuses to which the client is returning.

The general implication of this analysis is that other healers besides spiritists might well incorporate into their healing procedures explicit consideration of the kind of status transition their clients are undergoing, and the culturally defined statuses and associated role requirements that are available to each client at the termination of therapy. These considerations would enable the healer to help clients choose appropriate roles and then, through direct counseling, role play, and other forms of socialization, prepare them specifically for these roles and thus for incorporation into normal social life.

The approach I am suggesting seems to differ from that of most contemporary psychiatric therapies. Although none of these therapies ignores status issues entirely, such issues are rarely made an important focus of therapy, and specific training for reentry into old statuses or for admission to new ones is seldom undertaken. (Family therapy and behavioral modification seem to be important exceptions to this general rule.) In short, I am suggesting that, to the extent that all healing constitutes a transition rite, consideration of, as well as preparation for, the social statuses to which the client will pass at the termination of therapy should be integrated into the healing procedure.[11]

[11] Anne Parsons, in a brilliant analysis of her errors in treating an Italian American patient, comes to a similar conclusion and advocates what she calls "active treatment," in which "the therapist is actively concerned with the patient's possibilities for social reciprocity within the context of his own life. . . . The therapist should help the patient to seek his gratifications within the range of relationships socially available to him. The patient is then bound by the social norms of his environment, whatever these happen to be. . . . Active psychotherapy means, furthermore, that it is the responsibility of the therapist to know about his patient's social norms and to consider them as crucially relevant to the treatment process" (1969:322–323).

SUGGESTIONS FOR FURTHER RESEARCH

The research reported in this book was observational in nature, an attempt to comprehend and document spiritist beliefs and practices in a low-income Puerto Rican population. In the course of this research we uncovered a number of questions, an understanding of which would shed additional light not only on spiritist psychotherapy but also on healing in general. We have mentioned a number of these questions in passing but shall focus in this conclusion on four problems that seem most fruitful for further investigation. (See Fisch, 1968 for additional matters for research on spiritism as a therapeutic resource.)

1. As noted in Chapter 2, the need for social cohesion at certain stages in the development of *centros* leads to an emphasis on sorcery by rival mediums as the cause of clients' problems. To understand and evaluate this relationship between the social milieu and healing practices further, detailed investigation should be undertaken into the social composition and developmental cycle of spiritist *centros* as these factors relate to the diagnosis and treatment of clients. Further investigation into the effects of economic exchanges of various types on social relationships among *centro* members and on the power of head mediums would also aid considerably in understanding the social dynamics of spiritist groups.

2. An additional set of problems for investigation concerns the method by which *santero* mediums choose the protective spirits of their clients and the relation of the personalities of these protective spirits to clients' psychodynamics. As pointed out earlier in this chapter, the literature on hypnotic trance indicates that socially unacceptable behavior is most likely to emerge under trance; on the other hand, Pressel (1974:215, 222), in her study of a Brazilian spiritist cult, concludes that trance performances serve as a form of role play for behavior that trancers later evince in public. In view of these two claims, a detailed analysis of the process by which mediums "identify" their clients' protective spirits and by which the clients in turn learn to enact these spirits' personalities in a socially acceptable fashion would contribute greatly to understanding the relationship between clients' psychological states and their ultimate reincorporation into normal social roles.

3. More complete information on the process by which spiritist believers decide whether to take a particular problem to a spiritist or to another source of assistance would be valuable for two reasons: first, for better understanding the operation of the total, pluralistic medical system of this country; and second, for assisting people in helping-occupations of all types to understand the services provided by one of their

counterparts. This information would include patterns of referral and personal influence in decision making as well as criteria by which people decide the appropriate source of care.

4. A final and crucial problem for research concerns the comparative effectiveness of spiritist and psychiatric therapies for Puerto Rican clients. My research, since it was based on naturalistic observation, was not designed to evaluate rigorously the success of spiritist therapy relative to other modalities available to Puerto Rican patients. Provided ethical problems could be overcome (and these are many and weighty), a controlled experiment comparing cure rates of Puerto Rican spiritist patients who have been matched and assigned to spiritist and psychiatric forms of therapy would yield important evidence pertinent to the general question of the relative effectiveness of indigenous and psychiatric therapies. Although such studies have often been fraught with methodological problems in the past, recent work in developing standards and procedures for this type of evaluation (Bergin, 1971; Fiske, et al., 1970) promise much more reliable and useful studies in future.

In this period of United States history, when many of the values and norms of the society are being called into question and a more relativistic ethical system is apparently emerging, it seems appropriate for those in the helping professions to reevaluate their premises and techniques. This reevaluation is under way, and many workers are increasingly open to new forms of treatment and to viewing people in their sociocultural context before instituting traditional forms of psychotherapy. This book has described a therapeutic resource operating within the Puerto Rican sociocultural milieu and has examined its role within that milieu and in relation to the mental health resources of the wider society. In so doing, we hope to have contributed to the ongoing reevaluation of the nature of health and health resources in an increasingly pluralistic society.

APPENDIX

Selection and Training of Community Researchers

The specific aim of the research training program was to equip trainees, who were residents of the study area, with skills necessary to carry out an ethnography of their locale and to take jobs later in other social research operations. A more general function of the program was to introduce trainees to positive uses of social research and, in so doing, enable them to employ its techniques to their own ends. In addition, the program provided trainees with the opportunity to learn or review basic mathematical and communication skills, prepare for a high-school equivalency diploma, and develop greater confidence in their own abilities.

SELECTION OF TRAINEES

A brief description of the training program, research project, and associated jobs was mailed to civic organizations, churches, and other formally organized groups located within the target area. In addition, the medical personnel of the Health Center were informed of the program and encouraged to refer likely candidates from among their patients. Interested parties applied by coming to the Research Department office at the Health Center and were told on applying that there would be a group screening at a later time by members of the Community Advisory Board and myself. Of the 25 applicants, 18 appeared for the interview. Of the 5 male applicants, however, only 2 appeared.

The procedure used for screening applicants was modeled after that used by the training division of the Health Center, with specific additions designed to reveal the applicants' aptitudes for observing social interaction. All screening was done with myself and at least two members of the Community Advisory Board present.

The selection procedure involved an initial interview with five to eight applicants together, in which several social situations that might arise in the course of the research project were described. The candidates were asked to discuss what they might do if faced with these circumstances. The situations, which were devised jointly by three members of the Advisory Board and two members of the Research Department of the Health Center, raised such issues as respondents' rights to privacy, possible reactions to a prospective respondent's refusal to participate, and the researcher's flexibility in the participant observation situation. (The specific situations used are described in the complete outline of the screening procedure at the end of this appendix.)

Before one of these situations was presented for discussion, applicants were told that at the conclusion of the group interview they would be asked to write down "what had happened" during that particular discussion. By means of this exercise, the screening committee had an idea of each applicant's writing abilities as well as of the applicant's powers of observing a social situation while at the same time participating in it. After the group interview, while applicants wrote down their observations, members of the screening committee adjourned to share their opinions of the applicants based on the group discussion. After a coffee break applicants were called in individually to answer any questions raised by screening committee members during their postinterview discussion and to have an opportunity to express their feelings about social research and other matters. In no case were negative feelings about social research used as a basis for rejection from the program; on the contrary, given the screening committee's knowledge of the community, an expression of skepticism about research was considered honest and therefore valued more highly than a broadly approving position.

In all, three screening sessions were held. At the close of each session, the screening committee ranked applicants in terms of acceptability. After the third session three committee members who had been present during most of the interview sessions discussed all applicants. Eight of the 18 interviewed (44%) were chosen for the program, and an additional member transfered in from a part-time position with the regular Research Department of the Health Center. Ultimately one of the women chosen could not attend training sessions because of problems at home, so the final group came to consist of eight people in total, two males and six females, four of whom were Black and four Puerto Rican. The males were 32 and 34 years old and the females averaged 31 years, with a range from 19 to 43.

Although there was practically no difference of opinion between the members of the Community Advisory Board and myself in our final ranking of candidates, I think it important to note that we tended to differ in the importance we placed on various qualities in evaluating candidates. While I tended to focus on an applicant's ability to see through questions to the underlying issues and to get observations down on paper, community members placed primary emphasis on applicants' attitudes toward confidentiality. The amalgam of these different biases led, I think, to the selection of better trainees than if either one of these criteria was used exclusively.

THE TRAINING PROGRAM: AIMS AND INSTRUCTION

1. One of the principal aims of the first phase of the training program was to introduce trainees to basic concepts and methods of social science. This was done in a "Research Course" which centered as much as possible around the investigation of concrete problems.

To introduce interviewing techniques and the concepts of status, role, and formal vs informal structure, for example, trainees were presented with the problem of finding out about the structure of the Health Center. To do this, the group interviewed several key people (the Project Director, the heads of the Medical and Community Health Advocacy Departments, the acting head of the Training Department, and a member of the Health Advocacy staff who had been with the project almost since its inception.) In preparation for these interviews, trainees read and discussed a flier describing the program and received instruction on principles of interviewing and question formation. To concretize and illustrate points about research methods, instruction included mock interviews with members of the class taking parts as both interviewers and respondents. Since this investigation into the organization of the Health Center was done in the first weeks of training, it also served as an orientation to the agency.

Additional practice in formal interviewing was acquired with medical assistants at the Health Center, who were queried about their perceptions of doctor-patient communication. Since the medical assistants were frequently present during patient interviews with physicians, they were expected to be good sources of information on this topic. In fact, they proved unresponsive, answering queries in a general, often glowing manner. This interviewing experience enabled trainees to consider the reasons for this kind of response, and to discuss the value of gathering observations on interactions from people who are not directly involved.

A health fair sponsored by the Center provided an occasion for the introduction of participant observation techniques into the training program. Before the fair trainees discussed the sort of questions one might wish to answer about a gathering of this kind and the data one might collect to answer these questions. Some of the questions raised were: Who in different age, sex, and ethnic categories were present? How frequently did people of various social categories interact (for example, staff and community people, and people of different ethnic groups)? How was the food acquired and distributed? Methods of recording observations were also discussed.

After the fair, we read all trainees' observations aloud and discussed them. The group noticed certain things about the way the fair was organized which they felt impeded good communication between staff and community. A committee of two trainees and myself, therefore, wrote a memorandum to the department that had planned the event. The memo outlined the group's observations and made suggestions for improvement of future public functions sponsored by the agency.

An assignment to engage a stranger in conversation about his or her health provided trainees with an opportunity to practice participant observation in a less formal setting. Although the sample was select and small, it nevertheless yielded unexpected insights into ways in which medicines are procured in the area. Analysis and discussion of an experienced field worker's notes also gave trainees greater familiarity with the advantages and disadvantages inherent in participant observation as a method of social research.

In addition to formal training, a large part of the research course was spent in discussing various topics that arose spontaneously—attitudes toward marriage and divorce, folk medical remedies, ethnic food habits, race, and the like. These discussions helped trainees get acquainted and encouraged them to express their ideas openly. More academic topics, like the culture of poverty, the sociology of illnesss, and sampling, were interwoven among these dicussions.

2. Another main aim of the training was to introduce the future researchers to the specific purposes and design of the study. To do this, the class read the research proposal aloud and discussed questions and issues arising from it. They then did a considerable amount of role play, in which they explained the method and purposes of the research to would-be participants in the study.

To help the future field workers understand the importance of some of the data they would be collecting on the use of medicines, a pharmacologist on the Health Center staff conducted several classes on the effects that various commonly prescribed medicines have on the body and the implications for health of their improper use. These lectures, perhaps more than any others, impressed the trainees with the importance of the information they would be gathering.

3. The training program also included a number of "courses" that were introduced primarily to equip the future field workers with information and skills that could be used, with prudence, to assist participants in the research and thus offer something in return for the information they would be receiving. In addition, these courses provided knowledge that proved personally useful to the trainees, their families and friends. Courses that fell into this category were First Aid and Community Resources.

The first aid course was taught by a public health nurse and concentrated on management of emergency situations most likely to arise in the home. Thus, after a brief review of the systems of the body and general symptoms of illness, the first aid treatment of such conditions as loss of consciousness, bleeding, poisoning, and respiratory difficulty were covered in some detail.

The community resources course surveyed several local, nonmedical agencies that deal with problems characteristic of low-income urban areas. The trainees received background information into the function of these agencies and the procedures for referring clients to them. They were also encouraged to develop standards for evaluating community agencies. Included in the course were trips to a Youth Opportunity Center, which guided school dropouts to various training programs; LABOR, a local agency dealing with housing problems; and a Legal Services Corporation.

The latter trip, as well as two sessions on Welfare rights and budgets, was organized by a lawyer on the staff of the Health Center.

The teaching of first aid skills and knowledge of community resources, both of which equipped researchers to intervene in the lives of the population under study, naturally raises questions about the effects of such intervention on the data collected. For if the virtue of participant observation as a research technique is its ability to capture behavior in its natural context, intervention would seem to subvert this very virtue. To me this view ignores an important reality of social interaction: it assumes that participant observers, while on the job, are totally neutral objects. In fact they are always placed in a variety of roles by those they are observing, each role valued differently and each entailing certain expected behaviors. The important thing for observers, then, is not to ignore this fact in the supposed interests of detachment and objectivity but to know the statuses they are being placed in and to understand and document the way in which the people under observation construe their own positions with respect to these statuses. The observers' failure to live up to some of the behavior expected of them in their assigned roles may completely destroy their ability to gather naturalistic data on the very behavior they are most interested in observing. It is also important, of course, for them to exercise particular caution and restraint in intervening in the areas of their research interest.

In the context of this study, for example, one of the salient statuses in which researchers were frequently placed was "employee of the power structure." As a result, building residents from time to time sought help from them with various problems. To deny such aid might have destroyed the very relationship that allowed the researcher to observe medical practices.

In view of these considerations, considerable attention was focused in training on the use of information from the courses in first aid and community resources. Trainees were advised to analyze the status in which they were being placed when asked for help and to try to understand the request in terms of the family's dynamics—for example, to ask themselves if a mother were asking the research worker to help her son join a training program because she genuinely wanted this or because she wanted another proof of her son's unwillingness to work.

Trainees were advised to exercise particular caution in intervening in health and medical matters, since these were the areas of life we were most desirous of observing undisturbed. In cases where intervention or compliance with a request for help in these areas seemed necessary, however, the training program emphasized the importance of first documenting the family's perception of the situation and the alternatives open to them. A good deal of the discussion on this topic also concerned trainees' feelings about withholding advice or knowledge in the interests of research. This concern required repeated discussion as individual cases arose later on the job.

4. To increase trainees' skill in recording and working with data, as well as to prepare them better for employment at the end of the project, academic courses (remedial English, remedial mathematics, and high school equivalency preparation) were included in the program. Only two of the trainees had completed high school, and all but one of them had left school more than 10 years earlier. Two students also showed strong interest in learning to type and received daily instruction or practice in this skill. While these two were typing, the remainder of the group read and discussed Piri Thomas's *Down These Mean Streets,* a section of Oscar Lewis's introduction to *La Vida,* and an article by Robert Coles.

5. An important part of the first phase of the training program was to begin dealing with trainees' feelings about becoming and being researchers. Problems of identification with building residents, feelings about the value of research and about bringing information back to a White boss, attitudes toward racial and ethnic differences were all brought into the open at various stages of the training. In this regard a psychiatrist attached to the Health Center also spoke to the group about problems of observing social phenomena. He stressed the introduction of bias through overidentification, sexual interest in the informant, intrusion of private or cultural values and judgments into interpretations of behavior, among other topics. Although the encounter with the psychiatrist was probably more threatening than helpful, the more informal discussions of these attitudes and emotions during the training created an atmosphere of relative freedom to express and discuss feelings openly.

AGENDA FOR SCREENING APPLICANTS FOR POSITIONS AS SECRETARY AND RESEARCHER

1. Introduction of the Health Center staff and Community Advisory Board
2. Brief description of the Health Center and the relation of research project to it
3. Description of job
   a. Duties

   b. Starting date for orientation and training
   c. Salary

4. Group Interviews for Researcher Positions
   a. Explanation of written assignment—to describe what happened during the question 2 discussion
   b. Questions for discussion
      (1) How would you go about asking people in a building to participate in this project?
      (2) Mrs. Jones lives in the building you have been assigned to. She is on Welfare, getting assistance for herself and five children. While there, you have been introduced to Mr. Jones. One day a neighbor in the building asks you whether you have met Mr. Jones. What would you say?
      (3) Suppose you have been asked to make a list of the people living in all the apartments in the building to which you have been assigned. You go to one apartment several times. At first the people say they are busy, so you return again. Finally the people say they do not want to answer your questions. What would you do?
      (4) After you have been working in a building awhile, you stop by to talk to a woman. From past visits you have become friendly with the woman and her children. The woman says she would like to talk but must go shopping first. What might you do?

5. Discussion of Impressions (for interviewers); write-up of question 2 (for candidates)

6. Individual Interviews
   1. Questions
      a. What are you interested in?
      b. How do you feel about coming into this program?
      c. Do you feel that you have any special difficulties that would affect your participation in this program? Any special advantages to bring to the program?
      d. How do you feel about research?

FOR INTERVIEWERS: WHAT TO KEEP IN MIND DURING INTERVIEW

1. Are candidates alert, interested?
2. Are they nervous?
3. Are they defensive, hostile, unfriendly?
4. Do they adapt well to new people, new situations?

5. Are they able not to be judgmental?
6. Do they appear to have a sensitivity for people? Know how to listen and hear others?
7. Do they ask relevant questions?
8. Do they consider all possibilities in each situation?
9. How well do they organize their thoughts in speaking?

SUGGESTIONS

1. Take notes, so you will be able to remember.
2. Feel free to ask any questions, interrupt.

Bibliography

AARONSON, BERNARD S.

1973 ASCID Trance, Hypnotic Trance, Just Trance. *American Journal of Clinical Hypnosis* **16**.2:110–117.

ABU-LUGHOD, JANET

1961 Migrant Adjustment to City Life: The Egyptian Case. *American Journal of Sociology* **47**:22–32.

ACKERKNECHT, E. H.

1959 *A Short History of Psychiatry*. New York: Hafner.

BERGIN, A. E.

1971 The Evaluation of Therapeutic Outcomes. In *Handbook of*

Psychotherapy and Behavior Change. A. E. Bergin and S. L. Garfield, Eds. New York: Wiley. Pp. 217–270.

BERLE, BEATRICE

1958 *80 Puerto Rican Families in New York City: Health and Disease Studied in Context.* New York: Columbia University Press.

BETZ, B. J.

1962 Experiences in Research in Psychotherapy with Schizophrenic Patients. In *Research in Psychotherapy.* H. Strupp and L. Luborsky, Eds. Washington, D.C.: American Psychological Association.

BOLMAN, WILLIAM M.

1968 Cross-Cultural Psychotherapy. *American Journal of Psychiatry* **124**.9:1237–1244.

BOURGUIGNON, ERIKA

1974 Foreword to *Trance, Healing, and Hallucination: Three Field Studies in Religious Experience.* Felicitas Goodman, Jeanette H. Henney, and Esther Pressel. New York: Wiley.

BOURGUIGNON, ERIKA, ED.

1973 *Religion, Altered States of Consciousness, and Social Change.* Columbus: Ohio State University Press.

BRAM, JOSEPH

1958 Spirits, Mediums and Believers in Contemporary Puerto Rico. *Transactions of the New York Academy of Science* **20**:340–347.

BROOKE, RONALD

1968 An Audit of the Quality of Care in Social Medicine. *Milbank Memorial Fund Quarterly* **46**.3 (Part 1) :351–376.

CAPLAN, GERALD, AND RUTH B. CAPLAN

1967 Development of Community Psychiatry Concepts. In *Comprehensive Textbook of Psychiatry.* Alfred Freedman and Harold I. Kaplan, Eds. Baltimore: Williams & Wilkins. Pp. 1499–1512.

COHEN, ABNER

1974 *Two-Dimensional Man: An Essay on the Anthropology of Power and Symbolism in Complex Society.* Berkeley: University of California Press.

COURLANDER, HAROLD

1960 *The Drum and the Hoe: The Life and Lore of the Haitian People.* Berkeley: University of California Press.

DAVIS, KINGSLEY

1938 Mental Health and the Class Structure. *Psychiatry* **1**:55–65.

DENZIN, NORMAN

1970 *The Research Act: A Theoretical Introduction to Sociological Methods*. Chicago: Aldine.

DIRKS, ROBERT

1975 Ethnicity and Ethnic Group Relations in the British Virgin Islands. In *The New Ethnicity: Perspectives from Ethnology*. John W. Bennett, Ed. 1973 Proceedings of The American Ethnological Society. St. Paul: West.

DOUGHTY, PAUL L.

1970 Behind the Back of the City: "Provincial" Life in Lima, Peru. In *Peasants in Cities: Readings in the Anthropology of Urbanization*. William Mangin, Ed. Boston: Houghton Mifflin.

DOUGLAS, MARY

1967 Witch Beliefs in Central Africa. *Africa* **37**.1:72–80.

EL AKONI

n.d. Ayúdese espiritualmente: La voz de Orunla. (Publisher unknown.)

FENDALL, N. R. E.

1972 *Auxiliaries in Health Care: Programs in Developing Countries*. Baltimore: The Johns Hopkins University Press for the Josiah Macy, Jr. Foundation.

FERNÁNDEZ-MARINA, R.

1961 The Puerto Rican Syndrome: Its Dynamics and Cultural Determinants. *Psychiatry* **24**:79–82.

FERNÁNDEZ-MARINA, R., E. D. MALDONADO-SIERRA, AND R. D. TRENT

1958 Three Basic Themes in Mexican and Puerto Rican Family Values. *Journal of Social Psychology* **48**:167–181.

FIEDLER, FRED

1950 A Comparison of Therapeutic Relationships in Psychoanalytic, Non-Directive, and Adlerian Therapy. *Journal of Consulting Psychology* **14**:436–445.

FIRTH, RAYMOND

1956 *Elements of Social Organization*. 2d ed. London: Watts.

FISCH, STANLEY

1968 Botánicas and Spiritualism in a Metropolis. *Milbank Memorial Fund Quarterly* **46**.3 (Part 1) :377–388.

FISKE, D. W., H. HUNT, L. LUBORSKY, ET AL.

1970 The Planning of Research on Effectiveness of Psychotherapy. *Archives of General Psychiatry* **22**:22–32.

FORD, DONALD H., AND HUGH B. URBAN

1963 *Systems of Psychotherapy*. New York: Wiley.

FRANK, JEROME

1961 *Persuasion and Healing: A Comparative Study of Psychotherapy*. Baltimore: The Johns Hopkins University Press. (Schocken paperback edition, 1963.)

1964 Foreword to *Magic, Faith, and Healing*. Ari Kiev, Ed. New York: Free Press.

1967 Evaluation of Psychiatric Treatment. In *Comprehensive Textbook of Psychiatry*. Alfred M. Freedman and Harold I. Kaplan, Eds. Baltimore: Williams & Wilkins.

FREEDMAN, ALFRED M., AND HAROLD I. KAPLAN, EDS.

1967 *Comprehensive Textbook of Psychiatry*. Baltimore: Williams & Wilkins.

FREEDMAN, MAURICE

1961 Immigrants and Associations: Chinese in 19th Century Singapore. *Comparative Studies in Society and History* **3**:25–48.

FREIDSON, ELIOT

1961–1962 The Sociology of Medicine. *Current Sociology* **10–11**:123–92.

FREUD, SIGMUND

1959 Obsessive Actions and Religious Practices. In *The Standard Edition of the Complete Psychological Works of Sigmund Freud*, Vol. 9. J. Strachey, Ed. London: Hogarth.

FROMM, ERICH

1967 *Psychoanalysis and Religion*. New York: Bantam Books. (First published by Yale University Press, 1950.)

GARCÍA, CÉSAR

1956 Spirits, Mediums, and Social Workers. New York School of Social Work, Student Project #4570.

GARRISON, VIVIAN

1967 The Puerto Rican Spiritualist: A Model for Psychotherapy Among Low-Income Populations? Paper delivered at the 66th Annual Meeting of the American Anthropological Association, Washington, D.C.

1968 Faith Healers, Spirit Mediums, and Professional Psychotherapy in a Low-Income Urban Area. Unpublished research proposal.

1972 Social Networks, Social Change and Mental Health among Migrants in a New York City Slum. Ann Arbor: University Microfilms.

1973 *Espiritismo*: Implications for Provision of Mental Health Services to Puerto Rican Populations. Paper delivered at the 8th Annual Meeting of the Southern Anthropological Society, February 1972.

GEERTZ, CLIFFORD

1966 Religion as a Cultural System. In *Anthropological Approaches to the Study of Religion.* Michael Banton, Ed. ASA Monographs, No. 3. London: Tavistock.

GLAZER, NATHAN, AND DANIEL PATRICK MOYNIHAN

1970 *Beyond the Melting Pot.* 2d ed. Cambridge: M.I.T. Press.

GOFFMAN, ERVING

1967 The Nature of Deference and Demeanor. Reprinted in *Interaction Ritual: Essays in Face-to-Face Behavior.* Chicago: Aldine. (First published, 1956.)

GOLDSTEIN, ARNOLD, KENNETH HELLER, AND LEE B. SECHCREST

1966 *Psychotherapy and the Psychology of Behavior Change.* New York: Wiley.

GONZÁLEZ, NANCIE L.

1975 Patterns of Dominican Ethnicity. In *The New Ethnicity: Perspectives from Ethnology.* John W. Bennett, Ed. 1973 Proceedings of The American Ethnological Society. St. Paul: West.

GONZALEZ-WIPPLER, MIGENE

1973 Santería: *African Magic in Latin America.* New York: Julian.

GOODENOUGH, WARD H.

1963 *Cooperation in Change.* New York: Russell Sage.

1971 Culture, Language, and Society. McCaleb Module in Anthropology. Reading, Mass.: Addison-Wesley.

HALEY, JAY

1963 *Strategies of Psychotherapy.* New York: Grune & Stratton.

HALIFAX, JOAN, AND HAZEL H. WEIDMAN

1973 Religion as a Mediating Institution in Acculturation: The Case of Santería in Greater Miami. In *Religious Systems and Psychotherapy.* Richard H. Cox, Ed. Springfield, Ill.: Charles C Thomas. Pp. 319–331.

HANNERZ, ULF

1969 *Soulside: Inquiries into Ghetto Culture and Community.* New York: Columbia University Press.

HARPER, ROBERT A.

1959 *Psychoanalysis and Psychotherapy: 36 Systems.* Englewood Cliffs, N.J.: Prentice-Hall.

HARWOOD, ALAN

1970 *Witchcraft, Sorcery and Social Categories among the Safwa.* London: Oxford University Press for the International African Institute.

1971a The Hot-Cold Theory of Disease: Implications for Treatment of Puerto Rican Patients. *Journal of the American Medical Association* **216**.7:1153–1158.

1971b Housing and Health in the Area of the Dr. Martin Luther King, Jr. Health Center. In *Nutrition and Human Needs, Part 4*: Housing and Sanitation Hearings of the U.S. Senate Committee on Human Needs, 91st Congress, U.S. Government Printing Office.

HERSKOVITS, MELVILLE J.

1937a African Gods and Catholic Saints in New World Negro Belief. *American Anthropologist* **39**:635–643.

1937b *Life in a Haitian Valley.* New York: Knopf.

HILGARD, ERNEST R.

1975 Hypnosis. *Annual Review of Psychology* **26**:19–44. Palo Alto, Calif.: Annual Reviews.

HOLLINGSHEAD, AUGUST B., AND FREDRICK REDLICH

1958 *Social Class and Mental Illness.* New York: Wiley.

HUXLEY, F. J. H.

1966 The Ritual of Voodoo and the Symbolism of the Body. In *A Discussion on Ritualization of Behavior in Animals and Man.* Sir Julian Huxley, Convener. *Philosophical Transactions of the Royal Society of London, Series B*, **251**:423–427.

JONES, DELMOS

1972 Incipient Organization and Organizational Failures in an Urban Ghetto. *Urban Anthropology* **1**.1:51–67.

KAPLAN, SEYMOUR R., AND MELVIN ROMAN

1973 *The Organization and Delivery of Mental Health Services in the Ghetto: The Lincoln Hospital Experience.* New York: Praeger.

KARDEC, ALLAN

1960 Colección de oraciones escogidas. Mexico, DF: El Libro Español.

1963a El libro de los espíritus. 9th ed. Mexico, DF: Editorial Diana.

1963b El libro de los médiums. 9th ed. Mexico, DF: Editorial Diana.

1964 El evangelio según el espiritismo. 12th ed. Mexico, DF: Editorial Diana.

KIEV, ARI

1973 Magic, Faith, and Healing in Modern Psychiatry. In *Religious Systems and Psychotherapy*. Richard H. Cox, Ed. Springfield, Ill.: Charles C Thomas.

KIEV, ARI, ED.

1964 *Magic, Faith, and Healing: Primitive Psychiatry Today*. Glencoe, Ill.: Free Press.

KLEINMAN, ARTHUR

1973 Some Issues for a Comparative Study of Medical Healing. *International Journal of Social Psychiatry* **19**:159–165.

KOSS, JOAN D.

1964 Puerto Rican Spiritualism in Philadelphia: A Lady or the Tiger Dilemma. Paper delivered at the 63rd Annual Meeting of the American Anthropological Association.

1967 Therapeutic Aspects of Puerto Rican Cult Practices. Paper delivered at the 66th Annual Meeting of the American Anthropological Association, Washington, D.C.

n.d. Therapeutic Aspects of Puerto Rican Cult Practices. Revised, unpublished version of paper delivered at the 66th Annual Meeting of the American Anthropological Association. (Mimeograph.)

1970 Terapéutica del sistema de una secta en Puerto Rico. *Revista de Ciencias Sociales* (Rio Piedras) **14**.2:259–278. (Expanded version of above reference.)

1972 El porque de los cultos religiosos: El caso del espiritismo en Puerto Rico. *Revista de Ciencias Sociales* (Rio Piedras) **16**.1:61–72.

LAMBO, T. ADEOYE

1961 A Form of Social Psychiatry in Africa. *World Mental Health* **13**:190–203.

1964 Patterns of Psychiatric Care in Developing African Countries. In *Magic, Faith, and Healing*. Ari Kiev, Ed. Pp. 443–453.

1966 Patterns of Psychiatric Care in Developing African Countries: The Nigerian Village Program. In *International Trends in Mental Health*. H. P. David, Ed. New York: McGraw-Hill.

LANDY, DAVID

1959 Tropical Childhood. Chapel Hill, N.C.: University of North Carolina Press.

LAUER, ROGER M.

1973 Masters of Metaphysics. In *Religious Systems and Psychotherapy*. Springfield, Ill.: Charles C Thomas.

1974 A Medium for Mental Health. In *Religious Movements in Contemporary America*. Irving I. Zaretsky and Mark P. Leone, Eds. Princeton: Princeton University Press.

LEACH, EDMUND

1954 *Political Systems of Highland Burma*. Boston: Beacon.

1966 Ritualization in Man in Relation to Conceptual and Social Development. *Philosophical Transactions of the Royal Society of London, Series B*, **251**:403–408.

1968 Ritual. In *International Encyclopedia of the Social Sciences*, Vol. 13. New York: Crowell Collier Macmillan.

LEACOCK, SETH, AND RUTH LEACOCK

1975 *Spirits of the Deep: A Study of an Afro-Brazilian Cult*. Garden City, N.Y.: Anchor Doubleday. (First published by Natural History Press, 1972.)

LEDERER, WOLFGANG

1973 Primitive Psychotherapy. In *Religious Systems and Psychotherapy*. Richard H. Cox, Ed. Springfield, Ill.: Charles C Thomas.

LENNARD, HENRY, AND ARNOLD BERNSTEIN

1960 *The Anatomy of Psychotherapy*. New York: Columbia University Press.

LÉVI-STRAUSS, CLAUDE

1963 *Structural Anthropology*. Claire Jacobson and Brooke G. Schoepf, Trans. New York: Basic Books.

LEWIS, I. M.

1971 *Ecstatic Religion: An Anthropological Study of Spirit Possession and Shamanism*. Harmondsworth: Penguin Books.

LEWIS, OSCAR

1965 La Vida: *A Puerto Rican Family in the Culture of Poverty—San Juan and New York*. New York: Random House.

1968 *A Study of Slum Culture: Backgrounds for La Vida*. New York: Random House.

LITTLE, KENNETH

1965 *West African Urbanization: A Study of Voluntary Associations in Social Change*. Cambridge: Cambridge University Press.

LUBCHANSKY, ISAAC, GLADYS EGRI, AND JANET STOKES

1970 Puerto Rican Spiritualists View Mental Illness: The Faith

Healer as Paraprofessional. *American Journal of Psychiatry* **127**.3:312–321.

LUBORSKY, L.

1962 The Patient's Personality and Psychotherapeutic Change. In *Research in Psychotherapy*. H. H. Strupp and L. Luborsky, Eds. Washington, D.C.: American Psychological Association.

LUCE, GAY

1971 The Importance of Psychic Medicine: Training Navaho Medicine Men. In *Mental Health Program Reports—5*. Julius Segal, Ed. Washington, D.C.: National Institute of Mental Health, Department of Health, Education, and Welfare.

MACKLIN, JUNE

1974 Belief, Ritual and Healing: New England Spiritualism and Mexican-American Spiritism Compared. In *Religious Movements in Contemporary America*. Irving I. Zaretsky and Mark P. Leone, Eds. Princeton: Princeton University Press.

MAIR, LUCY

1969 *Witchcraft*. London: World University Library.

MALDONADO-SIERRA, E. D., R. D. TRENT, AND R. FERNÁNDEZ-MARINA.

1960 Neurosis and Traditional Family Beliefs in Puerto Rico. *International Journal of Social Psychiatry* **6**:237–246.

MANGIN, WILLIAM

1965 The Role of Regional Associations in the Adaptation of Rural Migrants to Cities in Peru. In *Contemporary Cultures and Societies of Latin America*. D. B. Heath and R. N. Adams, Eds. New York: Random House. Pp. 311–323.

MANNERS, ROBERT

1956 Tabara: Subcultures of a Tobacco and Mixed Crops Municipality. In *The People of Puerto Rico*. Julian Steward et al. Urbana: University of Illinois Press.

MASSERMAN, JULES H., ED.

1967 *Current Psychiatric Therapies*. New York: Grune & Stratton.

MEHLMAN, R.

1961 The Puerto-Rican Syndrome. *American Journal of Psychiatry* **118**:328.

MÉTRAUX, ALFRED

1959 *Voodoo in Haiti*. New York: Oxford University Press.

MIDDLETON, JOHN, AND E. H. WINTER, EDS.

1963 *Witchcraft and Sorcery in East Africa.* London: Routledge and Kegan Paul.

MINTZ, SIDNEY W.

1973 Puerto Rico: An Essay in the Definition of a National Culture. In *The Puerto Rican Experience: A Sociological Sourcebook.* Francesco Cordasco and Eugene Bucchioni, Eds. Totowa, N.J.: Rowman & Littlefield. (Originally published in *Status of Puerto Rico: Selected Background Studies for the United States–Puerto Rico Commission on the Status of Puerto Rico.* Washington, D.C.: U.S. Government Printing Office, 1966.)

MINUCHIN, SALVADOR, ET AL.

1967 *Families of the Slums: An Exploration of Their Structure and Treatment.* New York: Basic Books.

MISCHEL, WALTER, AND FRANCES MISCHEL

1958 Psychological Aspects of Spirit Possession. *American Anthropologist* **60**.2:249–260.

MITCHELL, J. CLYDE

1956 *The Kalela Dance: Aspects of Social Relationships Among Urban Africans in Northern Rhodesia.* Manchester: Manchester University Press.

MOSTELLER, FREDERICK, AND ROBERT R. BUSH

1954 Selected Quantitative Techniques. In *Handbook of Social Psychology,* Vol. I, Ch. 8. Reading, Mass.: Addison-Wesley.

OPLER, MARVIN K.

1967 *Culture and Social Psychiatry.* New York: Atherton.

PADILLA, ELENA

1956 Nocorá: The Subculture of Workers on a Government-Owned Sugar Plantation. In *The People of Puerto Rico.* Julian Steward et al. Urbana: University of Illinois Press.

1958 *Up from Puerto Rico.* New York: Columbia University Press.

PARSONS, ANNE

1969 *Belief, Magic and Anomie: Essays in Psychosocial Anthropology.* New York: Free Press.

PARSONS, TALCOTT

1951 *The Social System.* Glencoe, Ill.: Free Press.

1953 Illness and the Role of the Physician: A Sociological Perspective. In *Personality in Nature, Society, and Culture.* Clyde Kluckhohn and Henry A. Murray, Eds. New York: Knopf.

1958 Definitions of Health and Illness in the Light of American Values and Social Structure. In *Patients, Psysicians, and Illness.* E. Gartley Jaco, Ed. Glencoe, Ill.: Free Press.

PATTISON, E. MANSELL

1973 Exorcism and Psychotherapy: A Case of Collaboration. In *Religious Systems and Psychotherapy.* Richard H. Cox, Ed. Springfield, Ill.: Charles C Thomas.

PRESSEL, ESTHER

1973 Umbanda in São Paulo: Religious Innovation in a Developing Society. In *Religion, Altered States of Consciousness, and Social Change.* Erika Bourguignon, Ed. Columbus: Ohio State University Press.

1974 Umbanda Trance and Possession in São Paulo, Brazil. In *Trance, Healing, and Hallucination: Three Field Studies in Religious Experience.* Felicitas Goodman, Jeannette H. Henney, and Esther Pressel. New York: Wiley.

PRINCE, RAYMOND

1968 Possession Cults and Social Cybernetics. In *Trance and Possession States.* Raymond Prince, Ed. Proceedings of 2nd Annual Conference, R. M. Bucke Memorial Society. Montreal: Electra. Pp. 157–165.

1969 Psychotherapy and the Chronically Poor. In *Social Change, Poverty, and Mental Health.* J. Finney, Ed. Lexington: University of Kentucky Press. Pp. 20–41. (Paperback edition, 1970.)

PURDY, BEATRICE, RENEE PELLMAN, SARAH FLORES, AND HARVEY BLUESTONE

1972 Mellaril or Medium, Stelazine or Séance? A Study of Spiritism as It Affects Communication, Diagnosis, and Treatment of Puerto Rican People. In *On the Urban Scene.* Morton Levitt and Ben Rubenstein, Eds. Detroit: Wayne State University Press for the American Orthopsychiatric Association.

RAPPAPORT, ROY A.

1971 The Sacred in Human Evolution. *Annual Review of Ecology and Systematics* **2**:23–44.

REDLICH, F. C., AND D. X. FREEDMAN

1966 *The Theory and Practice of Psychiatry.* New York: Basic Books.

RENDON, MARIO

1974 Transcultural Aspects of Puerto Rican Mental Illness in New York. *International Journal of Social Psychiatry* **20**:18–24.

RIESSMAN, FRANK, JEROME COHEN, AND ARTHUR PEARL

1964 *Mental Health of the Poor: New Treatment Approaches for Low-Income People.* New York: Free Press.

ROGERS, CARL R.

1957 The Necessary and Sufficient Conditions of Therapeutic Personality Change. *Journal of Consulting Psychology* **21**:95–103.

ROGLER, LLOYD H.

1972 *Migrant in the City: The Life of a Puerto Rican Action Group.* New York: Basic Books.

ROGLER, LLOYD H., AND AUGUST B. HOLLINGSHEAD

1961 The Puerto Rican Spiritualist as a Psychiatrist. *American Journal of Sociology* **67**:17–21.

1965 *Trapped: Families and Schizophrenia.* New York: Wiley.

ROSEN, JOHN

1953 *Direct Analysis: Selected Papers.* New York: Grune & Stratton.

ROTHENBERG, A.

1964 Puerto Rico and Aggression. *American Journal of Psychiatry* **120**:962–970.

RUESCH, J.

1957 *Disturbed Communication.* New York: Norton.

SANDIS, EVA E.

1970 Characteristics of Puerto Rican Migrants to, and from, the United States. *International Migration Review* **4**:22–42. Reprinted in *The Puerto Rican Experience: A Sociological Sourcebook.* Francesco Cordasco and Eugene Bucchioni, Eds. Totowa, N.J.: Roman & Littlefield.

SARGANT, WILLIAM

1957 *Battle for the Mind: A Physiology of Conversion and Brain-Washing.* Garden City, N.Y.: Doubleday.

SCHEELE, RAYMOND L.

1956 The Prominent Families of Puerto Rico. In *The People of Puerto Rico.* Julian Steward et al. Urbana: University of Illinois Press.

SCHOFIELD, WILLIAM

1964 *Psychotherapy: The Purchase of Friendship.* Englewood Cliffs, N.J.: Prentice-Hall.

SEDA, EDUARDO

1973 *Social Change and Personality in a Puerto Rican Agrarian Reform Community*. Evanston: Northwestern University Press.

SEIPP, CONRAD, ED.

1963 Health Care for the Community: Selected Papers of Dr. John B. Grant. *The American Journal of Hygiene Monographic Series,* No. 21. Baltimore: The Johns Hopkins University Press.

SIMPSON, GEORGE E.

1962 The Shango Cult in Nigeria and Trinidad. *American Anthropologist* **64**.6:1204–1219.

1965 The Shango Cult in Trinidad. *Caribbean Monograph Series,* No. 2. San Juan: Institute of Caribbean Studies.

SOMERS, HERMAN MILES, AND ANNE RAMSAY SOMERS

1962 *Doctors, Patients, and Health Insurance: The Organization and Financing of Medical Care*. Abridged ed. Garden City, N.Y.: Anchor Books. (Unabridged edition published 1961).

ST. CLAIR, DAVID

1971 *Drum and Candle*. Garden City, N.Y.: Doubleday.

STEIN, MORRIS, ED.

1961 *Contemporary Psychotherapies*. New York: Free Press.

STEWARD, JULIAN, ET AL.

1956 *The People of Puerto Rico*. Urbana: University of Illinois Press.

STOECKLE, JOHN

1969 The Future of Health Care. In *Poverty and Health: A Sociological Analysis*. John Kosa, Aaron Antonovsky, and Irving Kenneth Zola, Eds. Cambridge: Harvard University Press. Pp. 292–318.

STRAUSS, ANSELM

n.d. Medical Organization, Medical Care and Lower Income Groups. Unpublished paper prepared for The Institute for Policy Studies, Washington, D.C.

1970 Medical Ghettos. In *Where Medicine Fails*. Anselm Strauss, Ed. Chicago: Aldine.

STYCOSE, J. MAYONE

1955 *Family and Fertility in Puerto Rico*. New York: Columbia University Press.

SUTTLES, GERALD D.

1968 *The Social Order of the Slum: Ethnicity and Territory in the Inner City*. Chicago: University of Chicago Press.

SWEARINGEN, CHRISTINE M.

1968 Study of School Health Services. Unpublished report prepared for the Dr. Martin Luther King, Jr. Neighborhood Health Center. (Mimeograph.)

TORREY, E. FULLER

1969 The Case for the Indigenous Therapist. *Archives of General Psychiatry* **20**:365–373.

1970 Mental Health Services for American Indians and Eskimos. *Community Mental Health Journal* **6**.6:455–463.

1972 *The Mind Game: Witchdoctors and Psychiatrists.* New York: Emerson Hall.

TRUAX, CHARLES, AND ROBERT CARKHUFF

1967 *Toward Effective Counseling and Psychotherapy.* Chicago: Aldine.

TURNER, VICTOR

1964 Symbols in Ndembu Ritual. In *Closed Systems and Open Minds: The Limits of Naivety in Social Anthropology.* Max Gluckman, Ed. Chicago: Aldine.

1968 *The Drums of Affliction: A Study of Religious Processes Among the Ndembu of Zambia.* Oxford: Oxford University Press.

1969 *The Ritual Process: Structure and Anti-Structure.* Chicago: Aldine.

1973 Symbols in African Ritual. *Science* **179**.4078:1100–1105.

1974 *Dramas, Fields, and Metaphors: Symbolic Action in Human Society.* Ithaca, N.Y.: Cornell University Press.

VAN DER WALDE, PETER H.

1968 Trance States and Ego Psychology. In *Trance and Possession States.* Proceedings of 2nd Annual Conference, R. M. Bucke Memorial Society. Montreal: Electra. Pp. 57–68.

VAN GENNEP, ARNOLD

1960 *The Rites of Passage.* Monica B. Vizedom and Gabrielle L. Caffee, Trans. Chicago: University of Chicago Press. (First published 1908.)

WAKEFIELD, DAN

1960 *Island in the City: Puerto Ricans in New York.* New York: Corinth.

WEIDMAN, HAZEL H.

1968 Anthropological Theory and the Psychological Function of Belief in Witchcraft. In *Essays on Medical Anthropology.*

Thomas Weaver, Ed. Southern Anthropological Society Proceedings, No. 1. Athens: University of Georgia Press. Pp. 23–35.

WEISS, FREDERICK A.

1962 Self-Alienation: Dynamics and Therapy. In *Man Alone: Alienation in Modern Society*. Eric Josephson and Mary Josephson, Eds. New York: Dell. (First published in *American Journal of Psychoanalysis*, 1961.)

WILL, OTTO ALLEN

1967 Schizophrenia. V: Psychological Treatment. In *Comprehensive Textbook of Psychiatry*. Alfred M., Freedman and Harold I. Kaplan, Eds. Baltimore: Williams & Wilkins.

WITTKOWER, E. D.

1970 Trance and Possession States. *International Journal of Social Psychiatry* **16**.2:153–160.

WITTKOWER, E. D., AND H. H. WEIDMAN

1969 Magic, Witchcraft, and Sorcery in Relation to Mental Health and Mental Disorder. In *Social Psychiatry*. N. Petrilowitsch and H. Flegel, Eds. *Topical Problems in Psychiatry and Neurology* **8**:169–184.

WOLF, ERIC R.

1956 San Jose: "Traditional" Coffee Muncipality. In *The People of Puerto Rico*. Julian Steward et al. Urbana: University of Illinois Press.

WOLF, KATHLEEN

1952 Growing Up and Its Price in Three Puerto Rican Subcultures. *Psychiatry* **15**.4:401–433.

YALOM, IRWIN

1970 *The Theory and Practice of Group Psychotherapy*. New York: Basic Books.

Index